The New
Professionals

Randy Rieland

A
REDEFINITION
BOOK

BASEBALL IN THE 1970s

The New Professionals

Four Hours of Magic
Two time-honored teams took a World Series game deep into the October night and lit up the sky.

4

Charlie O. and the A's
Traditionalists hated the gaudy uniforms, the horseplay and the hype, but Charlie Finley's Athletics proved they could play real baseball.

18

Big Money
Playing baseball had made few men rich, until a frustrated outfielder and a feisty lawyer challenged the owners and created a new era.

42

The Big Red Machine
Celebrating its second century of professional baseball, a powerhouse Cincinnati team charged headfirst to the top of the National League.

62

Made for TV   88
Could sitting at home in front of the tube replace an afternoon in the grandstand? Television ruled America in the 1970s and ushered in a whole new ballgame.

The Artificial Game   106
Floodlights and plastic turf threatened to replace sunshine on grassy fields. Purists kicked and screamed, but teams like the Kansas City Royals just slapped and ran.

Fire the Manager   120
Caught between capricious owners and overpaid players, some baseball managers changed uniforms as often as they changed lineup cards.

The Specialists   142
Pinch runners, designated hitters and relief pitchers turned baseball into a relay race. You could get a win on one pitch and play a whole game without a glove.

George, Reggie and Billy   160
Three world-class egos struck sparks behind the scenes and ignited explosive power on the field, as a Yankee dynasty flourished once again.

1970s Statistics   184   **Index**   187   **Credits/Acknowledgments**   190

Four Hours of Magic

After Carlton Fisk's game-winning blast (preceding page) in the 12th inning of Game 6 of the 1975 World Series bounced off the foul pole at Fenway Park, Fisk had to dodge exuberant Red Sox fans on his way home. Third-base coach Don Zimmer got the last handshake before Fisk disappeared into a sea of teammates.

For three days a steady rain had soaked Boston. It did wonders for the outfield grass at Fenway Park, but not much for the 1975 World Series. The Cincinnati Reds and the Boston Red Sox had played the baseball of little boys' fantasies—acrobatic catches, eleventh-hour rallies, and home runs that answered prayers. After five games, the Reds were up, three games to two. Then it started to rain.

Three times the sixth game was postponed, each delay frustrating television executives nervous about a dwindling audience and sportswriters stuck with neither a fresh story nor fresh clothes. The players, for their part, began to feel stale, and by the time the skies cleared on Tuesday, October 21, there was a sense that something had been lost.

"It's incredible how much of the edge is taken off this thing right now," Red Sox rookie Fred Lynn told reporters before the game. "It just doesn't seem the same as it did a few days ago. Now it's just like a regular-season game." This was one time that Lynn's instincts failed him. When the game ended four hours later, anyone watching knew that they had seen a classic, a game that is still known simply as *Game Six*.

The downpour brought one blessing, at least for the Red Sox. Boston manager Darrell Johnson had a chance to juggle his starting rotation and recycle his pitching ace, Luis Tiant. If anyone could get the Red Sox even, it was Tiant, the chunky Cuban right-hander who had already pitched both of Boston's victories. Tiant was an original. No one was sure how old he was. The official program had him as 34; rumor had him as much as five years older. Tiant was also partial to cigars—long black cigars. Occasionally he would smoke one during his post-game shower.

The spell Boston's Luis Tiant (above) cast over Reds hitters was broken in Game 6, as the wily right-hander was tagged for 11 hits and six runs in seven innings. But without Tiant, the Red Sox might not have made it to Game 6. He shut out the Reds in Game 1, then scattered nine hits and scored the winning run himself on the way to a complete-game, 5–4 win in Game 4.

In 1975 Boston outfielders Fred Lynn and Jim Rice formed the most potent one-two rookie punch in baseball history. Both topped the .300 and 100-RBI marks, and while Rice sat out the postseason with an injury, Lynn kept on plugging, leading the Red Sox in RBI in both the playoffs and the World Series.

On the mound, Tiant was no less quirky, his pitching motion a sideshow of jerks and contortions, exaggerated twirls and quick wiggles. In mid-windup he coiled his body, actually turning his back to the plate and facing left field; there were times when it seemed he had no choice but to deliver a high fastball to the third baseman. His gyrations helped him win 18 games during the regular season and the opening playoff game against the defending champion Oakland A's, after which Reggie Jackson described him as "the Fred Astaire of baseball."

In the opener, Tiant's syncopated motion baffled Reds batters, who managed only five hits and didn't score. He won Game 4, too, although his spell was clearly weakening. Tiant struggled through that game, working slowly, falling behind batters, giving up line drive outs, and holding a one-run lead into the ninth when the Reds' Ken Griffey, with two men on, knocked a pitch toward the center field wall. In keeping with the script, Fred Lynn, after a long run, was able to haul it down.

As Tiant walked out to the mound to begin Game 6, the fans greeted him with their familiar chorus, "Looo—eee . . . Looo—eee." He responded with his tango twists, and the Reds went down without harm to the Red Sox in the first. The batters, however, seemed to have figured out his motion. They were timing his pitches better and making good contact. But if Tiant was less than mystifying, Boston fans did not have much time to wring their hands.

In the bottom of the first, the Sox attacked Cincinnati's Gary Nolan as if they had spent their rain days locked in a small room. Carl Yastrzemski, the team's aging heart, singled, and Carlton Fisk did the same. That brought up

6' 2" 175 lbs.
BR TR

b 5/14/1942

TONY PEREZ
First Base

Tony Perez was the silent cog in the Big Red Machine that dominated the NL from 1970 through 1976. Although the spotlight often focused on his teammates—Pete Rose, Joe Morgan and Johnny Bench—it was Perez, nicknamed Big Dog for his ferocity at the plate, who consistently provided punch and power to Cincinnati's star lineup.

The Reds signed Perez out of a Cuban sugar mill in 1960. By 1965 he was a regular.

Dave Bristol, who managed Perez when he was with San Diego and Cincinnati, once said, "If the game lasts long enough, Tony Perez will win it." Those words often proved prophetic.

In the 1967 All-Star Game, Perez's first of seven, he slammed a game-winning, 15th-inning home run against Catfish Hunter. In the remarkable 1975 World Series, playing against Boston, Perez broke out of an 0 for 15 slump and blasted two home runs in Game 5. In the sixth inning of the seventh and deciding game, Perez shattered Bill Lee's shutout with a two-run shot over the left field screen, sparking the Reds to a world championship.

But consistency, not heroics, was the hallmark of Perez's game. From 1967 to 1977, he was the *only* major leaguer to knock in 90 or more runs for ten consecutive years.

"He could do it in the clutch," Joe Morgan noted. "Johnny Bench, Pete, me, we got the MVPs, but Tony was just as valuable as we were."

Only four years older than his number in 1975, Fred Lynn (19) continued his remarkable rookie season with a homer in the first inning of Game 6. Scoring ahead of him were Carl Yastrzemski (left) and Carlton Fisk (right).

Fred Lynn—the same Lynn who had complained of ennui a few hours earlier. A smooth hitter and often a spectacular fielder, Lynn had been the team's most productive batter during the season, with 21 homers and 105 RBI. His numbers had almost been matched by Jim Rice, the team's other rookie who, playing left field and DH, contributed 22 homers and 102 RBI, but his season ended in late September because of a broken wrist.

With two men on, Lynn could almost have been forgiven if he had turned overanxious and popped up. Instead, he acted as if he were in batting practice, drilling a Nolan pitch over the Red Sox bullpen and into the right-center field bleachers. The venerable rookie clapped his hands once as he glided around the bases, and the Sox were up, 3–0.

The Reds did not seem impressed. They had swaggered toward the Series, at one point winning 41 of 50 games and finishing with 108 wins, more than any NL team had in 66 years. They were an explosive team, one that could slug opponents senseless one day and run them silly the next. Sometimes they got carried away and did both in the same game. For a team that hit 124 homers and stole 168 bases during the season, it was not so much a matter of whether they would retaliate, but of how they would go about doing it.

Tony Perez's line single in the fourth was a good omen for the Reds. In the previous two games against Tiant, Perez had flailed at his pitches, out of sync and out of the offense. But even though he didn't score this time, his hit made one thing clear: Tiant was ripe for picking.

The harvest came an inning later. With one out, pinch hitter Ed Armbrister came to bat. A .185 hitter during the season, Armbrister had already become a World Series footnote. Most ballplayers do great things for their fame; Armbrister simply got in the way. At Riverfront Stadium in Game 3,

with a man on first in the tenth inning, he had bounced a sacrifice bunt high off the artificial surface. A right-handed batter, he charged across the plate in front of catcher Carlton Fisk, who was scrambling out to field the ball. The resulting collision was brief, but in his hurry to force out Cesar Geronimo at second, Fisk heaved a throw that sailed into center field, and Geronimo made it to third. The Red Sox screamed interference by the runner, but umpires Larry Barnett and Dick Stello saw the bump as having been accidental, one of those things that happen in the heat of a game. One out later, Geronimo scored the winning run on a single by Joe Morgan.

This time Armbrister found an easier way to first, drawing a walk. Pete Rose, after fouling off a half dozen pitches, followed with a single up the middle. That brought up Ken Griffey, a player who typified the Reds. He could hit with power—he led the team with nine triples—but it was Griffey's speed that unnerved opponents. He specialized in infield hits—he had had 38 the past season—and while that wasn't going to get him into the Hall of Fame, it helped reinforce the image of the Reds as a team never at rest. Facing Tiant, Griffey lashed a fly ball to the 379-foot marker in left center. Lynn gave chase and, in full flight, bounced off the wall. When the play ended, Griffey was on third, with two runs in, and Lynn was lying motionless in center like a puppet without strings, the top half of his body propped against the bottom of the wall and his head resting on his right shoulder. Some in the press box actually wondered if he had killed himself. Finally, he stirred, then rose and fought off suggestions that he leave the game. Boston fans cheered, more with relief than with joy, but that passed quickly. Joe Morgan popped out, but Johnny Bench smacked a single off the Green Monster in left, scoring Griffey with the tying run, three all.

Center fielder Fred Lynn was never wall-shy, especially in big games, but his run in with Fenway's center field wall in the fifth inning of Game 6 was nearly a knockout. The ball he was chasing came off the bat of Reds outfielder Ken Griffey (below), and scored the Reds' first two runs. Fortunately for the Red Sox, Lynn stayed in the game, and in the eighth he singled and then scored on Bernie Carbo's game-tying homer.

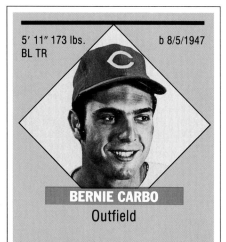

5' 11" 173 lbs.
BL TR

b 8/5/1947

BERNIE CARBO
Outfield

In 1970 rookie outfielder Bernie Carbo hit 21 home runs, drove in 63 runs, and batted .310 while helping Cincinnati win its first pennant since 1961. *The Sporting News* named Carbo its "Rookie of the Year."

Then the bottom fell out.

Carbo's sophomore slump was a whopper, and his batting average plummeted to an anemic .219. Just 19 games into the 1972 season, as Carbo's nosedive continued, Cincinnati dealt its former wunderkind, at this point hitting .143, to St. Louis. The move rejuvenated the brash Carbo, who hit .286 for the Cards in 1973, then was traded to the Red Sox at the close of the regular season. And it was with Boston, during the 1975 World Series against his former Cincinnati teammates, that Carbo had his second moment in the spotlight.

Late in Game 6 the outlook for Boston was bleak. The Red Sox were down three games to two and were behind, 6–3, when Carbo was called upon to pinch-hit with two on and two out in the bottom of the eighth. With two strikes against him, Carbo drilled a Rawley Eastwick fastball into Fenway's center field bleachers, tying the game and setting the stage for Carlton Fisk's game-winning, 12th-inning blast.

Carbo hit over .280 each year from 1977 through 1979 for Boston, Cleveland and St. Louis. But when he called it quits in 1980, his rookie stats were his career best.

Reds manager Sparky Anderson kept warm in Game 6 by wearing out a path between the dugout and the mound. Anderson went to the bullpen seven times in Game 6, and a record 23 times in the seven-game Series.

In the seventh inning, the Reds had Tiant looking in need of a cigar. With two out and Griffey and Morgan on base with singles, George Foster knocked a ball off the center field fence and the Reds took a 5–3 lead. Maybe it was loyalty that made Boston manager Darrell Johnson leave Tiant in the game; maybe it was wishful thinking. It did not appear to be baseball wisdom, particularly when Cesar Geronimo led off the eighth with a home run. That was the showstopper for Tiant, and as he started his walk to the clubhouse, the "Looo—eee . . . Looo—eee . . . Looo—eee" chant echoed off the bleachers one last time. That he left the field not a conquering king, but a tragic hero, was, of course, true to the Red Sox tradition. And as they joined the chorus, Boston fans sensed the inevitable: once again they had flirted with a championship, once again the team had only been kidding.

Yet Lynn led off the bottom of the eighth with a single off Pedro Borbon, the Reds' fifth pitcher, and third baseman Rico Petrocelli walked. Sparky Anderson—his pitchers called him Captain Hook—wasted no time bringing on Rawley Eastwick, who led the team in saves. All season Anderson had thrown waves of pitchers at opponents, using them like pinball flippers to stay in the games. He routinely used four or five in a game, and at one point, Reds starters went a record 45 consecutive contests without a complete game. Under Sparky the quick-change artist, starters were just starters.

Eastwick, pitcher number six, struck out Dwight Evans, then got shortstop Rick Burleson to fly out. Obviously, hope of a Boston rally had been one last, cruel tease. There was no designated hitter in this Series, and the next scheduled batter was reliever Roger Moret, so Johnson sent up Bernie Carbo to pinch-hit. Carbo had 15 home runs—third on the team—and already had a pinch-hit homer in Game 3. There was irony in Johnson's

choice, because Carbo had started his career with the Reds, drafted ahead of Johnny Bench in 1965. Bench, of course, had become the best catcher in baseball; Carbo had struggled to avoid mediocrity. Now he was struggling just to keep Boston breathing. He worked the count to two and two, then watched Eastwick's sinking fastball dip into the strike zone at the last instant. Carbo waved at the pitch clumsily, just nicking it foul. Sportswriter Roger Angell described him as looking "like someone fighting off a wasp with a croquet mallet."

Eastwick, sensing Carbo to be a strikeout waiting to happen, came back with another fastball, one that strayed a little too close to the heart of the plate. Carbo jumped on it, driving a shot that crashed into the center field stands. It happened so quickly that there was no time for the crowd's roar to build; it simply erupted. Fenway was in a frenzy as Carbo bounded around the bases, clapping his hands and plunging into the swarm of teammates at home plate. Tie game. The New England winter was on hold.

In the bottom of the ninth, Boston fueled the fantasy, loading the bases with nobody out and Lynn again at bat. Only the most cynical of Red Sox fans could have doubted that the game was about to be won. But Boston fans have a thousand reasons to be cynical, and the play that followed was destined to become another. Lynn, facing Reds reliever Will McEnaney, twisted a fly ball down the left field line. George Foster caught it at the grandstand, perhaps 90 feet beyond third base. The out was a setback for Boston supporters but not disastrous—until they realized that the play had not ended. Red Sox second baseman Denny Doyle had tagged at third and taken off, home plate in sight and glory on his mind. Waiting at the end of his mad dash, unfortunately, was Johnny Bench, ball in hand. Later, Red Sox third-base coach Don Zimmer

With one swing, Bernie Carbo went from the end of the Red Sox bench to a place in team history. His pinch-hit, three-run homer in the eighth was, according to Boston Evening Globe *writer Leigh Montville, "a giant electric jolt that brought 35,206 virtual cadavers out of their Fenway Park seats."*

Red Sox second baseman Denny Doyle
(above) sprouted goat horns halfway
toward home in the ninth inning of Game
6. Racing plateward with the potential
winning run, he came up 10 feet and 20
pounds short in his attempt to get by Reds
catcher Johnny Bench. The double play
killed the Boston rally.

claimed that Doyle heard his screams of "No! No! No!" as "Go! Go! Go!"
Zimmer said, "At first I thought Doyle was faking a break to the plate, but
when I saw him keep on running, I like to die."

It almost didn't matter that two runners were still on base—the Red
Sox, true to their tradition, had found a way not to win. When Petrocelli
grounded out to end the inning, Sox fans were forlorn, but not surprised. An
opportunity wasted, the balance of the game shifted a third time, now toward
the Reds, who threatened in the tenth but didn't score.

By this point, the players themselves were caught up in the drama, almost in awe of the event taking shape around them. Leading off in the 11th,
Rose couldn't contain himself. Turning to catcher Fisk, he said, "This is
some kind of game, isn't it." Fisk had to agree. Dick Drago, also feeling the
pressure, struck Rose with a pitch, sending him to first, where he was forced
out on Ken Griffey's bunt.

With one out and Griffey at first, second baseman Joe Morgan lifted a fly
toward the right field bleachers. Boston's Dwight Evans went after it, but it
looked as if he would need a seat to catch this one. Yet the ball seemed to die a
bit, and Evans, racing backward and following it over his shoulder, jumped up
and lunged to his left the instant before the ball cleared the fence. Evans'
momentum almost carried him over the low railing, but somehow the ball
stayed in his glove. Morgan, running to first, couldn't believe it. Neither
could Griffey, who was on his way to third. Like a convict caught in a spotlight, Griffey froze, then tried to retrace his steps. But Evans had bounced
off the bleachers and heaved the ball toward first. Yastrzemski retrieved it to
the right of the coaches' box and flipped it to shortstop Rick Burleson, who
had raced across the infield to cover first. It was an inning-ending double play

Everyone was stunned by Dwight Evans' acrobatic catch of Joe Morgan's 11th-inning drive, even Evans himself. The usually laser-armed Evans made a wild throw to first, but the Red Sox still had time to catch the Reds' Ken Griffey in a spectacular, inning-ending double play.

Cincinnati-Boston
October 21, 1975

Cincinnati	ab	r	h	rbi	Boston	ab	r	h	rbi
Rose 3b	5	1	2	0	Cooper 1b	5	0	0	0
Griffey rf	5	2	2	2	Drago p	0	0	0	0
Morgan 2b	6	1	1	0	f Miller ph	1	0	0	0
Bench c	6	0	1	1	Wise p	0	0	0	0
Perez 1b	6	0	2	0	Doyle 2b	5	0	1	0
Foster lf	6	0	2	2	Ystrzmsk lf-1b	6	1	3	0
Concepcion ss	6	0	1	0	Fisk c	4	2	2	1
Geronimo cf	6	1	2	1	Lynn cf	4	2	2	3
Nolan p	0	0	0	0	Petrocelli 3b	4	1	0	0
a Chaney ph	1	0	0	0	Evans rf	5	0	1	0
Norman p	0	0	0	0	Burleson ss	3	0	0	0
Billingham p	0	0	0	0	Tiant p	2	0	0	0
b Armbrister ph	0	1	0	0	Moret p	0	0	0	0
Carroll p	0	0	0	0	d Carbo lf	2	1	1	3
c Crowley ph	1	0	1	0	**Total**	41	7	10	7
Borbon p	1	0	0	0					
Eastwick p	0	0	0	0					
McEnaney p	0	0	0	0					
e Driessen ph	1	0	0	0					
Darcy p	0	0	0	0					
Total	50	6	14	6					

Cincinnati	000	030	210	000—6	
Boston	300	000	030	001—7	

None out when winning run scored.

a Flied out for Nolan in third. b Walked for Billingham in fifth. c Singled for Carroll in sixth. d Homered for Moret in eighth. e Flied out for McEnaney in tenth. f Flied out for Drago in eleventh. E–Burleson. DP–Cincinnati 1, Boston 1. LOB–Cincinnati 11, Boston 9. 2B–Doyle, Evans, Foster. 3B–Griffey. HR–Lynn, Geronimo, Carbo, Fisk. SB–Concepcion. SH–Tiant.

Cincinnati	IP	H	R	ER	BB	SO
Nolan	2	3	3	3	0	2
Norman	⅔	1	0	0	2	0
Billingham	1⅓	1	0	0	1	1
Carroll	1	1	0	0	0	0
Borbon	2†	1	2	2	2	1
Eastwick	1‡	2	1	1	1	2
McEnaney	1	0	0	0	1	0
Darcy (L)	2§	1	1	1	0	1

Boston	IP	H	R	ER	BB	SO
Tiant	7*	11	6	6	2	5
Moret	1	0	0	0	0	0
Drago	3	1	0	0	0	1
Wise (W)	1	2	0	0	0	1

* Pitched to one batter in eighth.
† Pitched to two batters in eighth.
‡ Pitched to two batters in ninth.
§ Pitched to one batter in twelfth.

HBP–by Drago (Rose). T–4:01. A–35,205.

on a ball that was headed out of the park. Sparky Anderson called it "just about the greatest catch I've ever seen." In the press box, the *Boston Globe's* Bud Collins, assigned to write a story on the game's hero, changed his pick for the 18th time.

The Reds didn't score in the twelfth inning either, although they rattled the Fenway crowd by putting two men on with one out. Rick Wise, a starter-turned-World-Series reliever, pitched out of the jam by getting Dave Concepcion to fly out and Geronimo on strikes. The Sox, still numb from their botched ninth-inning rally, sent six batters up in the tenth and eleventh against Pat Darcy, whose appearance as the Reds' eighth pitcher tied a Series record; none made it as far as first. By the bottom of the twelfth, it was nearly midnight and the Red Sox offense seemed to have called it a day.

Leading off for the Sox was Fisk, hitless since his first-inning single. It had been a comeback year for him. AL Rookie of the Year in 1972, he missed the last half of 1974 because of a knee injury and the first half of 1975 because of a forearm broken when he was hit by a pitch in a preseason game. Fisk didn't make it back into the lineup until the end of June, but he still hit ten homers and drove in 52 runs. He dug in against Darcy, taking a high, inside fast one for a ball. The next pitch was a sinker that moved outside. Fisk went after it, swinging upward. The ball rose into the night above the stadium lights, spinning in an arc toward the left field line, and it quickly became clear that the issue was not the ball's distance, but its direction. Fisk took a few steps toward first, then joined the 35,000 others gazing at the ball as it fell back down through the glow of the lights.

Fenway Park wasn't the only place they celebrated Carlton Fisk's game-winning homer in Game 6 (above). After midnight in Fisk's hometown of Charlestown, New Hampshire, church bells pealed in honor of the town's favorite son. The bells woke the church's minister, who thought it "was a hell of an idea."

Frantically waving his arms as he watched, he willed the ball fair, and when it finally came down, crashing into the wire mesh attached to the inside of the foul pole, Fisk bounced up and down like a boy on a pogo stick in a victory dance no Red Sox fan would ever forget.

Spectators poured onto the field, amazed that the four-hour marathon was finally over and incredulous that the Red Sox had actually won. Rounding the bases, Fisk weaved and pushed his way through them: "I straight-armed somebody and kicked them out of the way and touched every little white thing I saw." When he reached home plate, he landed on it with both feet and was swept away into the clubhouse by his teammates.

The stadium's organist broke into the "Hallelujah Chorus," then "Give Me Some Men Who Are Stout-Hearted Men," then "The Beer Barrel Polka." For a long time the fans, drained and delirious, stood in the aisles and sang along, savoring a sensation that usually didn't come with loving the Red Sox.

In the locker room, Fisk swore he had never played in a more emotion-filled game. In the other clubhouse, the Reds knew they had been part of something unique, a game that had ennobled all of them. "This is the greatest game in World Series history," said Pete Rose, "and if this ain't the national pastime, tell me what is." ◗

Fisk hit a pretty good sinking fastball from Reds reliever Pat Darcy, so he needed a good dose of body english (opposite) to keep the ball fair and the Red Sox' hopes alive. Somehow, for once, wishing made it so.

The Forgotten Game

In any other World Series, it would have gone down as a classic. Full of twists, turns and what-ifs, with enough second-guessing fodder to last the winter, it was everything you could want in the final game of a World Series. There was only one problem—it wasn't Game Six.

A TV audience of 75 million had tuned in to a continuation of the improbabilities of the night before. Despite Fenway Park's reputation as a graveyard for left-handed pitchers, two southpaws were picked to start Game 7. The Reds were banking on the well-rested fastball of 24-year-old Don Gullett—15–4 during the season—who hadn't pitched since his Game 5 win six days earlier. Boston went with junkballer Bill "Spaceman" Lee, who was coming off his third straight 17-win season. Lee had pitched well in Game 2 but hadn't worked in ten days because of three rain-outs.

As they had in five of the first six games, the Red Sox scored first. Gullett struck out the side in the third, but in between strikeouts he gave up a run-scoring single to Carl Yastrzemski and walked in two runs. Boston's 3–0 lead held through the fifth, but veteran Red Sox fans didn't have to look far for ominous signs. Boston had stranded nine runners in the first five innings, and the Reds were starting to make some noise, if only in their dugout. Pinch hitter Merv Rettenmund's reaction to grounding into a double play with one out and runners on first and third in the fifth got things going. "Most guys would go sit in the corner with their head hung low. Not Merv," said Pete Rose. "He got in the dugout and started cheerleading as loud as he could. It really picked us up. If he wanted to win that bad, that his personal failure didn't matter, then we wanted to win that bad."

With one out and Rose on first in the sixth, Johnny Bench hit what looked like a sure double play ball to shortstop Rick Burleson. But Rose's high, hard slide helped send second baseman Denny Doyle's relay throw into the Boston dugout. Then Tony Perez hopped on one of Lee's super-slow curveballs and deposited it on the Massachusetts Turnpike. Score: 3–2.

In the seventh, Lee left because of a blister on his pitching hand, and Rose tagged reliever Roger Moret with a game-tying single to center, his tenth hit of the Series. In the seventh and eighth, Reds relievers Jack Billingham and Clay Carroll set the Sox down without a whimper.

In the final inning of this amazing World Series —to no one's surprise—two rookies took the mound. Left-handed rookies. Boston's Jim Burton went first, with Red Sox fans braced for the worst. The Big Red Machine was rolling, and Fenway Park, wrote Roger Angell, "was like a waiting accident ward early on a Saturday night." Ken Griffey drew a leadoff walk, went to second on a sacrifice and to third on a ground out. Burton wisely walked Rose and got ahead of Joe Morgan on a ball and two strikes. The tall, skinny rookie then threw a great clutch pitch—a slider on the outside corner at the knees—but he threw it to the NL's Most Valuable Player, who got just enough of his bat on it to bloop a single in front of center fielder Fred Lynn. In Game 6 Lynn had crashed into the center field wall going back on a fly ball and, according to Reds manager Sparky Anderson, played deeper in Game 7. "He was a little shy of that fence. He didn't want to run into it again." Griffey, who had scored the tying run, now scored the go-ahead run.

In the bottom of the ninth, Reds rookie reliever Will McEnaney went for the quick kill. With two outs and none on, Yastrzemski came up as the

last hope of fans who could no longer afford to hope. Yaz swung for the seats but managed just a lazy fly ball to center, which Cesar Geronimo squeezed for the final out. A thousand miles away, Reds fans filled Fountain Square in Cincinnati for a wild celebration. In Boston, fans went home weary and disappointed, but defiant and proud. "They did not look bitter," Angell wrote, "and perhaps they felt, as I did, that no team in our time had more distinguished itself in the World Series than the Red Sox—no team, that is, but the Cincinnati Reds."

For the Reds, the game provided vindication. All season long they had lived with the pressure of being expected to win it all, and now they had chased the "can't lose" demon away for good. "Now we can say we're the best," Morgan said. "Before, we felt we were the best but couldn't say it because we hadn't won. Now, The Big Red Machine is the champion of the world." Rose may have been the happiest Red of all, and he expressed his joy in a manner all his own.

"I wish Opening Day was tomorrow," he said.

Reds second baseman Joe Morgan was denied a Series-winning hit by Dwight Evans' miraculous catch in Game 6, but he was undeterred, and in Game 7 his looping single in the ninth (above) gave the Reds a 4–3 lead. Reliever Will McEnaney slammed the door on the Red Sox with a 1-2-3 bottom of the ninth, then opened his arms wide for catcher Johnny Bench and the first post-Series hug.

Charlie O. and the A's

"Charles O. Finley is one of the most disreputable characters to ever enter the American sports scene. The loss of the A's is more than recompensed by the pleasure of getting rid of Mr. Finley. Oakland is the luckiest city since Hiroshima."

—Senator Stuart Symington
The Congressional Record, October 19, 1967

Billy Martin called him a liar. Bill Veeck said he was without class. Dick Williams said he treated employees like serfs. To Reggie Jackson he was "so cold-blooded he ought to make anti-freeze commercials." By most accounts, Charlie Finley was petty, slippery and tyrannical, yet his team was one of the few baseball dynasties of the 1970s and the last to win three straight world championships. "He has to be the biggest clown the game has ever known," concluded pitcher Denny McLain, who passed through Oakland near the end of his career. "But I am convinced it is Finley who keeps the A's together. The players have such a common bond in their collective hatred of the man that this hatred makes the A's an even better team when they cross the white lines."

Charles Finley made his fortune selling disability insurance to doctors, a business he dreamed up while recovering from tuberculosis in an Indiana sanitarium. Doctors, he reasoned, saw many people financially ruined by medical bills. They also had a lot to lose if they suffered the same fate. Physicians all over the country were swayed by his pitch, and their fear made Finley rich.

Finley wasted little time buying his way into big-league baseball, a fantasy he had had since washing out as a semipro player in the 1940s. In 1960 he picked up 52 percent of the Kansas City Athletics in an estate sale. Within a

Part huckster, innovator, sideshow barker and marketing whiz, A's owner Charlie O. Finley (opposite) was nothing if not colorful. And successful. Los Angeles Times *sportswriter Jim Murray called Finley "a self-made man who worships his creator."*

CHARLIE O. AND THE A'S **19**

In 1968 Finley moved the A's from Kansas City to Oakland and his promotional gusto exploded, leaving events such as Hot Pants Day (above) for baseball historians to ponder. Still, attendance was mediocre at best, totalling 837,466 that season.

few months he bought the rest. He swore to the people of Kansas City that The A's were in town to stay forever. Forever lasted seven years.

Charlie O. never met a manager he couldn't fire—his first, Joe Gordon, was gone in three months, and five more followed in six years. Admittedly, none of them made the Athletics winners. But managers were just props in Finley's stage show. Charlie O. intended to run the club, make all the trades, devise all the lineups. The A's were his toy, one he didn't intend to share.

In the name of promotion, no idea was too loony for Finley. The A's performed as miserably at the box office as they did on the field, pulling a dismal attendance of 636,000 in 1962. So like a circus barker without a center ring, Finley pushed the sideshow. He had folks milking cows and chasing greased pigs to warm up the crowd. He had caged monkeys beyond the fence in left, a sheep herd in right. He unveiled a mechanical rabbit named Harvey that popped up behind home plate and handed baseballs to the umpire. He hired Miss USA as bat girl. He offered discount tickets to every special interest group he could imagine—bald men one night, women in hot pants another. Finley's pièce de résistance was a mule he named Charlie O. The mule didn't talk, but he did give press conferences whenever the team arrived in a new town, with Finley speaking for the animal from a nearby platform.

Some of his gimmicks actually caught on—fireworks after home runs, scoreboards that flash messages to fans. Other notions—orange baseballs, multicolored bases, walks on three instead of four balls—were dismissed as the ravings of a heretic. Finley also had a fine appreciation for costume—he

Shortstop Bert Campaneris and pitcher Blue Moon Odom were among Finley's first key acquisitions with the Kansas City A's in the mid-1960s. Campaneris was an instant star, leading the AL in steals in each of his first four full seasons. Odom preferred the West Coast—he was 9–15 with Kansas City, 31–16 his first two years in Oakland.

clothed his club in outfits better suited to a bowling team with unusually bad taste. Uniforms came in a combination of "Kelly Green, Wedding Gown White, and California Gold." White shoes came later. The A's Norm Siebern was held out of the 1963 All-Star Game, reportedly because AL manager Ralph Houk thought his uniform would embarrass the rest of the team.

Baseball purists felt Finley was a graceless shill with no appreciation for baseball's understated charm, no patience for its unhurried rhythms. Yet for all his fast-buck buffoonery, Finley had savvy. Instead of filling his roster with used but recognizable players, he hired top scouts like Whitey Herzog and Hank Peters to find new stars.

By the early 1970s the A's were a team of ripening talent. At shortstop was Dagoberto "Bert" Campaneris, a swift, wiry, and occasionally ham-handed Cuban whom Finley had signed for $500. In left was Joe Rudi, a converted third baseman taught to catch fly balls by Joe DiMaggio, whom Finley hired as a special coach. At third and in center were two Arizona State teammates, Sal Bando and Rick Monday. Behind the plate was Dave Duncan, a Californian with a sturdy swing and an accurate arm. Among the pitchers were reliever Rollie Fingers and two prize recruits from the deep South, John Odom and Jim Hunter.

Odom, a flashy pitcher from Georgia with a 42–2 record and eight no-hitters in high school, had so excited Finley that he showed up at the teenager's home the night of his high school graduation and cooked a soul-food dinner for his family. Odom, who signed for $75,000, became known as "Blue Moon," so christened by Finley because he liked the sound of it.

Jim "Catfish" Hunter was a country boy with a tireless, precise arm, a willingness to act in Finley's pregame circuses, and another nickname coined

Third baseman and team captain Sal Bando steadied the volatile A's on and off the field. The clutch-hitting Bando averaged 22 homers and 93 RBI during the A's three world championship seasons and was one who led by example. "Sal always played in such a controlled fury, with so much heart, he just naturally evolved into the team leader," said pitcher Catfish Hunter.

The A's under Finley were full of free spirits —and free swingers. In 1968 outfielder Rick Monday struck out a whopping 143 times, second only on the team to Reggie Jackson, who led the AL with 171. But Monday managed just eight homers to Jackson's 29, and in 1971 he was traded to the Cubs for pitcher Ken Holtzman.

by Finley. But as precious as young pitchers with catchy names were for publicity, by 1969 Finley had something even better. He had Reggie. By early July, Reginald Martinez Jackson had 26 home runs and the first of many *Sports Illustrated* covers, prompting sportswriters to mention his name with the likes of Ruth and Maris. To say that Jackson liked the attention is like saying banks like cash. He thrived on it. So did Finley, who passed out "Reggie's Regiment" membership cards at the gate. Turned into instant contenders by the creation of two AL divisions that year, the A's surged into first place. But young Reggie was thrown off balance by the media whirlwind, and he spun into a cruel slump that helped pull the team out of the lead.

The A's were in Oakland by then, having abandoned Kansas City at the end of the 1967 season. Finley went into a promotional frenzy, reviving gimmicks from his KC days and adding new twists. For a team song he commissioned a country/western number titled "Charlie O., The Mule." It didn't catch on. He asked A's announcer Harry Caray to change his trademark "Holy cow!" for "Holy mule!" That didn't catch on, either. In fact, Oakland responded much as Kansas City had, which is to say, not at all. Catfish Hunter pitched a perfect game in that first Oakland season, while only 6,300 fans watched. The Coliseum was so hushed that the players called it "the Mausoleum." But the A's kept getting better. So did their sideshow.

Reggie and Charlie had their first big fight after Jackson's outstanding 1969 season. His 47 homers, Reggie figured, made him at least a $50,000 man. Finley offered $40,000 and didn't budge for three months, letting the high-strung slugger sit out spring training. Finally, just before the start of the

season, Finley raised his offer to $45,000. Too frustrated to hold out any longer, Jackson accepted, but his ill will festered through the 1970 season, eventually erupting into a very public feud.

That season Jackson played like a man dispossessed, tentative at the plate, confused and unfocused. He blamed Finley, who responded by benching Jackson against left-handers, telling the press that he might send his cover boy to the minors. Jackson, outraged, told the press that he wouldn't go. He didn't, but at one point late in the season he sat out 13 straight games before being sent up to pinch-hit against Kansas City. It was a classic setting —close game, bottom of the eighth, bases loaded, two out—and Reggie responded with a grand slam. He rounded the bases slowly, savoring each step, then as he crossed the plate, he raised a defiant fist toward the owner's box. Few in the Fan Appreciation Day crowd missed the meaning of the gesture, least of all the owner.

Finley demanded a written apology—he had prepared the document in advance. Reggie, in no mood to grovel, refused, but he soon realized that no one else—not manager John McNamara, not coach Charlie Lau, not even team captain Sal Bando—was going to come to his defense. Trapped and abandoned, Jackson broke into tears. Yes, he would sign, he sobbed. He never actually did, but his humiliation was good enough for Finley.

The A's finished at 89–73 in 1970, the best record yet for any Finley team, and again in second place behind the Twins. With its nucleus of Campaneris, Bando, Jackson, Rudi, Duncan, Hunter and Fingers, the team also had the promise of Vida Blue, a 21-year-old left-hander with a fastball that made major league hitters look inert. In September, in his fourth start of the season, Blue pitched a no-hitter against the division-leading Twins.

Like Sal Bando and Rick Monday, Reggie Jackson (above) played varsity baseball at Arizona State University. But Reggie was in a class by himself and, in 1969, at the tender age of 23, he exploded for 47 home runs and league highs of 123 runs scored and a .608 slugging percentage.

6' 165 lbs.
BR TR

b 4/18/1942

STEVE BLASS
Pitcher

Steve Blass's baseball nightmare began in 1973, his ninth season in the majors. For no apparent reason, his pinpoint control vanished. Forever.

Blass's descent into pitchers' hell was especially mysterious in light of his accomplishments. By 1968, his fourth year with the Pirates, he had a .750 won-lost percentage—the NL's best.

In 1971 Blass became a World Series hero. He tossed a three-hitter against Baltimore in Game 3 for Pittsburgh's first Series win, then clinched the championship by holding the Orioles to just one run for a 2–1 Pirate victory in Game 7.

The next season, 1972, Blass was an NL All-Star, with a career-high 19 victories for Pittsburgh. He pitched well in two playoff games against Cincinnati. But the next spring, he lost his ability to throw strikes. As the season progressed, so did his wildness. In a particularly awful outing against Atlanta, Blass surrendered seven runs, five hits, six walks, and threw three wild pitches—in 1⅓ innings! He closed the season at 3–9. His 9.85 ERA was the worst in the league.

Blass worked hard to regain control. He analyzed slow-motion films of his delivery. He consulted an optometrist, a hypnotist and, reportedly, a psychiatrist. He even tried transcendental meditation. Nothing helped.

Pitching for the AAA Charleston Charlies in 1974, Blass went 2–9, and his ERA approached double digits. The following spring, he retired.

The 1972 A's were a powerhouse, leading the AL with 134 homers to go with a sparkling 2.58 team ERA. But not even gimmicks like Moustache Day (above) could attract enough Bay Area fans. Attendance that year was under a million.

For 1971 Finley replaced McNamara with Dick Williams, the man who had engineered the "Impossible Dream" season for the Red Sox in 1967. Williams had a reputation as a disciplinarian who could—and would—spray a player's face with profanities. He was as smart as he was abrasive, a lineup tinkerer and a strategist of the Earl Weaver school, who kept detailed charts on players' performances in every conceivable situation.

The club stumbled through the first few weeks of the season, making Finley nervous. It was too early to fire the manager, which is what he usually did when he was nervous, so instead he jockeyed a big trade. He sent Don Mincher, a 27-homer man the year before, and long reliever Paul Linblad to the Washington Senators for first baseman Mike Epstein, a moody, but menacing hitter, and left-handed reliever Darold Knowles. It proved an inspired move. Epstein finished third on the team with 18 homers and Knowles became an ideal bullpen complement to right-hander Rollie Fingers.

But no matter how well anyone else played, the 1971 season was Vida Blue's. He struck out 301 batters, walked only 88, and his 1.82 ERA and eight shutouts led the league. The media shadowed him in packs all year, and Finley did little to protect his star from the press—Blue was a promotional godsend. Williams was ordered to reshuffle his starting rotation to insure that seven of Blue's last nine starts would be at home. Sadly, Blue won only two of the seven, and attendance still fell short of a million. Charlie O. threw a tantrum and canceled the traditional Fan Appreciation Day. Later, feeling contrite if no more appreciative, he rescheduled it.

Blue was a weary man come September, but he finished at 24–8 and the team clinched its first division title. The A's, however, had the bad luck of facing the Baltimore Orioles in the playoffs, a team that not only had a quartet

of 20-game winners—Dave McNally, Pat Dobson, Mike Cuellar and Jim Palmer—but also had won its last 11 games. Not even Vida Blue could slow the Orioles' surge. Oakland was swept in three games.

Still, the 1971 A's collected 101 victories, more than any of their championship teams of the next three years. And while the spotlight never left Blue, other A's quietly wound up among the league leaders. Catfish Hunter, winning nine of his last ten starts, recorded his first 20-win season. Jackson had 32 homers; Bando, 94 RBI; Campaneris, 34 stolen bases; Fingers, 17 saves. It was a template for the coming years.

The team was being transformed. For one thing, it became much hairier. A few players came to 1972 spring training wearing moustaches, and where others saw just facial hair, Charlie O. saw publicity. He offered $300 to any player who would grow a moustache by Father's Day. What better way to finish off the team's renegade look? "For $300, I would grow hair on my feet," said pitcher Ken Holtzman. By June 18, decreed Moustache Day by Finley, everyone on the team had enough lip hair to qualify for the award, although Blue shaved his off immediately after the pregame ceremony.

That season it seemed as if every healthy adult male in America would have a chance to play for the A's: 47 players wore the white shoes. Some, like Holtzman, who won 19 games, and Matty Alou, who lined key hits all over the field during the team's stretch drive, proved invaluable. Others were passing fancies. Former 30-game-winner-turned-heavyweight Denny McLain won one game and lasted a month; aging Orlando Cepeda lasted three at-bats.

Finley tampered with the team in other ways. Baseball needed more specialists, he insisted, so he created the many-headed second baseman. In midseason, Finley ordered pinch hitters for the team's weak-batting second

The Oakland A's dugout was a consistently lively place with a constantly changing cast in the early 1970s. First baseman Mike Epstein (above, left) and catcher Dave Duncan (standing on top step) combined for 45 home runs as the A's won it all in 1972, but both were gone by 1973.

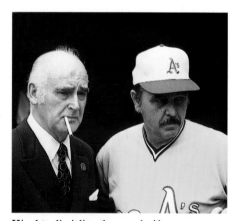

Hired to discipline the unruly A's, manager Dick Williams (above, right) was the right man for the job. The problem was, he couldn't control owner Charlie Finley (above, left). Williams resigned in 1973 after the A's second straight world title.

JIM HUNTER
PITCHER A's

Catfish Hunter

It's May 8, 1968. A cool breeze blows across the well-manicured fields of the Oakland Coliseum, home of Charles O. Finley's Athletics. James Augustus "Catfish" Hunter, the strong-armed 22-year-old farm boy out of Hertford, North Carolina, is on the mound for the A's, pitching the game of his life. His fastball and slider are dead on, and the Minnesota Twins can't touch him.

Again and again the Twins' potent lineup, including Rod Carew, Harmon Killebrew and Tony Oliva, goes down in order. The refrain of "three up and three down," echoes from the announcers' booth at the end of each inning. By the seventh-inning stretch, it's clear to the 6,289 fans in the stadium that they're witnessing something special. What they don't know yet is that they're witnessing one of baseball's rarest feats—the perfect game.

At the top of the ninth, John Roseboro steps into the batter's box. He grounds out. Pinch hitter Bruce Look goes down on strikes, Hunter's tenth strikeout victim of the night. With only one out between Hunter and the record books, the Twins send in Rich Reese, the American League's best left-handed pinch hitter. Reese fouls off a fastball for his first strike. The next two fastballs miss the plate. Reese swings and misses the next pitch. Then Hunter misses with a slider. Three and two. The fans are on their feet. Hunter's wife, Helen, watching from the stands, breaks down in tears. Reese fouls off the next pitch. Then another. After two more fouls, Reese swings at a fastball and misses. The A's win, 4–0, and Catfish gets his perfect game.

With 107 pitches, Hunter became the 11th man in major league history, and the first American Leaguer since 1922, to pitch a perfect game. While many would consider a perfect game the highlight of a career, Hunter said he was prouder of his five 20-win seasons. "There's a lot of luck in pitching a no-hitter," he explained. "When you win 20 games in a season everyone remembers that. They think you are a pitcher then."

From 1971 through 1975 Hunter posted seasons of 21–11, 21–7, 21–5, 25–12 and 23–14. He won the Cy Young Award in 1974 and was the fourth pitcher in history to win 200 games by the age of 31. He was also a good-hitting pitcher. In 1971, he became the last pitcher to win over 20 games and hit over .300 in the same season.

While his sturdy right arm brought him fame, Hunter's keen business sense brought him fortune. In 1974, after Finley reneged on a payment clause in Hunter's contract, the hurler sued Finley—and won. As baseball's first free agent, he was permitted to offer his services to the highest bidder. By the time the dust cleared—22 of the game's 24 teams made offers—Hunter had traded his garish green, white and gold A's uniform for the sedate pinstripes of the New York Yankees. In addition to the new threads, Hunter received $100,000 a year for 20 years plus bonuses, insurance annuities, legal fees, college endowments for his children and a new car every year for five years—a package worth about $3.75 million.

In his first season as a Yankee, Hunter had a league-leading 23 wins with a 2.58 ERA. Then he faltered, and while his team soared to three World Series, Hunter posted the worst marks of his career and retired after the 1979 season. Despite his poor finish, Hunter holds a lifetime record of 224–166 with a 3.26 ERA. In 1987 he was elected to the Hall of Fame.

CATFISH HUNTER

Right-Handed Pitcher
Kansas City Athletics 1965–1967
Oakland Athletics 1968–1974
New York Yankees 1975–1979
Hall of Fame 1987

GAMES		500
INNINGS		
Career		3,448⅓
Season High		328
WINS		
Career		224
Season High		25
LOSSES		
Career		166
Season High		17
WINNING PERCENTAGE		
Career		.574
Season High		.808
ERA		
Career		3.26
Season Low		2.04
GAMES STARTED		
Career		476
Season High		41
COMPLETE GAMES		
Career		181
Season High		30
SHUTOUTS		
Career		42
Season High		7
STRIKEOUTS		
Career		2,012
Season High		196
WALKS		
Career		954
Season High		85
NO-HITTERS (perfect game)		1968
WORLD SERIES		1972–1974, 1976–1978
CY YOUNG AWARD		1974

Amid the white-hot pressure of the deciding fifth game of the 1972 AL Championship Series against Detroit, A's manager Dick Williams (above, center, with Sal Bando, left, and catcher Gene Tenace, right) went to starter-turned-bullpen-ace Vida Blue in relief of Blue Moon Odom (behind Williams). Blue blanked the Tigers for the final four innings of a 2–1 A's win, the third one-run game of the Series.

basemen every time they came up with men on base. In one game, six different A's played second base, and some of their double play attempts suggested water buffalo ballet.

But as much as Finley meddled like some Little Leaguer's father, as much chaos as he created with his slapdash mentality, the A's kept winning. In spite of Finley's arrogance, Williams' surliness, and constant needling by Bando and Hunter on the team bus, the A's developed a kind of jagged edge that kept them dangerous. When a late-season slump dropped them behind the surprising White Sox, the A's regrouped as if Charlie O. himself had forbidden it. A's pitchers gave up only six runs in five straight September victories. In the last home game of the season, they fell behind the Twins, 7–0, rallied to tie the score, and in the bottom of the ninth, aging utility infielder Dal Maxvill—who had never hit much in his "pre-aging" days—knocked home the winning run with a double for the A's second straight division flag.

Appropriately, the playoffs began with one locker room fight—between Jackson and Epstein over free tickets—and ended with another, between Odom and Blue. In between the A's took on the Detroit Tigers, another team with a reputation for brawling, largely because of bantamweight manager Billy Martin. Bert Campaneris was hit by a pitch and responded by trying to pick off Tigers pitcher Lerrin LaGrow with his bat. Fortunately, LaGrow moved faster than the flying club, but Campaneris was suspended. Jackson tore a hamstring stealing home on a double steal. But the A's won in five tight, draining games, the decisive one pitched by the tandem of Odom and Blue. Odom pitched the first five innings but was so nervous he started gagging in the dugout. Blue finished up, holding the

Tigers to two harmless hits. They congratulated each other in typical A's fashion—a shoving match in the locker room after Blue made a "choke" sign with his hands.

Despite a league-leading 134 homers and a rotation of Hunter (21–7), Holtzman (19–11) and Odom (15–6), the A's went into their first World Series in 40 years a clear underdog to the faster, more famous, and certainly better-groomed Cincinnati Reds. The A's, with all their rowdiness, made Reds manager Sparky Anderson uneasy. "The Tigers are more predictable," he said. "Gee whiz, you don't know what these A's are going to do."

The A's went beyond unpredictable. A balding, 26-year-old catcher, Gene Tenace was not even a regular Oakland starter until August. He had managed only a .225 average and five homers during the season, went 1 for 17 in the playoffs, and made a crucial error as one of Finley's second basemen-of-the-moment. But for a week in October, he played the baseball of his dreams. In the opener against Gary Nolan, he hit home runs in his first two Series at-bats—something no one had done before—and drove in all three Oakland runs for the win. He hit another homer and scored a ninth-inning winning run in Game 4. In Game 5 Tenace reached the seats a fourth time, suddenly sharing space in the record books with Babe Ruth, Lou Gehrig, Duke Snider and Hank Bauer. But the Reds, down 3–1, rallied to tie it up in the eighth, then Pete Rose knocked in the winning run in the ninth. Cincinnati strolled to a third win in Game 6, but all that did was give Tenace another chance. In the first inning of Game 7, he bounced a bad-hop single off a seam in the artificial surface to knock in a run. In the sixth, he drove in another with a double into the corner for a nine-RBI Series; no one else on his team had more than one.

During the 1972 World Series against Cincinnati, A's catcher Gene Tenace hit almost as many home runs as he did the entire regular season. Tenace hit five regular-season homers, then hit four more in the Series and became the only player in history to homer in his first two Series at-bats. Both came off Reds starter Gary Nolan—a two-run shot (above) in the second and a solo shot in the fifth.

Oakland Coliseum

pening Day at the Oakland Alameda County Coliseum was pure Charlie Finley. It was April 17, 1968, and the pregame festivities were, well, festive. Charlie O., the A's mule mascot, arrived in his luxury van complete with a police escort and then paced around the diamond, stopping to bow at each base. Miss California was escorted to home plate by A's Rick Monday and Sal Bando. For the national anthem, the stadium went completely dark, except for a lone spotlight on the flag in center field, and fireworks accompanied "rockets' red glare, the bombs bursting in air." California's governor, Ronald Reagan, threw out the first ball, and the circus that was A's baseball in Oakland began.

Catfish Hunter got pounded by four Oriole homers in a 4–1 loss that day, but he knew that the Coliseum would be friendly to pitchers. There's little wind, so the ball just doesn't carry well there, especially at night, and the ballpark has the roomiest foul territory in baseball. "My job was getting hitters out," Hunter said, "and for that, the Oakland Alameda County Coliseum provided the perfect place to play." Perfect was the word less than a month later, when Hunter pitched a perfect game against Minnesota on May 8.

The Coliseum was a pitcher's paradise in the 1970s, when four no-hitters were thrown there. Oakland's Vida Blue no-hit Minnesota by himself on September 21, 1970, and combined with Glenn Abbott, Paul Linblad and Rollie Fingers to no-hit California on September 28, 1975. The A's were on the short end of the other two, including one in 1976 at the hands of Chicago's Blue Moon Odom, who had been a member of all three Oakland world championship teams from 1972 through 1974.

Whether it was the 1970s mini-dynasty, the Billy Martin teams in the early 1980s, or the powerhouse clubs of the late 1980s, baseball success in Oakland has always started and ended with good pitching, and the Coliseum is one reason why. The A's have always been an outstanding home team, and through 1989 had won 55.9 percent of their home games, compared with 46.7 percent on the road. In all three world championship seasons, the A's surrendered the fewest runs at home of any team in baseball.

The stadium itself is something of a lush green oasis surrounded by urban decay. The city of Oakland suffers in comparison to its across-the-bay cousin, San Francisco, but the Coliseum has it all over Candlestick Park. The stadium is part of a 120-acre entertainment complex that includes an enclosed arena and an exhibit hall. The field is symmetrical, and the huge foul area places fans far from the diamond, but the Coliseum offers other amenities, including three huge scoreboards beyond the outfield bleachers.

The A's have had their ups and downs since moving to Oakland in 1968, and attendance at the Coliseum has followed suit. A's fans were slow to react to Finley's great teams of the early 1970s, topping the million mark in just one of the three world championship seasons, 1973. Winners of 101 games in 1971, the A's hit the skids in 1979 with 108 losses and a total gate of just 306,763, including a season-low 653 on April 17. Manager Billy Martin brought excitement, victory and fans back to the Coliseum in 1981, and in 1989 the A's won their first world title since 1974. They did it with a typical Coliseum team —good speed, great pitching, and a solid dose of power.

Symmetrical and once described as a "concrete pillbox," the Oakland Coliseum has provided a relatively undistinguished backdrop for some of the game's most colorful characters, including Charlie Finley, Reggie Jackson, Catfish Hunter and Billy Martin.

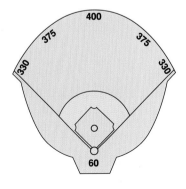

Oakland Alameda County Coliseum

San Leandro Boulevard and
  66th Avenue
Oakland, California

Built 1966

Oakland A's, AL
1968-present

Seating Capacity
48,219

Style
Multipurpose, symmetrical,
  grass surface

Height of Outfield Fences
8 feet

Dugouts
Home: 3rd base
Visitors: 1st base

Bullpens
Foul Territory
Home: 3rd base
Visitors: 1st base

400
375   375
330   330
60

The Reds were ready and waiting for A's base-stealing wizard Bert Campaneris in the 1972 World Series. A peg from Johnny Bench to Joe Morgan (right) erased Campaneris in the third inning of Game 1. The Reds stole 12 bases to Oakland's one, but this was Campy's only attempted steal in the Series.

Outfielder George Hendrick (25) hit just .133 in the 1972 World Series but scored three runs, and twice was the first run of the game for the A's. In Game 2 (above) he beat Pete Rose's throw home, scoring on a single by Catfish Hunter in a 2–1 A's win.

When Rose flied out to end the game with the tying run on base, Fingers had his second Series save, Catfish Hunter his second win, the A's the Series and Charlie Finley the last laugh. Finally, he was on top of the world that for so long had considered him its jester. That off-season, in an event no one in baseball could have visualized a few years earlier, *The Sporting News* named him its Man of the Year. In his hour of vindication, Finley turned soft, shelling out $1,500 per player for championship rings—a figure he announced with characteristic humility at a press conference—and promised even finer jewelry next year if the A's repeated.

It didn't matter that his team had won the championship. With Williams around as manager for another year, Finley needed to change something. Catcher Ray Fosse was bought from the Tigers, and old-timer Deron Johnson from the Phillies in the new role of designated hitter, a concept Finley had been pushing for years. From the Cubs came a young, flashy center fielder named Billy North, a part-time player with a .181 average in 1972. But he had speed. And he had an attitude. In May North came to bat against Kansas City reliever Doug Bird. What no one in the stands or on either bench knew was that three years earlier, in the minors, Bird had beaned North with a pitch. Facing him for the first time since, North swung at a pitch and let his bat go. Walking out to retrieve it, he stopped suddenly at the mound and decked Bird with a punch. The A's liked him.

With North's running—he stole 53 bases—and a team batting average up 20 points to .260, the 1973 A's were now a more balanced club. Their pitching, led by Hunter (21–5), Holtzman (21–13) and Blue (20–9), was as overpowering as ever. But still they struggled. At one point Jackson crit-

icized the coaches for criticizing the players, for which he was then criticized by manager Williams. Reggie responded in customary A's style. "Never talk to me again," he told Williams. "Just write my name in the lineup."

Williams had little choice because Jackson was in the middle of an MVP year—32 homers, 99 runs, 117 RBI and a .293 average. In August Jackson and Blue sparked a nine-game winning streak that carried the A's into first place for sure. Helping out were some players Finley had picked up in his annual stretch-drive shopping spree: outfielders Jesus Alou and Vic Davalillo and infielder Mike Andrews, who had played for Williams in Boston.

The A's outlasted the Orioles in the playoffs, and went on to meet the New York Mets. The Mets had Tom Seaver and reliever Tug "You Gotta Believe" McGraw, but at 82–79, they also had the worst won-loss record of any team in World Series history. For the A's, roles had been dramatically reversed: they were not just the favorites; they were—perish the thought—the establishment.

The A's won a sloppy Game 1 on two unearned runs, 2–1. But that only served to prepare observers for the gruesomeness of Game 2. New York's Willie Mays, then 42, twice fell down chasing fly balls; the A's made five errors; the teams stranded a total of 27 runners. By the end of nine, they had bungled their way to a 6–6 tie, which lasted until the 12th. Then Mays bounced his last major league hit through the middle to give the Mets a one-run lead, and the fun began. After another single, two Mets hit grounders right at second baseman Mike Andrews; the first rolled through his legs, the second he threw away. That led to three more runs and a Mets' victory.

Immediately after the game, the raging Finley ordered Andrews examined by the team doctor. Andrews felt no pain, but he quickly learned what

All hell broke loose for the A's in Game 2 of the 1973 World Series against the upstart Mets, and even steady third baseman Sal Bando played a part in the fiasco. Bando couldn't handle a bases-loaded roller in the sixth (above), allowing Cleon Jones to score the first of four Mets runs that inning. The A's committed five errors in a 10–7, 12-inning loss, but they recovered to win the Series in seven games.

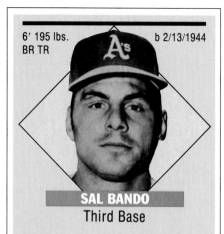

6' 195 lbs.   b 2/13/1944
BR TR

SAL BANDO
Third Base

In 1969, his second full season in the majors, 25-year-old Sal Bando was named captain of the Oakland A's by manager Hank Bauer. A few months later, Bauer was gone, a victim of owner Charlie Finley's revolving-door policy for managers. But Bando stayed on to captain the A's through their glory years, in which they won five AL West titles and three World Series.

Bando provided stability to a team that frequently tottered on the brink of chaos. There had been clubhouse brawls, an owner who publicly berated his players, and a dizzying succession of six managers in eight years. Through it all, Bando was the on-field leader and the off-field arbiter.

A three-time All-Star third baseman, Bando also had power at the plate. He averaged 90 RBI per season from 1971 to 1975 and, in 1973, his 32 doubles led the league. Bando single-handedly provided the muscle to beat Baltimore in the 1974 playoffs. He scored the first run in Game 2, the A's first win of the playoffs. In Game 3, a pitchers' duel between Jim Palmer and Vida Blue, Bando's homer was the game's only run. And in the fourth and final game, he scored both of Oakland's runs in a 2–1 victory.

In 1977 Bando signed as a free agent with Milwaukee. With an average of 82 walks in his 12 full seasons, he tied an AL record with five walks in a game on May 29, 1977. His last season, 1981, was the first for his brother Chris, a catcher with the Indians.

That they'd done it the year before didn't seem to dampen the A's enthusiasm for their second straight world championship in 1973. Oakland reliever Darold Knowles retired the Mets' Wayne Garrett to clinch the Series, and then got mobbed.

Finley was up to. After a brief physical, Andrews was summoned to the manager's office. Finley was waiting with a typed statement, signed by the doctor Andrews had just left, stating that, because of a chronic shoulder injury, Andrews would be disabled the remainder of the Series. That would allow Finley to call up Manny Trillo, who was a better fielder. The wily Finley was firing Andrews for the sin of bad hands. Andrews, a relative newcomer to the weird, wicked ways of the A's, was dumbfounded. At first he refused to sign the paper, then after a second browbeating in Finley's office, he caved in.

Even longtime Finleyologists were stunned by the pettiness of this ploy. Some of the team mumbled about going on strike in the middle of the Series. "It's the bushest thing I've ever seen," announced Sal Bando. But the most damning reaction was a private one by Dick Williams. Just before the start of Game 3, he told the team he would bend no more under the boss' heavy hand; win or lose, said Williams, he was resigning after the Series.

This was a curious way to inspire a team, but ultimately, it had that effect. After the initial shock—they barely won Game 3, then lost the next two—the A's, united against their owner, found their edge. They beat Seaver in Game 6 to even the Series. In the finale, they exploded for four runs in the third on two-run homers by Campaneris and Jackson, while Fingers and Knowles preserved the lead. Not since the 1961–1962 Yankees had a team repeated as champion. Shortly after Game 6, Williams announced that he was quitting. Several hours later, while out celebrating with teammates at a local restaurant, Jackson and Odom got into a fight.

And what of Andrews? He was reinstated with the A's for Game 4 by Commissioner Kuhn, who had quickly smelled out Finley's scam. In New

Alvin Dark (left) was the epitome of a journeyman—both as ballplayer and manager. He was traded six times as a player, then fired three times as a manager—once by Charlie Finley—before rejoining the A's in Oakland and leading them to their third straight world championship.

Though Reggie Jackson claimed to be the "bread and butter" of the A's, Charlie Finley (above, center) was the hub around which the team revolved. And what a team—clockwise, from top left, Rollie Fingers, Joe Rudi, Vida Blue, Gene Tenace, Bert Campaneris, Catfish Hunter, Sal Bando and Reggie Jackson.

York that night, in what turned out to be his last major league at-bat, Andrews grounded out as a pinch hitter. As he trotted back to the dugout, he received the only standing ovation of his career.

Always a dangerous man with a grudge, Finley struck swiftly to take revenge against his rebellious players. Based on his promise of the year before, they expected championship rings dense with diamonds; instead he gave them synthetic emeralds. "Trash rings," complained Reggie. "The new rings are horsemeat," added Catfish Hunter. The 1974 A's were off and running.

Finley's new man in the dugout was Alvin Dark, a retread of sorts who had lasted a year and a half as an A's manager back in Kansas City. Quieter and less combative than Williams, he was a deeply religious man quick to quote scripture, one thing that had been missing from the Oakland clubhouse repartee. His restraint seemed to make him an easy touch for Finley's machinations, and when Dark began yanking starting pitchers early, players suspected that he was doing the owner's work. "I knew Alvin Dark was a religious man," griped Vida Blue, "but he's worshipping the wrong god—Charles O. Finley." A few weeks later, Bando, annoyed at some managerial gaffe, stalked into the clubhouse and declared, "He couldn't manage a meat market." Dark, unfortunately, was standing right behind him.

Even with their doubts about their manager, even with their recurrent locker room slugfests—the best of 1974 was a North vs. Jackson two-rounder—the A's claimed first place in late May and stayed there. They had evolved into the best team in baseball, a fact often lost in the tales of follies and feuds. Oakland had the speed—a league-leading 164 stolen bases—to

The A's: Armed and Ready

From 1972 through 1974, Oakland demonstrated how far a team can go with a few big bats and a strong, well-balanced pitching staff. In each of their three world championship years, the A's had three solid starters and a bullpen with at least one right-handed and one left-handed reliever, which enabled them to get big outs late in a game no matter who was at bat. The constants were Catfish Hunter, Ken Holtzman and Rollie Fingers as the A's produced team ERAs of 2.58 in 1972, 3.29 in 1973 and 2.95 in 1974.

Starters

	Player	Won-Lost	Innings Pitched	Strikeouts	ERA
1972	C. Hunter	21-7	295	191	2.04
	K. Holtzman	19-11	265	134	2.50
	B. Odom	15-6	194	86	2.51
1973	K. Holtzman	21-13	297	157	2.97
	V. Blue	20-9	264	158	3.28
	C. Hunter	21-5	256	124	3.34
1974	C. Hunter	**25**-12	318	143	**2.49**
	V. Blue	17-15	282	174	3.26
	K. Holtzman	19-17	255	117	3.07

Relievers

	Player	Won-Lost	Saves	Appearances	ERA
1972	R. Fingers	11-9	21	65	2.51
	B. Locker	6-1	10	56	2.65
	D. Knowles	5-1	11	54	1.36
1973	R. Fingers	7-8	22	62	1.92
	D. Knowles	6-8	9	52	3.09
	H. Pina	6-3	8	47	2.76
1974	R. Fingers	9-5	18	**76**	2.65
	P. Lindblad	4-4	6	45	2.05

Boldface indicates league leader.

win one-run games. They had the power to come from behind—Jackson, Tenace, Rudi and Bando all had at least 20 homers. They had the fielding to bail their pitchers out of bad innings—Rudi was a model of defense in left, as were Dick Green at second and Ray Fosse behind the plate. And they had the pitching—a league-leading 2.95 ERA—to stave off long losing streaks. Vida Blue, after all, was merely the third starter. But slowly, with little notice, a crack was forming in the foundation. Finley read the fine print in Catfish Hunter's contract a little differently than Hunter and his lawyer did, but Charlie O. figured it was a problem that could wait until after the World Series. So did Catfish.

After losing the first playoff game, the A's made short work of the Orioles, allowing a total of one run in the last three games. They then turned to the Los Angeles Dodgers—a club that was young, clean-cut, almost reverent, a team that seemed like a walking Wheaties commercial next to the woolly A's. After winning three out of four against the Pittsburgh Pirates in the playoffs, the Dodgers dared to be cocky; outfielder Bill Buckner suggested that some of Oakland's big names couldn't make his team's starting lineup. Buckner, of course, had no way of knowing that the day before Game 1, Blue Moon Odom had started teasing Rollie Fingers about his marital problems, and that Fingers took a swing at Odom, and that Odom pushed Fingers into a locker, and that Fingers needed five stitches in his head. From that point on, the Dodgers were doomed.

It was a West Coast whirlwind. In Los Angeles, the A's were at their opportunistic best, using Dodger errors, timely hitting, and one stunning play after another by Dick Green at second to win Game 1. Los Angeles managed to win the second game, 3–2, on a two-run homer by catcher Joe Fergu-

The A's weren't particularly frightening at the plate in 1974, but they still had a solid starting rotation and the game's best relief pitcher—Rollie Fingers. Of the four one-run games in the World Series against the Dodgers, Fingers won one and saved three.

son. The A's swept the final three at Oakland. Fingers—with one win, three saves and five stitches—was the Series' MVP. Finally, no one dared not to take the A's seriously. They were the third team in history to win three straight World Series and the first that wasn't the Yankees.

Little more than a month later, the dynasty began to crumble. Hunter won his arbitration case, freeing him from his contract. Bidding for Hunter reached staggering levels, and for the first time other A's had an idea of what the market thought they were worth. Although Hunter's case was unique, they thought they finally had some leverage in negotiating with Finley. Not so, said Finley: Hunter was an aberration. He intended to treat his team the way he always had, meaning he would continue to fight for every penny.

A year later, baseball's reserve clause was overturned and Charlie Finley's world began to come undone. His team had done better than expected in 1975, winning its division for the fifth consecutive time, before being swept by the Red Sox in the playoffs. But past glories had little hold on the Oakland players; free agency gave them an opportunity to escape Finley and to make big money at the same time. No one was surprised when almost all of the A's starters chose to play out their options in 1976, meaning that they could sell their services to any team after the season. It also meant that Finley would get nothing in return. To cut his losses, Finley traded Reggie Jackson and Ken Holtzman to the Orioles for outfielder Don Baylor and pitchers Mike Torrez and Paul Mitchell. Trying to build up a cash reserve, he sold Vida Blue to the Yankees for $1.5 million and Joe Rudi and Rollie Fingers to the Red Sox for $1 million each. Commissioner Kuhn, how-

Free agency made it too expensive to hold on to great talent, and so it signalled the demise of Charlie Finley's dynasty. By 1979 the A's lay in ruins. Oakland lost 108 games that season and was so pathetic that on April 17, only 653 fans could bear to watch (above).

Catfish Hunter, now a rich, young New York Yankee, got together with former A's teammates Reggie Jackson (left), Paul Linblad and Joe Rudi (far right) after beating Oakland for the second time in five days during August of 1975. "I tried to show Mr. Finley I could still pitch," he said.

ever, overturned the sales, saying they were "inconsistent with the best interests of baseball" and would devastate the A's and upset the league's competitive balance.

But the dominoes had already toppled. After the 1976 season, Rudi and Fingers were free agents, as were Bando, Campaneris, Tenace and Baylor. Even Charlie O. the mule died that off-season, victim of a liver ailment; the players joked that he drank himself to death. On Opening Day, 1977, Billy North was the only regular left from the starting lineup of a year earlier. The rest of the team was a collection of eager rookies and worn veterans. As such teams often do, it plunged to last place.

As his team became more inept and attendance more pathetic, Finley worked out his final deal. On August 23, 1980, came the announcement that Finley had sold the team to officers of Levi Strauss & Co. for $12.7 million. "During the time we were winning championships," he said, "survival was a battle of wits. It is no longer a battle of wits, but how much you can have on the hip. I can no longer compete." After 20 years, three championships, and too many pratfalls to remember, the Charlie O. Show had closed. ◑

Fireworks were in order after the A's beat the Dodgers, 3–2, in Game 5 of the 1974 World Series (opposite). The win made the A's the first non-Yankee team ever to win three straight world championships.

Vida Blue

n 1971 Vida Blue, the high-kicking, hard-throwing Oakland Athletics pitcher, could do no wrong. The 22-year-old thrilled fans and terrorized batters—his fastball was clocked at 95 mph—as he racked up a 24–8 season with a 1.82 ERA. Brimming with energy and enthusiasm, he ran everywhere—to the mound, from the mound, to the plate, and when he struck out, he even ran back to the dugout. When pitching he barely slowed down, pausing just long enough to get the catcher's signal before throwing. Usually, he threw fastballs. Usually, they were strikes.

Blue arrived at the 1971 All-Star game with a 17–3 record. The Reds' Johnny Bench, preparing to face Blue for the first time, said, "They tell me that he can throw a ball so fast he can put it through a car wash without even getting the ball wet."

Blue's skill and magnetism captivated all who saw him. Oakland's attendance shot up whenever he started a game. On the road, his appearances doubled gate receipts. In New York a record crowd turned out to celebrate "Blue Tuesday," a night game in which even the scorecards were printed in blue. A's owner Charlie O. Finley jumped on the promotional bandwagon and presented his superstar with a flashy wardrobe and a baby-blue Cadillac equipped with the license plates "BLUE."

Blue popped up on the covers of *Time* and *Sports Illustrated,* traded quips with Bob Hope on national television, and made small talk with President Richard Nixon at the White House. The media had a field day with baseball's hottest new prospect, and it surprised no one when Blue won both the Cy Young and the AL's Most Valuable Player awards in 1971. He was the fifth pitcher, and the youngest ever, to win both awards in the same year. Vida Blue was baseball's fastest-rising star.

But Blue's star fell almost as quickly as it had risen. Dissatisfied with his $14,750 salary, he sat out training camp and the start of the 1972 season. Although he finally signed for $63,000, vicious negotiations with Finley had scarred him. "Charlie Finley has soured my stomach for baseball," said Blue. "He treated me like a damn colored boy." Oakland fans watched in dismay as their falling star struggled through a 6–10 season.

Although Blue came back to win 20 games in 1973 and 22 in 1975, much of the old Blue magic was gone. Both his fastball and his image had been damaged by the constant bickering with Finley. In 1978 Blue was traded to the San Francisco Giants for seven players and $390,000. His fortune improved; he went 18–10, the best won-lost record on the Giants' staff, with a 2.79 ERA. But in the next three years, he averaged just 12 wins a season and was traded to Kansas City.

By 1983 the superstar had sunk to a miserable 0–5 record and was released by Kansas City while under investigation for drug use. Blue and three other Royals were arrested for possession of cocaine, and on January 1, 1984, Blue began serving a 90-day sentence at the Fort Worth Federal Correctional Institute. He went through a drug treatment program and returned to San Francisco for the 1985 and 1986 seasons, where he pitched his last major league game.

In September 1989, Blue returned to the mound at Candlestick Park for his wedding. Orlando Cepeda and Willie McCovey stood with the bride and groom.

At 22, Vida Blue won 24 games and became a nationwide phenomenon. "It's a weird scene," he said. "You win a few baseball games and all of a sudden you're surrounded by reporters asking things about Vietnam and race relations and stuff about yourself. I'm only a kid."

VIDA BLUE

Left-Handed Pitcher
Oakland Athletics 1969–1977
San Francisco Giants 1978–1981,
 1985–1986
Kansas City Royals 1982–1983

GAMES	**502**
INNINGS	
Career	3,344
Season High	312
WINS	
Career	209
Season High	24
LOSSES	
Career	161
Season High	19
WINNING PERCENTAGE	
Career	.565
Season High	.750
ERA	
Career	3.26
Season Low	1.82
GAMES STARTED	
Career	473
Season High	40
COMPLETE GAMES	
Career	143
Season High	24
SHUTOUTS	
Career	37
Season High	8
STRIKEOUTS	
Career	2,175
Season High	301
WALKS	
Career	1,185
Season High	111
NO-HITTERS	**1970**
WORLD SERIES	**1972–1974**
CY YOUNG AWARD	**1971**
MOST VALUABLE PLAYER	**1971**

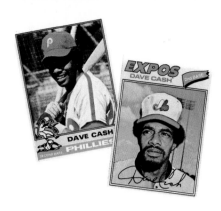

Big Money

*" . . . the Club shall have the right by written notice to the Player to
renew this contract for the period of one year on the same terms . . . "*

During the 1970 season, ten major league ballplayers earned
more than $100,000—exalted players like Henry Aaron,
Frank Robinson, Carl Yastrzemski, Roberto Clemente, Bob
Gibson and Willie Mays. They played with an artistry that
others could only imitate. They were the mythic figures at
the heart of baseball and the fans did not begrudge them their big money.
But not everyone agreed. As their stars' salaries spiraled upward, some
owners figured, so would everyone else's—next, utility infielders would
expect $50,000 a year. August "Gussie" Busch, patriarch of the St. Louis
Cardinals, snarled about "greedy players." In 1970, after wrangling
over money with pitcher Steve Carlton, Busch moaned, "I can't understand
it. The player contracts are at their best, the pension plan is the finest and
the fringe benefits are better than ever. Yet the players think the owners
are a bunch of asses." Cubs general manager John Holland complained,
"we have reached the saturation point. If our payroll goes any higher, we
just can't make it."

By the end of the decade, the *average* major league player's salary was
$121,000, Houston's Nolan Ryan was making $1 million a year, and utility
infielders were buying stock options. The Cubs, somehow, were still around.

In the interim, baseball's dirty little secret—money—became public.
Baseball had always been a business disguised as a boys' game, but in the
1970s the mask of innocence fell away. The change was initiated by one man

*Players who became free agents in the late 1970s often suffered under the pressure of
million-dollar contracts, but not the irrepressible Luis Tiant. He was 13–8 in 1978 with
Boston, signed a lucrative contract with the Yankees (opposite), and was 13–8 in 1979.*

Detroit great Ty Cobb would have felt right at home in the labor turbulence of baseball in the 1970s. Cobb (above, with Commissioner Kenesaw Mountain Landis) refused to report to training camp in 1913 when his salary demands—an increase from $9,000 to $15,000—were denied by Tigers owner Frank Navin. Navin suspended him, but when the suspension led Congress to start investigating baseball's antitrust exemption, an $11,332.55 compromise was quickly reached.

and the vague wording of a single clause in a contract. In keeping with the spirit of the times, it all came down to a technicality.

The first shot in the money wars came from Curt Flood, an agile, consistent center fielder who helped make the St. Louis Cardinals a dominant team in the late 1960s. He had batted over .300 for six seasons and, in the Cards' championship year of 1968, *Sports Illustrated* proclaimed him "Baseball's Best Center Fielder." But after a mediocre season in 1969, Flood went to the Philadelphia Phillies in a seven-man deal that brought slugger Richie Allen to the Cardinals. At first, Flood was upset most with the way the news had been delivered—a call from an underling in the office of Cardinal general manager Bing Devine and a notice that read: "Dear Mr. Flood: You have been Sold/Traded/Released/Optioned." The "traded" box was checked off.

Flood had two choices: he could go along with the trade or he could quit baseball. He didn't like either one. Moving from St. Louis would undoubtedly hurt the thriving photo studio he had established there. Retirement made even less sense. At 32, he may have been beyond his peak, but he knew he was still among baseball's top outfielders. Besides, with a salary of $90,000 in 1969, he finally was making good money.

If Flood had been an accountant or a lawyer or a plumber, he could have tried to land a job with another firm. But in baseball's standard contract, a string of legalese known as the "reserve clause" prevented him from shopping his services to other teams. Dating back to the 1880s, the reserve clause was created to keep players from team hopping. If one owner with deep pockets could lure away all the best talent, the reasoning went, the entire league would fall apart. That became accepted wisdom, a gospel so sacred that to challenge it was to challenge baseball itself. Through two world

St. Louis center fielder Curt Flood (far left) had a true legal heavyweight—former Supreme Court Justice Arthur Goldberg—go to bat for him in his case against baseball's reserve clause, which tied a player to one team until it decided to cut him loose. Flood lost the case and sacrificed his career, but his actions hastened the onset of free agency and million-dollar contracts for players.

On August 19, 1968, Sports Illustrated proclaimed St. Louis' Curt Flood "Baseball's Best Center Fielder." By 1971 Flood's playing career was over. He remains a hero of baseball's labor movement, though he never benefitted from the salaries his court challenge helped create.

wars, and in spite of militant unionism and Supreme Court scrutiny, the reserve clause endured. Curt Flood didn't buy it. He saw it as a way for owners to keep a lid on salaries and "to play God over other peoples' lives."

Marvin Miller warned Flood. Miller, the savvy labor negotiator and executive director of the Players' Association since 1966, knew that any player who challenged the reserve clause in court was begging to be blacklisted. Forget about being the major league's first black manager, Miller told Flood. Forget about being a coach or even a scout. Be prepared for a legal battle that could last years and cost hundreds of thousands of dollars. Be prepared to lose $200,000 or more in salary. For a week, Flood wrestled with the possible consequences; then he made up his mind: he was going to take on professional baseball.

Initially, other players figured it was just a ploy to get more money or to finagle a big out-of-court settlement. But after Flood appeared before the Players' Association's executive board and swore "I can't be bought," the Association—a union in all but name—agreed to help pay his legal fees. Miller persuaded former Supreme Court Justice Arthur Goldberg to represent Flood.

On Christmas Eve, 1969, Flood sent a letter to baseball commissioner Bowie Kuhn pointing out that he wasn't a piece of property to be traded like livestock and requesting that the commissioner let other major league teams know he was available. Kuhn agreed that Flood wasn't property but said he didn't see how that was relevant. As expected, he refused Flood's request. So Flood filed his suit. Kuhn and the owners, nervous about what might happen, offered a last-minute deal: Kuhn gave Flood his blessing to work out a

For 13 days in April, 1972, Fenway Park and all other major league stadiums lay empty as baseball's first players' strike put the game on hold.

contract with any National League team. But Flood knew that if he did, his case would lose its teeth. The holdout went on.

The trial started in late May in a New York City courtroom, where witnesses from Commissioner Kuhn to former player and TV funnyman Joe Garagiola insisted that without the reserve clause, baseball was ruined. Flood's case, presented by Goldberg, argued that the clause was unconstitutional and violated antitrust laws, despite past Supreme Court decisions that allowed baseball to operate as a monopoly. Times had changed, Goldberg argued, pointing out that professional sports like football and boxing did just fine without antitrust exemptions. Former stars Jackie Robinson and Hank Greenberg testified in Flood's behalf, but no active players even showed up at the trial. It was too risky.

In August Flood lost the first round. The Association expected as much, and Goldberg immediately filed an appeal. Flood still had a case. What he didn't have was money. But after the 1970 season, Washington Senators owner Robert Short acquired rights to Flood's contract and offered him $110,000 for a year no matter what happened. After being assured that he wouldn't weaken his case, Flood signed. "Heck, I'm a baseball player," he said. "I don't know anything else."

But something had been lost during Flood's year of rebellion. His reflexes had softened, his rhythm had gone ragged. After only 13 games in the 1971 season, the sham ended. Curt Flood could no longer play in the major leagues. In trying to save his career, he had lost it. More bad news came in April, when the appeals court upheld the decision. Now only the U.S. Supreme Court could vindicate him, but on June 18, 1972, the Court voted 5–3 to keep the reserve clause intact. It hardly provided a ringing endorsement,

In veteran union negotiator Marvin Miller, the players finally had a serious weapon with which to battle the owners on any number of issues—pensions, insurance and salaries. Players like Tom Seaver and Rusty Staub (second and third to Miller's right, respectively) at last felt their collective power and put it to work.

however. Baseball's exemption from antitrust laws was an "aberration," conceded Justice Harry Blackmun in his assenting opinion, but the Court was not offended enough to do anything about it. That dirty bit of business, they suggested, was a job for Congress.

Flood's gambit had failed; baseball had not been forced out of its safe harbor. But the tide was shifting. Not only had the Supreme Court reminded the owners that they were on shaky legal ground, but public opinion had also turned against them. One poll showed eight opponents of the reserve clause for every supporter. In the end, Curt Flood, the man, had not won the fans' hearts, but his cause had. A year later, the owners conceded that any veteran of ten major league seasons who had spent at least five years with his current club had the right to veto any proposed trade. It became known as the "Curt Flood rule."

Curt Flood's private war with baseball had another effect, one that dramatically rearranged the balance of wealth and power: it served as a rallying point for players. By the time of the Supreme Court decision, the Players' Association had become a unified and increasingly militant group that had already staged its first general strike.

The strike began on April Fools' Day, 1972, a date *The Sporting News* called "the darkest day in sports history." For 13 days America was treated to the sight of baseball players walking in circles with strike signs. The sports world had gone mad. At least that's the way the media played the story. Dick Young, a caustic columnist for the *New York Daily News,* spat venom at union leader Marvin Miller: "He has a steel-trap mind wrapped in a butter-melting voice," wrote Young. "He runs the players through a high-pressure spray the

Roberto Clemente

Roberto Clemente, who played his entire 18-year career with the Pittsburgh Pirates, was originally signed by the Brooklyn Dodgers in 1954 and sent to their Montreal farm club to work on his hitting. He hit only .257 that season, but a Pirate scout watched him throw and remembered his remarkable throwing arm at draft time. Left on the Dodgers' unprotected list, Clemente was snatched up by Pittsburgh for $4,000.

Clemente attributed his powerful arm to the boyhood sports he had played in his native Puerto Rico. Clemente, the youngest of seven children born to a sugarcane cutter, participated in neighborhood baseball games and javelin competitions. "It made my muscles strong," he said, "and I also learned to be accurate."

In 1955 the Pirates put Clemente in right field, where he became one of the best fielders ever, winning 12 Gold Gloves and leading NL outfielders in assists a record five times. Noted one writer, "Fans will never forget his basket catches, his ballet leaps, his shoestring plays."

Clemente once crashed headlong into the Astrodome outfield fence to snatch a potential game-winning line drive from Houston's Bob Watson. He bloodied a knee, bruised an elbow and an ankle—but held on to the ball. "When Clemente was out in right field," Pirate pitcher Steve Blass explained, "there was nothing more a pitcher could want. . . . With him it was like having four outfielders."

The graceful fielder was also a power at the plate. For 13 seasons, he hit over .300. He had a .317 lifetime average, won NL batting titles in 1961, 1964, 1965 and 1967, and was named MVP in 1966. And he came through when it mattered most.

Clemente played in two World Series: in 1960 and in 1971. Both Series ran seven games, and he had at least one hit in every game. For his two homers and .414 average in the 1971 Series, Clemente was named Series MVP. The following year, in the last game of the season, he racked up his 3,000th hit: a double off New York's Jon Matlack.

Clemente's speed on the basepath complemented his success at the plate. In nine seasons he hit ten or more triples, with a personal best of 14 in 1965 and a league-leading 12 in 1969.

After the 1972 season, Clemente volunteered to help deliver food, clothing and medical supplies to earthquake victims in Nicaragua. He flew to Puerto Rico, and on December 31 boarded a DC-7 laden with supplies. The plane took off, but within minutes developed engine trouble and fell into the ocean. Clemente, the Pittsburgh right fielder who many claimed was the best player of his era, was dead. Some called it "the day baseball died."

His death was front-page news throughout the Americas. Shocked by the loss of the island's folk hero, Puerto Rico canceled its gubernatorial inaugural ceremonies. President Richard Nixon, a keen Clemente fan, sent a personal check for $1,000 to a memorial fund. The Pirates donated $100,000. Thousands of businesses and fans chipped in to the fund, which was established both to aid Nicaragua's earthquake victims and to set up baseball clinics in Puerto Rico.

As a special tribute to his greatness, the National Baseball Hall of Fame Committee waived its five-year admittance requirement and voted Roberto Walker Clemente into Cooperstown just 11 weeks after his funeral. He was the first Latin American admitted into the Hall of Fame.

Roberto Clemente playing baseball—whether at the plate or in right field—is one of the game's most graceful and indelible images. "He was the most complete ballplayer I ever saw," said former Dodger general manager Al Campanis.

ROBERTO CLEMENTE

Outfield
Pittsburgh Pirates 1955–1972
Hall of Fame 1973

GAMES	**2,433**
AT-BATS	**9,454**
BATTING AVERAGE	
Career	**.317**
Season High	**.357**
SLUGGING AVERAGE	
Career	**.475**
Season High	**.559**
BATTING TITLES	**1961, 1964,**
	1965, 1967
HITS	
Career	**3,000**
Season High	**211**
DOUBLES	
Career	**440**
Season High	**40**
TRIPLES	
Career	**166**
Season High	**14**
HOME RUNS	
Career	**240**
Season High	**29**
TOTAL BASES	**4,492**
EXTRA-BASE HITS	**846**
RUNS BATTED IN	
Career	**1,305**
Season High	**119**
RUNS	
Career	**1,416**
Season High	**105**
WORLD SERIES	**1960, 1971**
MOST VALUABLE PLAYER	**1966**

6' 190 lbs.   b 1/5/1951
BR TL

DON GULLETT
Pitcher

In 1976 it looked as if 25-year-old Don Gullett was one of the best free agent deals of the decade. He had a dynamite fastball, a forkball and a slider. In seven years with Cincinnati, he had posted a 91–44 record. Reds manager Sparky Anderson predicted, "He's going to be a Hall of Famer."

But Gullett had one crucial weakness: a susceptibility to injuries. He accumulated them almost as steadily as victories. In 1974 he suffered chronic back spasms. In 1975 he broke a thumb. And in 1976 he developed chronic shoulder soreness, a pinched nerve in his neck, and a dislocated ankle tendon.

In spite of this litany of ills, the Yankees signed free agent Gullett to a six-year, $2.1 million contract in November 1976. Yankee president Gabe Paul touted Gullett as "the next Whitey Ford." But the Yankees never recouped their investment.

Gullett went 14–4 for the Yankees in 1977. But in July 1978 his chronic shoulder pain worsened. He was placed on the disabled list and underwent rotator cuff surgery that September. For the next two years, Gullett struggled to return to form. His shoulder and arm, however, were damaged beyond repair.

Yet when the Yankees released Gullett on October 24, 1980, his record stood at 109–50. Among pitchers with 100 or more decisions in the 1970s, Gullett's .686 winning percentage remains the best.

Opening Day 1972 arrived, but stadiums across the country stayed silent and empty because of the 13-day players' strike. Especially disappointed were fans of the newly created Texas Rangers (above), who had to wait until April 15 for Opening Day.

way an auto goes through a car wash, and that's how they come out— brainwashed. With few exceptions, they follow him blindly, like zombies."

During spring training that year, Miller accused the owners of bad-faith bargaining on increased pension benefits. It was a relatively minor conflict, but both players and owners were spoiling for a fight. Under Miller's shrewd direction, the PA had begun to chip away at the owners' baronial rule. Besides a minimum salary of $15,000, the players had won the right to take non-salary disputes to outside arbitrators and to use agents in salary negotiations. Owners grumbled that the whole thing was starting to get out of hand. It was time to get tough.

So, what began as a fight about pensions quickly escalated into one about power. Soon, between shagging flies and perfecting pickoff moves, players were casting strike votes. By mid-March, the vote to call a strike was 349–0 and growing. Dissenters spoke up, among them Carl Yastrzemski, who said he could go for a one-day boycott but thought a strike had no place in baseball. "You'd think we've been working in a factory these past five or six years," he declared. But 663 players disagreed. That many major league players ultimately voted for a strike, while ten opposed it and two abstained.

The owners held their own war council, working themselves into a labor-baiting frenzy. Gene Autry, the singing cowboy-turned-team owner, reminded his brethren that unions had turned Hollywood into a ghost town, and Gussie Busch let it be known that owners were not going to take it anymore: "We voted unanimously to take a stand. We're not going to give them another God damn cent. If they want to strike—let 'em."

The player reps took Busch at his word. A few days later, after an intense six-hour meeting at which even apple-pie players like Johnny Bench

swore allegiance to the union, the Players' Association Executive Board voted 47–0 for a strike, with one abstention. The holdout was Dodger first baseman Wes Parker, who gave the owners a small moral victory when he suggested that unions were ruining the country. "I love baseball and I love the Dodgers," he said. "It's an image, a pedestal I've put baseball on. This strike takes some of the magic away."

Many fans assumed that things would be worked out before the traditional opener in Cincinnati on April 5. Those hopes faded when the owners refused to take the issue to arbitration. "We don't want an outside party running our business," declared Red Sox general manager Dick O'Connell. Predictably, Miller charged the owners were trying to break the union. Predictably, the owners countercharged that Miller was power-mad and the players were greedy. Before long, President Richard Nixon entered the fray—after all, this was baseball. He asked that both sides meet with a federal mediator. That meeting led to a compromise on the pension issue and by April 13, the fighting was over. Play resumed two days later.

By then, however, the season had lost 86 games. After some squabbling, the owners decided not to make them up, a decision that gave Red Sox fans yet another reason to curse their wretched fate: the Sox ended up playing one game less than Detroit and ended the season half a game behind. Overall, the strike cost the owners roughly $200,000 per team in lost ticket sales and TV revenue. It cost each player about five percent of his salary.

In 1973 the Association drained even more power from the owners, negotiating the right to take salary disputes to outside arbitration. That meant the owners would no longer have final say in setting players' salaries. The arbitrator would select either the player's final demand or the owner's

In 1972, under the leadership of Players' Association representative Marvin Miller, the players united against the owners, and made short-term sacrifices for long-term gains. The strike was on, and teams like the Baltimore Orioles (above) lined up for expense money from their union to tide them over during the layoff.

After a 3–6 record in 12 starts in 1975, pitcher Dave McNally called it quits, and even though in December he won his battle to be declared a free agent, he opted to stay retired. "I've been proud of the things I've accomplished in baseball," said McNally, a four-time 20-game winner with the Orioles. "I didn't want to drag them down."

Andy Messersmith played for the Dodgers without a contract in 1975, then in December was declared a free agent by an arbitrator in a decision that marked the formal opening of baseball's era of free agency. Braves owner Ted Turner bid highest for Messersmith—$1 million over three years, almost twice as much as the Dodgers' final offer.

last best offer—the difference could not be split. This resulted in some bizarre proceedings, such as Oakland A's owner Charlie Finley explaining in great detail to an arbitrator the ineptness of his star third baseman and team captain Sal Bando. And Finley won his case. In 1974, 29 players took salary complaints to arbitration. Only 13 won their cases, but that was enough to make owners realize that unless they wanted arbitrators setting their payrolls, they would have to keep salaries rising. It was only the beginning.

Marvin Miller liked a challenge and there remained one last, imposing hurdle: the reserve clause. The Supreme Court had failed to kill it, and Congress would probably study it for years before doing anything to change it. Maybe, just maybe, thought Miller, he could lawyer it to death. He went looking for a loophole in the standard player contract, and he found one in a section that read: "If . . . the Player and the Club have not agreed upon terms of such contract . . . the Club shall have the right . . . to renew the contract for the period of one year on the same terms."

This had always been interpreted to mean that the team could renew the contract for that year, and then the next year, and then the next year, in perpetuity. But Miller contended that it meant exactly one year—after that, a player should be free to negotiate with any team he wanted. To test his premise, he needed someone to play a year without a contract, declare himself a free agent and, when his team objected, file a grievance to force arbitration. In 1975 two players qualified: Andy Messersmith and Dave McNally.

Messersmith, a tall, curly-haired right-hander, had paced the NL champion Dodgers in 1974 with a 20–6 record and a 2.59 ERA. In 1975, playing without a contract, he was almost as effective with 19 wins and a 2.29

Twenty-two teams drafted pitcher Catfish Hunter (left, wearing Yankee cap) when he was declared a free agent in 1974, and his contract offers included such incentives as insurance annuities and a partnership in five new Wal-Mart stores.

Ferguson Jenkins won 20 or more games seven times from 1967 through 1974, all but once with the Cubs. In 1974, his first year with Texas, he set team records that still stand, with 25 wins, 29 complete games, 328 innings pitched and six shutouts. He became a free agent in 1981 and finished his career with the Cubs.

ERA. He was a legitimate star who, in a free market, could probably name his price. Not so with Dave McNally. A linchpin of the overpowering Orioles starting rotation of the late 1960s, he won at least 20 games in four straight years, 1968 through 1971. In 1974 he won 16 games for the Orioles, but Baltimore nonetheless traded him to the Montreal Expos. Because the trade was without his consent, McNally refused the deal and initially intended to sit out the 1975 season. He then decided to start with the Expos without a contract. In midseason, with a 3–6 record and a sore shoulder, he retired from baseball. His grievance, however, stayed active.

Miller had his men, and he joined them in arbitration. For his part, Messersmith claimed he was neither martyr nor mercenary. "I didn't do this for myself, because I'm making a lot of money," he explained. "I did it for the guys sitting on the bench who couldn't crack our lineup, but could make it elsewhere. These guys should have an opportunity to go to another club."

The owners, aware of the potential menace, took evasive action. They first argued that an arbitration panel had no business hearing the Messersmith and McNally grievances and asked a court to block the hearings. Neither tactic worked and, in November, 1975, a three-man arbitration panel took the fate of the once-omnipotent reserve clause in its hands. The panel included Marvin Miller, the players' man; John Gaherin, the owners' representative; and Peter Seitz, a 70-year-old lawyer and professional arbitrator. Seitz, the swing vote, made the owners nervous, because the year before he had ruled in Catfish Hunter's favor in a contract dispute with Oakland A's owner Charlie Finley, allowing Hunter to become a free agent.

Desperate to protect what they called "the backbone of baseball," the owners dusted off all their old arguments. Get rid of the reserve clause, they

Kiss and Tell

Jim Bouton didn't mean to cause so much trouble. At least that's what he told everyone later. All he meant to do, he swore, was to tell people what a major league player's life was really like. But the world was not ready for that—at least the baseball world wasn't—and when Bouton's *Ball Four* came out in 1970, fans of America's pastime went into shock. With its stories of sexual escapades and late-night carousing by heroes as sacred as Mickey Mantle, the book became baseball's *Fanny Hill,* vilified by the sport's establishment as profane and distasteful. Members of the San Diego Padres burned a copy of it in their clubhouse. Bouton himself was scorned as baseball's Judas, a "social leper" unfit to even be invited to play in an old-timers' game.

Only six years earlier, Bouton had been hailed as one of baseball's star pitchers. A right-hander who threw so hard his hat often fell off during his delivery, Bouton won 21 games for the Yankees in 1963 and 18 the following year, plus two more in the 1964 World Series. But his arm went bad in 1965, and he spent the rest of the decade trying to prop up his career by throwing knuckleballs. The Yankees finally unloaded him to the expansion Seattle Pilots in 1969. In spring training that year Bouton began keeping a diary.

The idea was to write a book in collaboration with sportswriter Leonard Shecter. Bouton told readers things that rarely showed up on the sports pages—insights on the pressures, frustrations, and complex personal lives of men worshipped one year and abandoned the next. The press played up the juicier stories about players' voyeuristic escapades, peeping into hotel windows, and about Mantle shutting a bus window on kids' hands as they waited for his autograph. Commissioner Bowie Kuhn enthusiastically denounced the book. The public enthusiastically bought it. More than 200,000 hard-cover copies were sold, the most ever for a sports book.

The controversy made Bouton a bigger celebrity than his pitching ever had. After finishing the 1970 season with the Astros, he became a sportscaster in New York, then starred in a television series based on his book. Baseball's powers took some consolation in the series' dismal failure. By then, though, baseball players were media stars, and every publishing house wanted its own play-and-kiss-and-tell book. Throughout the decade, books about players with adventurous off-the-field lives rolled off the presses, beginning with Bill Freehan's relatively tame *Behind the Mask* to autobiographies by uninhibited spirits like Joe Pepitone, Denny McLain and Bo Belinsky to Sparky Lyle's *The Bronx Zoo,* a diary of the Yankee's wild 1978 season. None of them came close to matching the popularity of *Ball Four.* Nor did any of them permanently sully baseball's reputation. If anything, they helped make fans less naive about players' less-than-heroic behavior.

For his part, Bouton followed up *Ball Four* with *I'm Glad You Didn't Take It Personally,* which stirred up far less agitation and far fewer sales. He drew more attention when he persuaded Braves owner Ted Turner to let him try a comeback. Working his way through the minors, Bouton made it back to the majors in 1978. Opposing players ridiculed his slow pitches and said they were humiliated when he got them out, but he did win one of the five games he pitched that year. After the season, he returned to television. Baseball, he said, had become boring.

A glitzy 91–44 lifetime record made Don Gullett one of the free agent market's hottest properties after the 1976 season, and he signed an equally glitzy contract with the Yankees—$2 million over six years. He pitched two years with New York, upping his lifetime mark to 109–50.

Free agency made salaries explode, but also turned players into profit-and-loss statements. One who hit the black immediately was reliever Bill Campbell (above), who won 13 games and led the AL with 31 saves in his first year of a lucrative contract with the Red Sox in 1977.

warned, and the top players would sell themselves each year to the top bidder, guaranteeing a championship for the owner with the biggest bankroll. "If he (Messersmith) wins his case, baseball is dead," insisted Dodgers manager Walter Alston. At the very least, testified NL president Charles "Chub" Feeney, competitive bidding could kill the World Series. This was wild speculation, countered Marvin Miller, pointing out that the reserve clause had not done such a good job of insuring competitive balance: in three-quarters of a century, 60 percent of the pennants had been won by only four teams, the Yankees far in the lead.

On December 23, 1975, Seitz recast baseball. Siding with the union, he made Andy Messersmith a free agent. The owners appealed Seitz's decision in federal court. They lost. Then, in the middle of negotiating new rules to control free agency, they locked the players out of spring training. With the help of a public relations firm, the owners convinced most of the media and the public that their action was only a precaution against a threatened strike. But Commissioner Kuhn knew he was facing another tainted season and, in a rare show of moxie, ordered the camps re-opened on March 17.

It was the middle of July before the owners and players finally reached an agreement on what should be done about free agency: First, a player could become a free agent only after six years in the major leagues. Second, a re-entry draft would be held every November to decide which teams could negotiate with a free agent: a maximum of 12 teams—13 beginning in 1977—could draft one player. Third, following a championship season, a player with five years in the majors could demand a trade, and if he wasn't traded by the next spring, he could become a free agent. It seemed so cut-and-dry. In truth, the owners were horrified at what it all meant. But

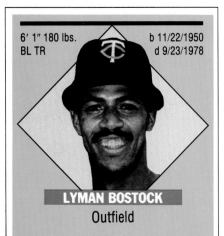

6′ 1″ 180 lbs.
BL TR
b 11/22/1950
d 9/23/1978

LYMAN BOSTOCK
Outfield

He was a perpetual-motion machine. Lyman Bostock Jr., a hard-hitting outfielder with the Minnesota Twins, earned the nickname "Abdul Jibber Jabber" for his exuberant displays of energy. The Birmingham, Alabama, native, son of former Negro league great Lyman Bostock Sr., signed with the Twins in 1975 and promptly made his presence known by hitting .282 in his rookie year. He followed with season averages of .323 and .336 in 1976 and 1977.

Bostock, understandably dissatisfied with his $20,000 Twins paycheck, signed a five-year, $2.25 million contract with the California Angels as a free agent in late 1977. After going only 2 for 39 his first month with the Angels, Bostock felt so ashamed that he offered to return his first month's salary to the team. When the Angels management refused his offer, he gave the money to charity. The gesture seemed to do the trick, and Bostock returned to form, hitting about .320 for the rest of the season as he labored to get his average for the year over .300.

He never reached his goal. Two weeks before the end of the season, while Bostock was visiting friends and relatives in Gary, Indiana, he was shot to death. The gunman was apparently attempting to kill his estranged wife, who was in the car with her sister, Bostock and Bostock's uncle. Cruelly cut down in his prime, the 27-year-old had played just four years in the big leagues and had earned a lifetime batting average of .311.

The day before Thanksgiving, 1976, infielder Bobby Grich (above, right) looked pretty thankful as Angels owner Gene Autry gave him a uniform and a five-year, $1.75 million contract. In June Grich broke his hand, and the Angels finished fifth.

there was no turning back. Free agency was officially part of baseball; it was in the rules.

Andy Messersmith was ready to cash in on his freedom. He knew the outrageous offers that had been thrown at Catfish Hunter the year before and waited for the bids to come rolling in. And he waited. For two weeks after the owners lost their last appeal, Messersmith's phone was curiously silent. His agent, Herb Osmond, smelled collusion. What Osmond didn't know until months later was that Dodger owner Walter O'Malley had let the other owners know that he would not be signing any free agents from other teams, the unspoken message being that they shouldn't try to sign his—Messersmith.

But the lure of a 20-game winner is powerful, and two teams—the Chicago White Sox and the California Angels—could not control themselves. They went after Messersmith, checkbooks in hand. Six other teams joined the chase. Messersmith ended up signing a "lifetime contract" with the Atlanta Braves. Actually, it was a three-year package for $1 million, a $400,000 signing bonus, and a no-trade clause. "Andy Messersmith will be with the Braves as long as I am," vowed the team's owner, Ted Turner, "until death or old age do us part."

It was a brief life together. Messersmith was no better than a .500 pitcher for the Braves that year, winning only 11 games. In 1977 he established a tradition followed by many free agents who came after him: he suffered a career-ending injury. In 1978 he was sold to the Yankees, for whom he didn't win a game, and then closed out his career back with the Dodgers, for whom he won two games as an occasional starter.

But in 1976 Messersmith symbolized the new age of million-dollar contracts. Anxious to follow him into the promised land, 62 players still hadn't

Twins owner Calvin Griffith was fast becoming a dinosaur in the late 1970s, as his hard line against high salaries and free agents doomed his team to mediocrity. Losing the likes of Rod Carew, Larry Hisle, Lyman Bostock and Bill Campbell, the Twins went on a slide that hit bottom in 1982 when they lost 102 games.

signed contracts with their teams by May 15. "I'll soon be an overpaid athlete," conceded Reggie Jackson. "I'll probably get a million more than I should, but I didn't make the rules. I'm just taking advantage of them." Jackson, at that point, was passing the time with the Orioles, the result of a preseason trade. Knowing that he would lose both Jackson and Ken Holtzman at the end of the season and get nothing in return, A's owner Charlie Finley had traded both to cut his losses. The Twins did the same thing in June, trading unsigned pitching ace Bert Blyleven to the Rangers for four players.

By the time of the first re-entry draft in November, 24 free agents remained and the owners had broken down into two groups: those willing to spend small fortunes and those who watched. Former movie star and Angels owner Gene Autry topped the first group by shelling out a total of $4.9 million for Joe Rudi from the A's at $418,000 a year, Bobby Grich from the Orioles at $350,000, and Don Baylor from the A's at $170,000. Yankee owner George Steinbrenner kept pace by paying $3 million—roughly $680,000 a year—for Jackson and $2 million, or $330,000 a year, for former Reds pitcher Don Gullett. Spending with almost as much vigor was hamburger czar and Padres owner Ray Kroc, who paid $3.42 million for Oakland escapees Gene Tenace, $363,000 a year, and Rollie Fingers, $266,000 a year.

The first player actually signed that fall was Bill Campbell, a relatively unknown reliever who had won 17 games and saved 20 for the Twins in 1976, earning $22,000. Red Sox general manager Dick O'Connell gave him a four-year contract worth $1 million, prompting one baseball executive to crack, "They ought to shoot Dick O'Connell." More stunning was the deal Cleveland made with Wayne Garland, a 20-game winner for the Orioles the year before. He was offered a ten-year, $2.3 million contract. When told of

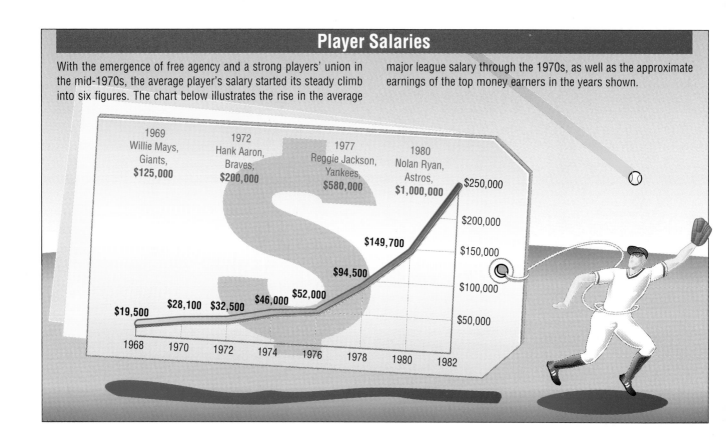

Player Salaries

With the emergence of free agency and a strong players' union in the mid-1970s, the average player's salary started its steady climb into six figures. The chart below illustrates the rise in the average major league salary through the 1970s, as well as the approximate earnings of the top money earners in the years shown.

1969
Willie Mays,
Giants,
$125,000

1972
Hank Aaron,
Braves,
$200,000

1977
Reggie Jackson,
Yankees,
$580,000

1980
Nolan Ryan,
Astros,
$1,000,000

$250,000

$200,000

$149,700

$150,000

$94,500

$100,000

$52,000

$50,000

$46,000

$19,500 $28,100 $32,500

1968 1970 1972 1974 1976 1978 1980 1982

the terms, Garland responded, "You gotta be kidding. Quick, gimme a pen before they change their mind." Indians general manager Phil Seghi explained his generosity with the comment, "We could not afford not to sign him."

That twisted logic dumbfounded owners who couldn't handle the stakes. "These million dollar salaries could easily price us out of the market," moaned Kansas City Royals owner Ewing Kauffman. "Reasonable entitlement to a good wage is one thing; greed is another." Twins owner Calvin Griffith was more succinct: "Sports today are sick. If I'm going to stay in business, I need a rich partner." Even before the draft, Reds owner Bob Howsam announced that he would not go after any free agents, in deference to his current players. Then again, his team was the reigning world champion, so he wasn't exactly short of talent.

Though they were tactful enough not to express it publicly, the have-nots must have felt some glee the following season when few of the new millionaires paid dividends. No one got less for his money than the Angels' Autry, who, after signing Rudi, Grich and Baylor, sat back and waited for glory. Rudi started like a dynasty maker, knocking in 27 runs in April, but in late June he broke his wrist and ended the season with only 53 RBI and a .264 average. Grich was even less productive. He hurt his back in early June and batted only 181 times all season. His paltry numbers: seven homers, 23 RBI and a .243 average. Baylor at least stayed healthy; he was simply an underachiever. He did hit 25 homers and drive in 75 runs, but he batted only .251.

Elsewhere, other free agents fizzled. Wayne Garland proved that his shock at how much the Indians were willing to pay him was not false modesty. He won 13 games but lost 19, then developed a sore arm that kept him from winning more than six games in any of his four remaining seasons with the

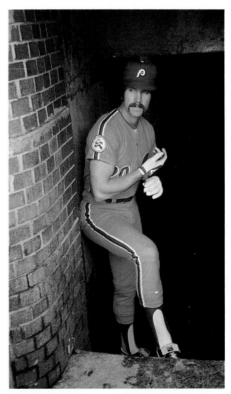

One player whose performance suffered under big money pressure was California's Don Baylor (left). Baylor struggled early in his first season with the Angels, saying "I think I've been trying too hard because of the money. The best thing would be for me to forget about the contract, but it can't be done."

Phillie third baseman Mike Schmidt was an eight-time NL home run champ, including three straight from 1974—1976. But in the age of free agency, a more impressive feat may have been staying with the same club for his entire 18-year career.

Tribe. Gene Tenace hit 15 homers for the Padres, but his average fell to .233 and went even lower the following year. Bill Campbell seemed a savior his first year in Boston, winning 13 games and saving 31, but he developed arm trouble and quickly dropped out of the Red Sox' plans. The same was true of Don Gullett, who went 14–4 with the Yankees in 1977. His arm went bad, and he lasted one more season. Rollie Fingers proved to be a prize—he saved 35 games—but he was not a miracle worker—the Padres finished next-to-last, losing four more games than they had the year before. The only player who truly lived up to his paycheck was Reggie Jackson. His bat and his mouth helped make the Yankees a championship team and a first-rate sideshow.

If middling performances by most of the new millionaires made owners skittish about the second free agent draft, they didn't want anyone to know. Once again, money flowed like cheap beer and some players found themselves making ten times as much as they had the year before. Larry Hisle, a rising star with the Twins, saw his salary leap from $47,200 to $525,833 when he moved to the Milwaukee Brewers. He responded with 34 homers and 115 RBI, until he was injured and never again came close. Another Twin, Lyman Bostock, went from $20,000 to $450,000 when he switched to the Angels. Before the season ended, however, he was murdered, an innocent party in a messy lovers' quarrel. Others handed staggering increases included Rich "Goose" Gossage—from $46,800 with the Pirates to $458,000 with the Yankees, Richie Zisk—from $54,000 with the White Sox to $295,000 with the Rangers, and Rawley Eastwick—from $23,200 with the Reds and the Cardinals to $220,000 with the Yankees.

The wild-salary spiral continued. In 1978 Dave Parker of the Pirates became the first $900,000-a-year player. Soon thereafter, Nolan Ryan

The Cubs paid $1.375 million over five years to get Dave Kingman's booming bat to make Wrigley Field its home. And in order to encourage his crowd-pleasing power, they inserted an attendance incentive clause in his contract. Kingman was to receive an extra $50,000 each season the Cubs drew at least 1.6 million fans. Kingman collected the bonus just once in three years.

In the era of free agency, one good season—at the end of a player's contract—could mean financial independence. Outfielder Oscar Gamble (above) hit .297 with 31 homers for the White Sox in 1977, then signed a six-year, $2.85 million contract with San Diego. In 1978 Gamble's average dipped to .275, his homers to seven, and in 1979 he was dealt to Texas.

Money was foremost on players' minds during the 1972 strike, but Atlanta pitcher Ron Schueler and shortstop Marty Perez (opposite) also kept their minds on baseball, working out in Atlanta's Fulton County Stadium during the strike.

crossed the $1 million barrier. The owners' worst nightmare had come true. Their other great fear, or at least the one they always fretted about—that free agency would destroy competitive balance—proved unfounded. A case could be made that George Steinbrenner bought back-to-back championships in 1977 and 1978 with his purchases of Jackson, Gullett and Gossage. But the Yanks were unseated in the American League the next year by the Orioles, a team known for modest salaries and strong farm teams. Nor did star players necessarily bounce from team to team in search of the perfect contract. Many, such as Mike Schmidt, George Brett and Steve Garvey, stayed with their teams, although at much higher salaries.

Maybe the most profound effect of free agency was on the fans. It took a while for them to adjust to the idea that grown men blowing bubbles and giving each other high fives were getting paid half a million dollars. And invariably, any time a runner was picked off first, half the people in the stadium screamed, "We pay him $400,000 for that?" The players became less endearing, more deserving of scorn or envy. Everything about the game seemed more jaded.

Yet the people who had grown up with a different game did not abandon baseball. On the contrary. They poured into stadiums and watched it on television in record numbers. Why? At least one reason had a lot to do with free agency. With so much news about player signings, re-entry drafts and salary talks in the off-season, baseball never left the sports pages. And while million-dollar contracts had made the players less likeable, less worthy of the wide-eyed adulation of childhood, they had also made them more famous. In America then, as now, nothing draws better than a celebrity. ◗

The Big Red Machine

He should have stopped at third. But Pete Rose didn't even hesitate. He rounded the base, stubby legs driving into the glistening green carpet and pushing his cement block of a body toward home. In center field, Amos Otis fielded Jim Hickman's single cleanly and cocked his arm to make the throw. At the plate, catcher Ray Fosse settled in at the corner in Rose's path. It was the 1970 All-Star Game in Cincinnati and not only was Rose the hometown hero, but the game was being played in the Reds' new home, Riverfront Stadium, which had opened only two weeks earlier. With the score tied at 4–4 in the 12th inning, what could be more fitting than Rose scoring the winning run?

The ball was already in Fosse's glove by the time Rose reached the plate. But Rose had no intention of going into one of his headfirst slides; it was too late for that. Rose lowered his head, his left shoulder found its mark, and Fosse reacted as if he had taken a small car in the ribs. He rolled over backwards, separated from his glove, the ball, and his senses. Rose, who also had been knocked aside, scrambled back to touch the plate. Other players were stunned. This wasn't done in All-Star Games; someone could get hurt. In fact, Fosse was hospitalized with a separated shoulder, missed part of the season, and never quite regained his All-Star form.

But Pete Rose had scored the winning run, the new stadium had been christened. And the Big Red Machine had run its first crash test.

The Reds' Pete Rose always took the shortest path home, even if it meant flattening Cleveland catcher Ray Fosse in the 1970 All-Star Game. Coming in a game that didn't count, Rose's play (opposite) shocked the baseball world. But it was the winning run.

General manager Bob Howsam fashioned the clean-cut, family-oriented image of everything connected with the Reds. He wanted the interior of Riverfront Stadium to smell like a bakery—apparently because studies show it makes people happy and hungry—but failed to find a spray scent that duplicates the aroma.

For much of the 1970s, the Big Red Machine ran without an off switch. It was a team that had winning credentials: two world championships, four National League pennants, six Western Division flags, and a mythic lineup—Pete Rose, Johnny Bench, Joe Morgan, Tony Perez, George Foster—good enough to prompt comparisons with baseball's greatest teams. From 1970 to 1977, the Reds averaged 96 wins a season, including their dark year of 1971, when they had only 79 victories and finished fourth. In those eight seasons, the team produced the NL Most Valuable Player six times—Bench and Morgan twice each, and Rose and Foster once apiece. They were arguably the most richly balanced team of modern times, a team of hitters who could field and fielders who could hit, and most of them ran as if they were paid by the base.

In 1975, their first world championship season, they led the NL with 840 runs scored, 168 stolen bases, 50 saves, and only 102 errors. The next year, when they became the first NL team since the 1921–1922 Giants to repeat as world champions, they set even more standards, leading the league with 857 runs, 271 doubles, 63 triples, 141 home runs, a .280 team batting average, 210 stolen bases, 45 saves, and 102 errors, again the fewest in the league. That year five Reds, as many as the mighty 1927 Yankees and their infamous "Murderers Row," hit over .300—Rose, Morgan, Foster, Ken Griffey and Cesar Geronimo.

The Reds were a team of stars that didn't play like prima donnas, which made them that much more impressive. They ran bases aggressively. They complemented one another on defense. And for all the potential crowding of egos, they never fought, at least not in public. Every team likes to describe itself as one big happy family, but the Reds actually seemed to be one.

Which was just the way Bob Howsam wanted it. Howsam was a shrewd baseball man, and in early 1967 he became the Reds' general manager. He had successfully steered the Cardinals the previous three seasons, and before that he had made the minor league Denver franchise so successful that it occasionally drew more people than some major league teams. He also was one of the founders of the old American Football League; his contribution was the Denver Broncos.

Howsam had learned a basic rule in those early years: know your market. And Cincinnati was not all that hard to read. The Reds' home region—from Columbus to the north, Louisville to the south, Indianapolis to the west and Huntington, West Virginia, to the east—was Midwestern heartland. Reds fans would not take well to a player like Bill Lee, who said he liked to have marijuana with his pancakes, or Reggie Jackson, who liked to stand at home plate and savor his home runs. They wanted players who were modest, who were conformists, ballplayers who seemed perfectly happy playing ball.

The team Howsam began reshaping in the late 1960s radiated traditional values. Troublemakers and free spirits were weeded out in the minors. "We preferred players who were happily married and were settled," said Howsam. "We wouldn't touch an athlete who used drugs in high school or college." His Reds looked clean—each player had nine uniforms to insure neatness—and were clean-cut—no long hair and absolutely no beards or moustaches. The Reds, like most other teams, wore new double-knit uniforms, but they wore them the traditional way. Shoes were black, and red stirrup socks were not covered with pant legs. Some Reds speculated that they had fewer low strikes called on them because the bottom of their pants

In terms of position players only, few teams have ever put together a more impressive lineup than the Cincinnati Reds of the mid-1970s. Four of them—catcher Johnny Bench, left fielder George Foster, second baseman Joe Morgan and Pete Rose, who played all over—won MVP awards during the decade. Manager Sparky Anderson (far right) had an enviable job.

With runners in scoring position, Tony Perez was the last person a pitcher wanted to face. He never won an RBI title, but his 1,652 RBI rank 16th on the all-time list, and when Pete Rose was asked whom he would want at the plate with a runner on and the game on the line, his answer was simple: "Perez."

defined the strike zone just below their knees. If that was so, it was a bonus. What Howsam wanted was uniform uniformity. There was even a photo of shortstop Woody Woodward displayed in the clubhouse to remind everyone of the way a Cincinnati Red should look.

"I was working in a market that wanted clean-cut athletes," Howsam explained. "If I was promoting something in Aspen, Colorado, I'd say everyone should have long hair and beards." Howsam was also enamored of artificial turf, and Riverfront Stadium was more artificial than any other ballpark. Only the pitching mound and the sliding areas around the bases escaped the carpet. Not even the basepaths were dirt. "It's neat, clean and it always looks good," explained Howsam, who found the bright green surface a "pleasing color in contrast to the ball."

Of course, no one would have cared much about the stage had the show been lousy. But Howsam paid just as much attention to molding talent. Admittedly, some elements of the Big Red Machine were already in place when he arrived. Clubhouse leader Tony Perez was turning into an RBI virtuoso, and Johnny Bench had sailed through the minors and was about to make his Reds debut. Also awaiting Howsam was Pete Rose, who was by then a Cincinnati idol.

Rose was a local boy, a graduate of Cincinnati's Western Hills High School, and a player of more energy than skill. Right away, he annoyed the Reds' veterans with his rah-rah style, running out a base on balls in his first major league at-bat. It didn't help that he had also pushed Don Blasingame, the popular second baseman, out of the lineup. The old-timers disliked Rose so much that they tried to smear him with the nickname "Charlie Hustle." The name stuck, but hardly as an insult. He hustled all year, managed to hit

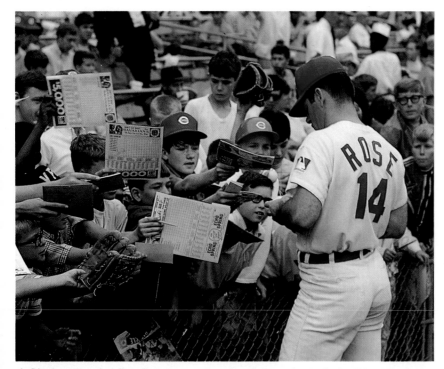

A Cincinnati native, Pete Rose was a promotional dream for the Reds. His enthusiasm for the game and everything connected with it was boundless. "For me, playing baseball for $3,000 a week is a license to steal," he said.

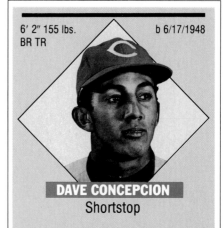

6' 2" 155 lbs.   **b 6/17/1948**
BR TR

DAVE CONCEPCION
Shortstop

In 1970 Dave Concepcion was a young kid from Venezuela who won the shortstop job in Cincinnati with his glove. By 1979 Concepcion had become one of the best all-around players in the game.

The Reds never questioned his glove. Concepcion invented the one-hop throw on artificial turf and won the Gold Glove five times in six years. "On his good nights," manager Sparky Anderson once said, "and that means all of them, Davey looks as if he's playing shortstop on roller skates."

At the plate, Concepcion improved every year. In 1978 he hit .301 with a slugging percentage of .405, a far cry from .205 in 1971 and .209 in 1972. In 1979 he hit .281 with power—16 home runs and 84 RBI—and helped the Reds win the NL West title.

As his batting improved, his personality evolved, and Concepcion became a clubhouse clown. "Now he's a .280 hitter, which is more than you should expect from any shortstop," Pete Rose noted, "and he's a .300-plus joker."

In 1976 Cincinnati rewarded Concepcion with a five-year contract, the longest of any Red. And in 1981 they made him baseball's first million-dollar shortstop.

Former star shortstop Pee Wee Reese summed up Concepcion's talent: "Mark Belanger may be a little smoother. Bowa is very quick. Rick Burleson is a leader type. Bill Russell has an accurate arm. But no one does everything as well as Concepcion. It's possible that no one ever has."

.273—second to only Vida Pinson among the regulars—and ended up NL Rookie of the Year.

From then on, Rose was the man who sparked the team's potent lineup. In 1965 he batted over .300 for the first of nine straight seasons, earning NL batting titles in 1968, 1969 and 1973. He was noted for his headfirst slides—which, he acknowledged, helped get his picture in the paper—and for his spray hitting, which helped make him baseball's first $100,000 singles hitter. If Rose had balked at Howsam's dress code or ridiculed his obsession with order, the image of the Reds as a team dedicated to old-fashioned values might never have taken hold. But Rose went along, although he admitted that "I always wondered what would have happened if the whole team showed up one day with shaved heads. That wasn't against the rules."

Early in 1968, it was clear that rookie Johnny Bench was not just another catcher with a hard head and soft stats. He had 15 homers and 82 RBI that year, and his huge hands, quick feet, and daunting arm made all the lunging and blocking and scrambling behind the plate look easy. Almost immediately, he became a new model for catchers. Like Rose, he was named NL Rookie of the Year, and the following spring, when Bench asked Ted Williams for an autograph, Williams inscribed the ball: "To Johnny, a Hall of Famer, for sure." Bench was celebrity material, a handsome, wholesome bachelor, but he kept his ego in check and replaced Rose as the darling of the Reds' fans.

With his two main cogs meshing, Howsam treated the rest of the team like spare parts, trading away old favorites and adding new talent to the roster. Certainly no one predicted and few applauded his hiring in 1970

Dave Concepcion's quick feet and strong arm fit the artificial turf at Riverfront Stadium like a glove. Concepcion (above, right, with third baseman Pete Rose) was the NL's Gold Glove shortstop five times, including 1975 and 1976, the Reds' two world championship seasons.

George "Sparky" Anderson, a minor league managerial wizard who had never been more than a third-base coach in the majors. But the gamble worked. Anderson neither coddled nor overmanaged his stars, but he did defer to their skills and knowledge of the game, all the while downplaying his own wisdom. "There ain't no genius who ever managed in this game," said Anderson, who never heard a double negative he didn't like. "I ain't no genius. No one is." Early on, Pete Rose sought him out and told him, "Look, I'm the highest paid player on this team and if you need anything done, come to me and I'll see it gets done."

As his stars ran interference, Anderson steered the Big Red Machine through a season of luck and long balls. It was a team that hitting coach Ted Kluszewski liked to say "had the bop," especially in batter-friendly Crosley Field, where the Reds started the 1970 season. Tony Perez hit ten homers in April, had 29 by the All-Star break, and ended up with 40 home runs and 129 RBI. First baseman Lee May added 34, part-time left fielder Bernie Carbo hit 21, and center fielder Bobby Tolan drove in 80 runs. But Bench was the biggest bruiser, finishing with 45 homers and 148 RBI. It was his best offensive season, and one of the best ever for a catcher. Once the team moved to the open spaces of Riverfront Stadium, the long balls were less frequent, but by that point it didn't matter. Except for one day early in April, the Reds were in first place all year and closed 14½ games ahead of the Dodgers. They swept the Pirates in the playoffs, but in the World Series they could overcome neither the Orioles' superior pitching nor the fielding artistry of Brooks Robinson.

The next year, almost nothing went right. Injuries knocked Tolan out for the season and crippled pitcher Jim Merritt, who went from 20 wins

Jack Billingham was the most consistent of the Reds' starting pitchers in the 1970s. Obtained in a trade from Houston, Billingham averaged 14.5 wins per season from 1972 through 1977, and he was nearly unhittable in three World Series—allowing one earned run and just 14 hits in 25 ⅓ innings.

to one. Things got so bad that Johnny Bench was booed. But Howsam knew he couldn't blame the team's plunge to fourth place solely on injuries. In the first full season in their new park, the Reds hit 53 fewer homers than the year before; obviously, they could no longer rely on power hitting to pummel other teams. It was time to make an adjustment. But this time Howsam didn't just tinker; this time he pulled off what Reds fans for years simply called "The Trade."

The deal just didn't seem to make any sense. Lee May, with 39 homers and 98 RBI in 1971, was one of two Reds' regulars who had improved on his 1970 numbers. Tommy Helms, a two-time All-Star second baseman, was the other. Howsam traded both, along with utility man Jimmy Stewart, to Houston. In return, he got Joe Morgan, Cesar Geronimo, Jack Billingham, Denis Menke and Ed Armbrister. Morgan was one of the better second basemen in the league, but rumors pegged him as a troublemaker. The players who came with him seemed even more of a mystery. In right field, Geronimo had an overpowering arm and great speed, but he also had an awful swing and a dismal average. Pitcher Billingham seemed destined for mediocrity, Menke was closing out his career, and Armbrister was strictly an extra. Howsam had promised the Reds' fans a good show; now, it seemed, he meant a farce.

Anderson wasn't dismayed. One of his first moves was to give Morgan a locker next to Rose's. Both were hyperactive leaders who spit out equal measures of insults and wisdom. Anderson needed them to be allies, not rivals, and his ploy paid off. In no time, they became brothers in banter, and with Morgan, clubhouse ragging became as much a part of the Reds'

A hypnotist helped George Foster (above) overcome his fear of getting hit by a pitch—he had been beaned twice early in his career—and soon it was the pitchers who were scared. Nicknamed "the Destroyer," Foster hit 13 career grand slams.

Joe Morgan

The Big Red Machine just started to roll when Joe Morgan came to Cincinnati in 1972. Morgan arrived as part of an eight-player trade that sent the right side of the Reds' infield, Lee May and Tommy Helms, to the Houston Astros. The Reds had reached the World Series in 1970, then fallen to fourth place a year later. Manager Sparky Anderson decided some new parts were necessary, and Morgan, at 5' 7" and 150 pounds, became the main cog in the rebuilt machine. Over the next five years, the Reds won four division titles, three pennants and two World Series.

"Little Joe" started his major league career with Houston in 1963 when he was just 19. His first big play came in a September game against the Phillies, when he singled to drive in the winning run. Phillie manager Gene Mauch yelled at his team for "getting beat by a guy who looks like a Little Leaguer."

In his seven years with Houston, Little Joe established himself as a steady fielder, a smart baserunner, and a solid hitter with an excellent eye for the strike zone. But the Astros never finished above fourth place. When he came to Cincinnati, Morgan got his chance to shine with a winning team. In 1972 he scored a league-leading 122 runs with 115 walks and 58 stolen bases. In 1973 he hit 26 homers, scored 116 runs and stole 67 bases. Both years Morgan led NL second basemen in putouts and, in 1973, in double plays. Both years Cincinnati finished first in the NL West.

"The difference between playing for Houston and this club is the guys on this club know what it takes to be a winner," Morgan said. "In Houston, people emphasize individual statistics, and that puts the team second. In Cincinnati, starting with the front office, they emphasize what the team has done. You feel it all through the ball club."

From 1972 through 1977, there was no better Big Red than Little Joe. In that six-year span, Morgan averaged .300, 22 home runs, 84 RBI, 113 runs scored, 118 walks, 157 hits and 60 stolen bases. In 1973 he became the first player to steal 60 bases and hit 25 homers in a season, and he did it again in 1977. Every year from 1973 through 1977, he appeared in the All-Star Game and won a Gold Glove Award. In 1976 he became the seventh player in history to win back-to-back MVP awards.

"You have to watch him every day to realize what a great ballplayer he is," Anderson said. "He can control a one-run game just by the things he does on the basepaths. Our success with an attack keyed by Morgan has changed a lot of other clubs' thinking."

After the Reds won World Series in both of Morgan's MVP seasons, they slipped to second place for two years. Morgan's production slowed because of injury in 1978, then nosedived in 1979. It signaled the end of his stay in Cincinnati.

As a free agent, Morgan returned to Houston in 1980, where he led the league in walks and the Astros to the division title. Then Morgan was traded to the Giants. He had a poor 1981 before rejuvenating in 1982 to become NL Comeback Player of the Year. Still, he was traded again, this time to the Phillies, who went to the Series. He played his final season with the Oakland A's in 1984.

"He has a quiet leadership quality," said pitcher Joe Sambito, who played with Morgan in Houston in 1980. "But the big thing is, he's done it. He's won. He's been there. He has to be one of the smartest men ever to play the game."

Joe Morgan's abilities ran so deep and so wide that you had to hang around a while to see everything he could do for a ballclub. "Every time I look up," said Reds catcher Johnny Bench, "Morgan's on base."

JOE MORGAN

Second Base
Houston Colt .45s 1963–1964
Houston Astros 1965–1971, 1980
Cincinnati Reds 1972–1979
San Francisco Giants 1981–1982
Philadelphia Phillies 1983
Oakland Athletics 1984

GAMES	**2,650**
AT-BATS	**9,281**
BATTING AVERAGE	
Career	**.271**
Season High	**.327**
SLUGGING AVERAGE	
Career	**.427**
Season High	**.576**
HITS	
Career	**2,518**
Season High	**167**
DOUBLES	
Career	**449**
Season High	**35**
TRIPLES	
Career	**96**
Season High	**12**
HOME RUNS	
Career	**268**
Season High	**27**
TOTAL BASES	**3,963**
EXTRA-BASE HITS	**813**
RUNS BATTED IN	
Career	**1,134**
Season High	**111**
RUNS	
Career	**1,651**
Season High	**122**
WORLD SERIES	**1972, 1975–1976, 1983**
MOST VALUABLE PLAYER	**1975, 1976**

Cincinnati's Johnny Bench was a little late trying to score past Pirates catcher Manny Sanguillen in the 1972 NL Championship Series, but his consistent postseason power was demonstrated throughout the 1970s. In 45 games over six NLCS and four World Series, Bench slammed ten home runs and went without a homer in only one of the ten postseason series.

personality as bullying offense and hairless faces. No ego was sacred. "Seaver is pitching today. Aren't you sick or something?" Morgan would needle Bench, who could never hit the Mets pitcher's hard slider. He'd tell Dave Concepcion, "Get away from here, Davey. We're talking about hitting and you ain't no hitter." In return, someone would ask Morgan why he made so much money when all he could do was steal bases. For all the profanity, all the deliberate disrespect, the ribbing became a locker room leveler, keeping the big names from taking their stats too seriously and the lesser ones from feeling invisible.

On the field, Morgan found other ways to agitate. Motivated by the work ethic of stars like Rose and Bench, he drilled himself on every part of his game. But more than anything else that first year, he showed the Reds how to steal bases. He had made a science of it, studying the motions of every pitcher, looking for gestures that would tip him off on when to make his move. Morgan was a menace to pitchers, just the kind of distraction they didn't need with Bench and Perez coming up to bat next. When he wasn't tormenting other teams, he was giving lessons on how to do it. In 1972 the Reds stole 140 bases, compared with 59 the year before. The Machine had shifted gears.

The Reds surged to the top of the Western Division in late May and never slowed down, winning 65 of 95 games at one point. Everything was clicking again—Bench hit 40 homers, Rose batted over .300, Perez knocked in 90 runs, and Morgan scored a league-leading 122 runs. Bobby Tolan was not slowed by his Achilles tendon injury of the year before, contributing 82 RBI and 42 Morgan-inspired stolen bases. Anderson still lived by his quick-hook philosophy, relying on starters for five or six innings, then turning the

game over to the bullpen. Only one Reds pitcher, Jack Billingham, worked more than 200 innings, and two relievers, Clay Carroll and Pedro Borbon, appeared in at least one out of every three games, with Carroll setting a major league record of 37 saves.

Reconstituted and rejuvenated, the Reds rolled to another NLCS date with the Pirates, whom they had swept two years before. The Pirates were a team of free swingers—behind Willie Stargell, Al Oliver, Manny Sanguillen, Richie Hebner and their longtime leader, Roberto Clemente, the team had nine players with at least 100 hits and a league-high .274 batting average. But it was strong pitching, by Steve Blass in Game 1 and Nelson Briles in Game 3, that gave the Pirates a 2–1 edge in the playoffs. Ross Grimsley pitched a two-hitter to get the Reds even.

In the fifth and deciding game, the Pirates, behind Blass, held a 3–2 lead into the ninth, when Pirates manager Bill Virdon called on palmball maestro Dave Giusti to save the game. Unfortunately for Giusti, Bench led off and answered every Reds fan's prayer by smashing the fourth pitch into the right field seats to tie the game. Giusti was stunned and gave up singles to Perez and Denis Menke. In desperation, Virdon brought in Bob Moose, the Game 2 starter who hadn't retired any of the five batters he had faced. This time, Moose got two outs on fly balls, then faced Reds utility outfielder Hal McRae. Moose threw a strike, then a ball, then a sinker that dipped too soon and rolled under catcher Manny Sanguillen's glove. Pinch runner George Foster sprinted in from third and the Reds were back in the World Series.

Cincinnati was confident that the team they had just beaten was better than the A's they were about to face. The A's, with their outlandish uniforms and backbiting attitudes, made the Reds look polished and professional,

Ken Griffey (above, right) was chosen so low in the 1969 player draft by the Reds, they didn't even call to tell him he'd be drafted. By 1975 he was one of the best hitters in the NL, an excellent right fielder, and the fastest wheel on the Big Red Machine.

Powerhouses of the 1970s

The decade was dominated by three teams that hoarded the world championship for seven straight years. Oakland, led by the power of Reggie Jackson and a stable of fine pitchers, won three straight from 1972 through 1974. Cincinnati, with its big bats and scrappy baserunners, bumped off the A's in the 1975 Series and beat the Yankees in 1976. Then the Yankees, now led by Jackson's bat and another outstanding pitching staff, took world titles in 1977 and 1978. Below is a look at each team's best years during the 1970s. Totals are for regular season only.

	Year	Won-Lost	Pct.	Batting Ave.	Stolen Bases	HRs	Total Runs	Opponents' Runs	ERA
A's	1972	**93**-62	**.600**	.240	87	**134**	604	457	2.58
	1973	94-68	.580	.260	128	147	**758**	615	3.29
	1974	90-72	.556	.247	**164**	132	689	**551**	**2.95**
C	1973	**99**-63	.611	.254	**148**	137	741	621	3.43
	1975	**108**-54	.667	.271	**168**	124	**840**	586	3.37
	1976	**102**-60	.630	**.280**	**210**	141	**857**	633	3.51
NY	1976	**97**-62	**.610**	.269	163	120	730	**575**	**3.19**
	1977	**100**-62	.617	.281	93	184	831	**651**	3.61
	1978	**100**-63	**.613**	.267	98	125	735	**582**	3.18

Boldface indicates league leader.

but the A's pitchers—mainly Catfish Hunter, Ken Holtzman and Blue Moon Odom—kept the Reds' troublemakers, Rose and Morgan, off the bases. While the Series lasted the full seven games, Cincinnati couldn't stave off the upset. People started to joke that the Big Red Machine came equipped with a choke.

In 1973 the Reds again won their division, this time by only 3½ games over the Dodgers. Rose had an MVP year, Perez drove in 101 runs, Morgan stole 67 bases and hit 26 homers, almost twice as many as he ever had before. Two starting pitchers, Billingham at 19–10 and Gullett at 18–8, were threatening to break Sparky Anderson tradition and become aces. So in the playoffs, when Cincinnati came up against the New York Mets, a team that had won only three more games than it had lost during the regular season, a rout seemed in order. Once more, however, the Reds sputtered at the plate. With his team far behind in Game 3, Rose tried to break up a double play with a hard slide into Mets shortstop Bud Harrelson. Rose and Harrelson ended up rolling on the ground, flailing away, and both benches emptied. Then both bullpens emptied. Then Reds reliever Pedro Borbon slugged Mets reliever Buzz Capra. Then Borbon, realizing he had placed a fallen Mets cap on his head, tore the hat off, took a bite out of it, and ripped it to bits as he stalked off the field.

When Rose went out to left field the next inning, he was pelted with all kinds of garbage, including a whiskey bottle. Anderson responded by pulling his team off the field, and Mets manager Yogi Berra had to lead a peace delegation with Tom Seaver and Willie Mays out to plead with the New York fans to show better manners. Sanity prevailed and so, ultimately, did the Mets, who went on to win that game and the pennant-clinching Game 5.

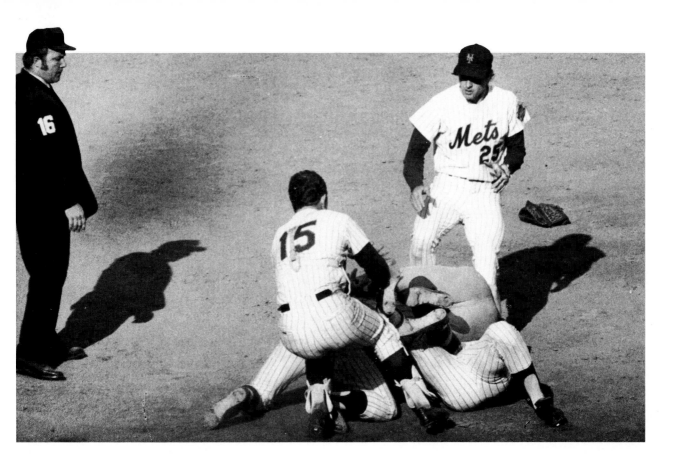

In 1974 the Reds chased the Dodgers all season without catching up. The following April, Anderson swore that 1975 would be his year. It was not idle optimism. For one thing, Joe Morgan had become the most complete player in baseball. Howsam called him the "best all-around offensive player I have ever seen." Morgan was now also a standout fielder, analyzing field positioning on batters as intently as he did base-stealing tip-offs. Shortstop Dave Concepcion had likewise become superb, adjusting to artificial turf as well as any infielder in the league. His nimble, fluid motion and powerful arm allowed him to play deep and to cut off balls bouncing into the hole or up the middle. In center field, Cesar Geronimo's deceptively quick gliding gait seemed perfectly suited for the plastic pastures of Riverfront. With Bench, everybody's model catcher, the Reds were unsurpassed at the four most crucial defensive positions.

Ken Griffey, a replacement for Bobby Tolan in right field, added more speed to the lineup. Tolan and left-handed starter Ross Grimsley wanted to grow facial hair, but had to find other places to do it. In Cincinnati, some rules were not meant to be broken. Anderson once wondered what would have happened if Bench had tried to grow a moustache, but fortunately none of the core four—Bench, Rose, Morgan and Perez—challenged Howsam's grooming guidelines. In fact, the quartet had become almost another set of coaches: Morgan was the baserunning expert, and he and Rose freely provided batting tips; Bench worked with young catchers, and Perez was guardian of the team's Latin players, advising Concepcion on media relations, chastising Geronimo for chasing bad pitches.

So the Red Machine seemed primed for the 1975 season. The only big question marks were Gary Nolan, the young right-hander who had missed

The frustration of losing 9–2 in Game 3 of the 1973 NLCS took its toll on the fiercely competitive Pete Rose, so Rose decided to take his frustration out on 160-pound Mets shortstop Bud Harrelson. Sprinting out to break things up were Mets catcher Jerry Grote and second baseman Felix Millan (25).

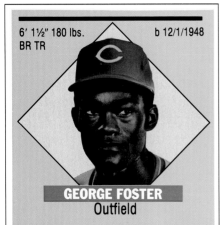

6' 1½" 180 lbs.
BR TR

b 12/1/1948

GEORGE FOSTER
Outfield

Cincinnati might not have dominated the 1970s if Sparky Anderson hadn't made a bold move in May of 1975. He needed more offense, so to add power to his lineup, Anderson moved Pete Rose from left field to third base and turned George Foster from a part-time player into the starting left fielder.

Foster was the final ingredient in the most powerful lineup of the decade. He hit .300 in 1975 with 23 home runs and 78 RBI. In 1976 he hit .306 with 29 home runs, and he led the league with 121 RBI.

In 1977 Foster exploded for 52 home runs—the most since Willie Mays in 1965—and became the tenth player to hit more than 50 homers in a season. He led the NL in RBI (149), runs scored (124), slugging percentage (.631), hit .320 and was named the league's MVP. And again in 1978, he led the league in homers and RBI.

Not only did Foster hit often; he also hit long. Of the 12 balls ever to reach Riverfront Stadium's upper deck, five were off Foster's bat. Comparing Foster to Morgan, Rose and Perez, Johnny Bench said, "George was a bigger offensive weapon than any of them."

In 1979 injuries hindered his bid to become the only player to lead the league in RBI for four consecutive seasons, but he still managed to get 98 RBI in just 121 games.

Foster was traded to the Mets in 1982 but was not the savior New York had hoped for, recording four average seasons. In 1986, after 18 seasons in the majors, Foster retired.

Center fielder Cesar Geronimo anchored the Reds' fine middle defense. In 1975 and 1976 Geronimo, second baseman Joe Morgan, shortstop Dave Concepcion and catcher Johnny Bench each won two Gold Gloves.

most of the past two seasons with shoulder problems, and third base. There, hard-swinging Dan Driessen simply made too many errors. Anderson turned to John Vukovich, a slick fielder picked up from the Milwaukee Brewers, whose weak bat, Sparky hoped, could be carried by the rest of the team. The Reds charged ahead, swept the first three games from the Dodgers, but then turned ordinary. By the end of April, they were 12–11, the Dodgers were building a lead, and Vukovich had already become a trivia answer. In the ninth game of the season, Anderson saw Vukovich coming up with the bases loaded and sent up a pinch hitter. The fact that it was only the second inning didn't seem to matter. Vukovich threw a tantrum and lost his job. Anderson next tried rookie Doug Flynn and veteran Darrel Chaney at third, but neither of them hit, a real problem because none of the Reds were hitting. In the first month, Bench had stranded almost 100 runners on base, Perez, only a few less. Anderson considered drastic action.

On May 2, during batting practice, he noticed that Rose was catching throws at first. Actually, Rose was trying to break in his daughter's new softball glove. Anderson approached him. "I wish you were over there."

"Over where?" asked Rose.

"Over there," said Anderson, pointing to third.

"You want me to play third?"

"Yep."

"When?"

"Tomorrow too soon?"

So began the move that many say made the Reds champions. Rose had tried third back in 1966 and responded by going into a batting slump. The next season, he became an outfielder, eventually an All-Star outfielder. But the

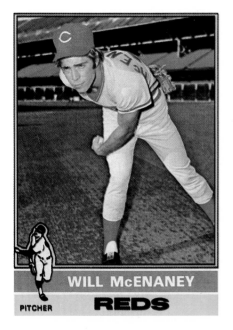

WILL McENANEY PITCHER **REDS**

RAWLY EASTWICK PITCHER **REDS**

PEDRO BORBON PITCHER **REDS**

move to third, said Rose, made him feel "like a kid with a new toy." It also allowed Anderson to get George Foster into the lineup. A part-time player for the past few years, Foster had a strangely high, squeaky voice, but he always seemed to hit the ball hard, and after several visits to a hypnotist, no longer was afraid of getting hit by pitches. His time had come and Anderson knew it.

The Reds spurted to 18–13, but Anderson thought that some of the younger players still seemed tentative, anxious about making mistakes. Part of the problem, he assumed, was that they were afraid of being roasted in the pregame rag sessions. So he ordered a gag rule: no more insults. In their next series, against Philadelphia, the Reds behaved well and exhibited good manners. They lost four straight. Then they lost to Montreal, their sixth defeat in a row. To make matters worse, Morgan was badly spiked in that game, and no one was sure how much time he would miss.

The next day, Morgan limped into the locker room, 14 stitches in his leg. With a smile on his face, he cursed Perez, then Rose, then Bench, then Anderson. The locker room was jolted to life. But Morgan wasn't through. "When you gonna hit a home run?" he challenged Perez.

"When you gonna play again?" Perez fired back. "The little scratch on your leg going to keep you out for a month?"

"I'm playing today," came the response.

The spark caught. "That right there, when Morgan came into the clubhouse and began shouting. That was the turning point," Anderson said. The Reds won 41 of the next 50 games, despite losing starter Don Gullett for two months with a broken thumb. Anderson juggled his relievers as never before. "There's always action in the Cincinnati bullpen," the joke went. He settled on a rotation of four relievers—two veterans, Carroll and Borbon,

Will McEnaney (above, left), Rawley Eastwick (center) and Pedro Borbon formed three-fourths of the Reds' bullpen committee in 1975. Along with Clay Carroll, the relief quartet combined for 49 of the Reds' league-leading 50 saves. The highest ERA of the group belonged to Borbon at 2.95.

Riverfront Stadium

Although Cincinnati's Riverfront Stadium didn't officially open until 1970, it had been a gleam in the Queen City's eyes for more than 20 years. A 1948 Riverfront Redevelopment Plan called for a new stadium nestled between downtown and the Ohio River, as well as a highway distributor system allowing easy access from all directions. On June 30, 1970, a crowd of 51,050 was on hand as the plan was finally realized and a new era dawned for the Reds.

Riverfront Stadium—which sits atop the former site of Rat Row, a notorious collection of saloons and bawdy houses in the 1800s—was exactly what Cincinnati and its team needed in 1970. The stadium provided a focal point for the city's downtown revitalization, and attracted fans and their money from nearby Indiana and Kentucky, as well as all of southern Ohio. A series of pedestrian bridges also made Riverfront an easy walk from the central business district.

Riverfront is in the same mold as other symmetrical, concrete multi-use stadiums built in the 1970s, like Three Rivers in Pittsburgh and Veterans in Philadelphia. It is the seventh home for the Reds, baseball's oldest all-professional team. Tradition dictates that the first game each season be the Reds' home opener. Part of the ceremony surrounding the opener is the various means of transportation used to bring the ball to the stadium—once it arrived by canoe up the Licking River; another time by bicycle in a Tupperware container from Washington, D.C.

Despite an opening-game 8–2 loss to the Braves on June 30, as Hank Aaron hit the stadium's first home run, the Reds and Riverfront hit it off immediately. On August 8 Tony Perez was the first to send a ball to the fifth-level red seats, 480 feet from home and 50 feet above field level, and the Reds powered their way to their first NL pennant since 1961. The team and its stadium were an instant hit with fans, as well; 1970 saw a team record attendance of 1,803,568. Although Cincinnati is among major league baseball's smallest cities, the Reds topped the two million mark in attendance every year from 1973 to 1980.

The 1970s Reds were strong, fast and aggressive—a team that was able to take advantage of the stadium's hard, fast artificial surface. Despite the perfect match of a team with their stadium, one of Riverfront's most memorable moments was provided by a visiting player. On April 4, 1974, Hank Aaron tied Babe Ruth's career home run record of 714 with a line drive to left field. The Reds reclaimed sovereignty over their stadium, and all of baseball, in 1975 and 1976, their world championship years. The only detour in their 1976 season came during a Saturday afternoon game when a swarm of 10,000 bees between third base and home caused a delay against the Giants.

More milestones were reached at Riverfront during the late 1970s and the 1980s. In 1978, Pete Rose got his 3,000th career hit on May 5, and Tom Seaver pitched his only no-hitter on June 16. On April 18, 1981 Seaver made Riverfront the site of his 3,000th career strikeout. But the stadium's most historic moment came four years later, as Cincinnati native Pete Rose lined a single off San Diego's Eric Show for his 4,192nd hit, breaking Ty Cobb's all-time record.

Riverfront Stadium's proximity to the Ohio River provides a picturesque setting as well as the potential for flooding. The stadium was built to be safe even if the river reached the same levels as the Great Flood of 1937, during which Crosley Field, the Reds' previous home, was under water.

Riverfront Stadium

Pete Rose Way and
  Mehring Way
Cincinnati, Ohio

Completed 1970

Cincinnati Reds, NL
1970-present

Seating Capacity
52,392

Style
Multipurpose, symmetrical,
  artificial surface

Height of Outfield Fences
8 feet

Dugouts
Home: 1st base
Visitors: 3rd base

Bullpens
Foul territory
Home: right field
Visitors: left field

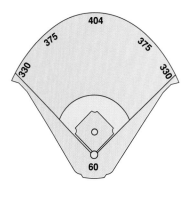

Reds manager Sparky Anderson (above, pointing) never met a starter he couldn't replace. In 1975, when the Reds won 108 regular-season games, their starters completed just 22 games—dead last in the majors.

and two youngsters, Will McEnaney and Rawley Eastwick, who had begun the season in the minors. At the first sign of trouble, sometimes before, Anderson called for help. Carroll was used least, and he got into 56 games. The Reds' starters went 45 straight games without a complete game; the team won 32 of them.

During the streak, Rose had 70 hits, Morgan batted .351, Bench hit 12 homers and drove in 47 runs, and Foster batted .308 with nine home runs. The Reds also went 15 straight games without an error. They were playing on a level no other team could approach, and they clinched the Western Division on September 7, the earliest date in NL history. They never lost their edge, sweeping the Pirates in the playoffs and outlasting the Red Sox in a World Series in which fortunes never stopped shifting, and each game had not one, but a handful of scene-stealing moments. Ultimately, the Reds won with their resourcefulness and will. In all seven games they fell behind, and three of their four wins came in either the ninth or extra innings. In the finale, a hard slide by Rose to break up a double play and a game-winning bloop single by Morgan on a tough pitch made the difference. Finally, the Reds were champions. Gone were the jokes about chokes.

In 1976 the Reds surprised no one when they repeated as champs. Their efficiency had become both devastating and predictable. They hit consistently, ran aggressively, fielded artfully, and seemed in control even when they were behind. No team adjusted as quickly or with as much authority to artificial turf, and no team was better at unnerving opponents with its speed. "With the Reds, the first baseman on the other team always has to hold the man on first," observed broadcaster and former Yankees shortstop

Tony Kubek. "And the shortstop and second baseman have to cheat towards second in case of a steal. That opens up room for hits to get through, something the Reds take advantage of."

The 1976 National League All-Star squad looked like the Reds with a few extras; of Cincinnati's starters, only Cesar Geronimo didn't make the team. At season's end, the Reds, propelled by Morgan's best year ever, finished ten games ahead of the Dodgers and rolled into the playoffs to face the Philadelphia Phillies. The Phillies were in some ways a scaled-down model of the Red Machine. They mixed power—Mike Schmidt led the league with 38 homers, Greg Luzinski added another 21—with speed—Garry Maddox had 29 stolen bases. Philadelphia even had something the Reds lacked—a stopper in the starting rotation, Steve Carlton, who ended up 20–7. They opened the season with a Reds-like streak, winning 52 of their first 73 games and finishing with one fewer victory than Cincinnati. None of it mattered. Rallying from behind in each game, the Reds swept in three, the last win coming on a characteristic bottom-of-the-ninth, three-run rally on back-to-back homers by Bench and Foster.

Next came the Yankees. It was their first World Series in 12 years, straight from a dramatic playoff win over the Kansas City Royals. None of that mattered either. The Reds took four straight, as everyone in Cincinnati's starting lineup, except Rose and Griffey, batted over .300. This was the stuff of dynasties, sportswriters declared. And somehow it was only fitting that the Reds, a team steeped in traditional values right down to the black polish on their shoes, should win in America's bicentennial year and the centennial year of the National League. It was also fitting because baseball was about to rush into a new age; free agency had arrived.

After winding up on the short end of the 1970 and 1972 World Series, the Reds come-from-behind win in Game 7 of the 1975 Series against Boston was cause for celebration. They repeated in 1976.

In 1979, after 16 seasons playing in his hometown of Cincinnati, Pete Rose pedaled his headfirst slides and Charlie Hustle image to the talented but unproven Philadelphia Phillies. Rose was given a great deal of credit for leading the Phillies to a world title—the team's first—in 1980.

A stalwart on the Reds' much maligned starting rotation, Gary Nolan (above) was a consistent winner, with a 110–70 lifetime mark and a 3.08 ERA. All but three of his decisions came as a member of the Reds.

Reds manager Sparky Anderson (opposite) was fired after consecutive second-place finishes in 1977 and 1978. Anderson went on to Detroit, where he fashioned another well-oiled machine. In 1984 he became the first person ever to manage world champions in both leagues.

Not surprisingly, Bob Howsam tried to hold back the tide; he would not soil his hands in a bidding war for players, he announced. But as much as Howsam wished it, the Reds could not be kept in a protective bubble. That off-season, Don Gullett, the team's top starter, jumped to the Yankees, an act Sparky Anderson termed a "defection." Then Rawley Eastwick, the star of Anderson's hyperactive bullpen, refused to sign a contract and early in the 1977 season was traded to the Cardinals. Other damage was self-inflicted. After the second World Series win, Howsam, anxious to make Dan Driessen the starting first baseman, traded Tony Perez to the Montreal Expos. Perez was near the end of his career, Howsam thought; he seemed expendable. Howsam was very wrong. Perez played ten more years and knocked in more than 90 runs twice. Even so, Doggie, as his teammates called him, was missed most in the Reds' locker room. "Morgan and Rose were the obvious leaders. But only when Perez left did I realize he was the leader," said Anderson. "He did the most to keep all those egos in harmony. Doggie could handle them all."

After the 1978 season, Pete Rose left, enticed from his beloved Cincinnati to Philadelphia by a contract so fat that "I should be playing two positions." A year later, after the Reds were swept in the playoffs by the Pirates, Joe Morgan bailed out for his old team, the Houston Astros. The Big Red Machine had come apart. ◗▮

Johnny Bench

From the beginning, the other Cincinnati Reds knew Johnny Bench was different. It wasn't just his huge hands—hands so large that he could hold seven baseballs in one of them. And it wasn't just his unorthodox one-handed catching style, in which he held his bare hand beside his knee and away from the cruel spin of foul tips. It was his attitude. Johnny Bench was never a rookie.

He entered the major leagues in 1967 as self-assured as any player on the team, a 19-year-old who neither feigned modesty nor deferred to veterans. Once, during his first full year in the league, Bench was catching for a pitcher named Jerry Arrigo, whose fastball wasn't nearly as fast as he thought it was. Bench signaled for a curve. Arrigo shook it off. Bench signaled for the curve again. Arrigo refused. After a third rejection, Bench let Arrigo throw his fastball. But to show that he wasn't impressed, Bench reached out and caught the pitch with his bare hand.

Nicknamed "the Little General" by his teammates, Bench was given the Reds' catching job by manager Dave Bristol over three veterans, including the popular Johnny Edwards. He had glided through the minors in three years after being drafted out of high school in Binger, Oklahoma, a town of less than 700 people. There he had been class valedictorian and star athlete—a high school All-American honorable mention in basketball, a leading pitcher, 30–1, and slugger, batting .675, on the school's championship baseball team. But Bench's father, Ted, had drilled him to become a catcher, and by the end of his rookie season with the Reds, he was already being compared to the game's best. Managers and other catchers were amazed by his speed and grace behind the plate, whether he was spinning back under a pop-up, pouncing on a bunt or sweeping a tag across a sliding runner. And they were awed by his powerful arm. "Every time Bench throws, everybody in baseball drools," said Baltimore executive Harry Dalton. The first time they faced him that year, the sprinting Dodgers tested Bench. He threw out three of them in one inning.

Bench was such an exceptional defensive catcher that he would have been forgiven a timid bat. But he quickly became the biggest menace in the Reds' lineup, and by the end of 1968, at his suggestion, he was batting cleanup. He finished with 15 home runs and 82 RBI and, to no one's surprise, was voted Rookie of the Year. It was just the first of a career full of plaudits. Two years later, he was selected Most Valuable Player after having one of the best offensive seasons of any catcher in history: .293 average, 45 homers, 148 RBI. He nearly matched those figures two years later when he hit 40 homers and knocked in 125 runs. Again he was chosen the Most Valuable Player. Starting with that year, Bench had more than 100 RBI in five of six consecutive seasons. In fact, during the 1970s, he drove in 1,013 runs, more than anyone else in the majors. That he did all this while playing the most physically demanding position on the field made his achievements that much more impressive. He was durable enough to catch more than 120 games in each of his first ten seasons,

When the game was on the line, few runners dared to test Bench's quick release and cannon arm (above). Mickey Rivers' stolen base in Game 4 of the 1976 World Series, was only the second off Bench in his 42 postseason games. Bench made up for the theft with two home runs and five RBI as the Reds swept the Yankees.

As tough as he was talented, Bench blocked the plate against all comers, even 200-plus pounders like Pittsburgh's Willie Stargell (above).

and talented enough to win Gold Glove Awards for ten consecutive years.

But his career was not all glory. He was booed regularly by Reds fans in 1971 when he held out for more money and then slumped badly, his average plunging to .238, his RBI to 61. His detractors, noting his off-season travels to Vietnam with Bob Hope and his new friendships with celebrities like Chuck Connors and Bobby Goldsboro, said he had gone Hollywood. An embittered Bench vowed never again to tip his hat after a home run. His stats fell again in 1973 after off-season surgery to remove a benign tumor from his chest. And later in his career, Bench, always a remarkable natural athlete, had to accept his inadequacies as a third baseman. Although he no doubt could have prolonged his career as a designated hitter in the American League, Bench retired in 1983

when the cumulative effect of his many injuries began to dull his skills. "I want to be able to walk when I'm 50," he explained.

Through the 1970s, however, he had not only been the engine of the Big Red Machine, but had also redefined catching. "Bench was picture-perfect. A marvelous mechanical catcher," said Ted Simmons, another expert at the position. "Bench did so many things almost perfectly that it almost seemed robotical," added Carlton Fisk. The greatest compliment, however, came from Sparky Anderson, the Reds' manager and Bench's sometime father figure. When, after Bench was named the Most Valuable Player in the 1976 World Series, Anderson was asked to compare the Yankees' Thurman Munson with his catcher, he simply replied, "Don't ever embarrass anyone by comparing him to Johnny Bench."

Unusually agile for a catcher, Bench took pride in his all-around ability. "I liked being able to win a game four different ways," he said. "Call a good game, throw out runners, get base hits and block the plate."

JOHNNY BENCH

Catcher
Cincinnati Reds 1967–1983
Hall of Fame 1989

GAMES	2,158
AT-BATS	7,658
BATTING AVERAGE	
Career	.267
Season High	.393
SLUGGING AVERAGE	
Career	.476
Season High	.587
HITS	
Career	2,048
Season High	177
DOUBLES	
Career	381
Season High	40
TRIPLES	
Career	24
Season High	4
HOME RUNS	
Career	389
Season High	45
TOTAL BASES	3,644
EXTRA-BASE HITS	794
RUNS BATTED IN	
Career	1,376
Season High	148
RUNS	
Career	1,091
Season High	108
WORLD SERIES	1970, 1972, 1975–1976
ROOKIE OF THE YEAR	1968
MOST VALUABLE PLAYER	1970, 1972

Made for TV

When Carlton Fisk came to bat in the 12th inning of Game 6 of the 1975 World Series, about 62 million people were watching him. One of them was a man he had never met but who was to change his life. His name was Lou Gerard, and at the moment Fisk was walking out into the glow of the stadium lights, Gerard was standing alone behind the Fenway Park scoreboard. He was intent on the television camera in front of him, trying to ignore the dank corners nearby where he could hear rats moving. A few minutes later, as everyone else followed the flight of the ball arcing down toward the left-field line, Gerard kept his eye and the camera focused on Fisk, who was pleading with waving arms and body English that the ball stay fair and, then, when it did, bouncing in the air in a moment of pure boyish joy. In NBC's control booth, director Harry Coyle noticed what the scoreboard camera was capturing and beamed. It was, he said later, "a director's dream."

Soon, 62 million other people saw what Lou Gerard had seen: the wave of hope, the dance of jubilation. The replay showed it all, a scene so vivid, so joyous that it transformed hitting a home run into a lasting symbol of triumph. Long after the stadium emptied, long after the score was forgotten, the image of Fisk's waving and bouncing endured, and even after he had played for the Chicago White Sox for many years, people thought he was still with Boston, so strong was the memory of his heroic night in Fenway.

New York's WPIX had been televising Yankee home games since the early 1950s, with famous on-the-air voices such as Mel Allen and Red Barber. But in the 1970s more and better cameras gave fans a closer look (opposite).

The theory that increased television exposure would keep fans in their living rooms instead of putting them in ballpark seats was exploded in the 1970s, as fans flocked to stadiums in record numbers in both leagues.

Even without television, Fisk would have been a hero. Because of it, he became a myth. Only television could capture Fisk's moment of glory, slow it down, and play it over and over until it became a slice of American folklore. Only television, it sometimes seemed, could truly celebrate baseball.

Then there were the other times. A year later, the American League playoffs between the Yankees and the Royals were carried on ABC and described by a trio of announcers—Keith Jackson, Reggie Jackson and Howard Cosell. It was an odd broadcast team for a major baseball event. Not only was Cosell an icon of ABC's Monday Night Football, but he had made no secret of his disdain for baseball, which he considered a dull, stodgy sport that even he might not be able to save. Keith Jackson was also a gridiron man, his voice so associated with college football that sports fans listening to the game expected him at any moment to get excited and scream "Fum-bo-o-o-o-le." And while Reggie Jackson obviously knew baseball, he didn't know broadcasting, and he and Cosell talked during pitches, during plays, and during the time the other was talking during pitches and plays. The low point, however, came during interviews with a parade of celebrities who just happened to drop by the broadcast booth. There was a chat with singer Frank Sinatra, another with Olympian Bruce Jenner, a third with Secretary of State Henry Kissinger, highlighted by a brief debate between Cosell and the Secretary over whether Kissinger had indeed been present at the reopening of renovated Yankee Stadium the past spring. In the background, a championship baseball game was in progress.

That was the way it was in the 1970s, a decade in which baseball and television could seem made for each other and yet totally ill-suited. But even when the medium demeaned or distorted the game, baseball needed televi-

It was big news when Frank Robinson (above, right) became baseball's first black manager in 1975, and NBC's Joe Garagiola (left) brought the story to millions during a "Game of the Week" broadcast. Garagiola's self-deprecating humor and knowledge of the game and its players made him a Saturday-afternoon fixture from 1976 through 1988.

sion, both for the money it offered and for its connection to a generation that had outgrown newspapers and radio. It was a reversal of the way things had been in the 1950s, when television, a new communications medium desperate to become a part of Americans' everyday lives, pursued baseball, the established national pastime. The courtship had sputtered through the 1960s, as TV executives were enticed by other sports—particularly professional football—that offered more continuous excitement, more concentrated action, more constant viewer gratification. A game as unevenly paced and flavored by nuance as baseball seemed too seamless, too unfocused, too uncontrollable. But by the 1970s, America had learned to depend on television for its entertainment. If team owners and promoters expected to use the power of television to reassert baseball in popular culture, baseball would have to adapt.

So the game began to contort and reshape itself as it fell under TV's manipulative pull. Baseball changed in many ways in the 1970s and almost every one of them was caused, to some degree, by television—the schedule meddling that brought World Series games on freezing October nights, the enormous player salaries befitting TV celebrities, the show-business mentality that spawned exploding scoreboards, ball girls in hot pants, and grown men strutting around in chicken costumes.

Television helped bring about the designated hitter as an effort to "liven up the game." It insisted on, and got, commercial-length breaks between innings, to slow down the game. It brought electric carts to haul relievers in from the bullpen, to speed it up. It encouraged expansion of both leagues into populous urban areas with huge television markets. TV even had a hand in draining the talent pool feeding major league baseball. First, it helped

Ballparks and Boob Tubes

Fears that baseball's television boom in the 1970s would keep fans away from the ballpark turned out to be unfounded. Attendance rose throughout the decade, and in 1978 each league topped the 20 million mark for the first time. The big jump in the AL in 1977 is due in part to the addition of two teams, the Seattle Mariners and the Toronto Blue Jays.

Major League Attendance

In Millions

American League
22,372,820

National League
21,178,491

225
200
150
100
50

1970 1971 1972 1973 1974 1975 1976 1977 1978 1979

Television mandated night World Series games starting in 1971, so players, like Yankee reliever Sparky Lyle (below), donned winter gear to stay warm.

to build up other sports, such as football and basketball, which lured away young athletes who in times past might have made a career of baseball. And it slowly subverted the minor leagues. Bush league teams, which used to be a part of life in small cities and towns all over the country, just couldn't draw crowds anymore, once people could stay home and watch big league games for free.

What offended baseball purists most was the conversion of the game into prime-time entertainment. Baseball, after all, was meant to be played outdoors in daylight. High TV viewer ratings, however, were to be had at night, and that, ultimately, is what really mattered. It was bad enough to have more night games in the regular season, but beginning in 1971, television made night baseball a part of the World Series. The following year, a TV-friendly schedule was set: the first two games of the World Series would be played on weekend afternoons, then there was a day off, three night games, another day off, and, if needed, the final two games were to be played the next weekend.

In time, even weekend games weren't sacred. Beginning in 1976, Commissioner Bowie Kuhn accepted $700,000 from NBC to allow the network to move a World Series game to Sunday night. The reason? Pro football had Sunday afternoon locked up. "When are we going to stop letting TV tell us when we are going to play," Yankee manager Billy Martin complained before the game. "This is asinine, playing night games in October. It's damn near freezing out there." Technically, it wasn't freezing, but it was 43 degrees in Cincinnati that night. Kuhn insisted that the weather was perfectly acceptable and spent the entire game sitting in his box without an overcoat. But

Yankee third baseman Graig Nettles was not fooled. He spent the game holding a hot water bottle to his bat to keep it warm.

Baseball fans blanched when a network producer suggested that the major leagues could get away with staging games only on weekends. Writer Roger Angell went so far as to predict that one day the World Series, like the Super Bowl, would be contested only in warm-weather cities. It could be called Superweek and would be better than the Super Bowl because it had seven games. "It will be an unbeatable television property," he suggested sarcastically, "the first All-American sports show truly worthy of Howard Cosell."

Even though West Coast baseball players didn't risk frostbite, prime-time scheduling created other problems in that part of the country. To keep advertisers and millions of East Coast viewers happy, West Coast games started at 5:30 or 6:00 p.m., Pacific time, which, because of lengthening shadows and fading light, happens to be the worst time of day to try to hit a baseball. Teams that played in Atlanta had the same problem, but for a different reason. Braves owner Ted Turner broadcast all of Atlanta's games on the cable network he owned and, for a time, scheduled games at 5:30. With luck, they would be over by 8:30, when the channel's nightly movie was supposed to start.

Other owners may have questioned Turner's priorities, but they had no problem with the concept of pay TV. For many of them, it was a financial godsend, though most did not cash in on it until the 1980s. But even before the cable bonanza, television money accounted for almost one-third of baseball's gross revenue. The new source of income increased the value of baseball franchises, but also gave networks and local stations that much more lever-

White Sox owner Bill Veeck would do just about anything to put fans in the seats, from outfitting his players in short pants—modeled here by pitchers Ken Kravec (above, left) and Goose Gossage—to exotic promotional events like "Disco Demolition Night."

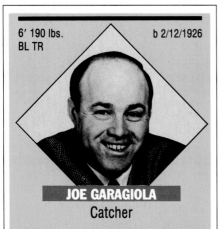

6' 190 lbs.
BL TR

b 2/12/1926

JOE GARAGIOLA
Catcher

Although he always dreamed of being a .300 hitter, Joe Garagiola is more at home in front of the camera than he was in his nine years on the field. Since the start of his second career in 1955, he has been an announcer for the Cardinals and Yankees, and a familiar face on game shows and commercials. But sportscasting's most famous bald man is best known to baseball fans for his announcing on NBC's Game of the Week from 1976 through 1988.

In 1950 Garagiola's season with the St. Louis Cardinals was cut short by a shoulder separation, and he was forced to consider what he would do if he was unable to continue playing ball. When he returned to the playing field the next season, he began to prepare for a future slot in the broadcasting booth. He began writing down anecdotes and practicing his announcing with a tape recorder. Once he even did the play-by-play call from his catcher's crouch, while a confused Roy Campanella looked over his shoulder at Garagiola from the batter's box.

On the air, one of Garagiola's favorite comic targets is Joe Garagiola the player. In fact his performance, though spotty, was at times outstanding. As a Cardinal rookie in 1946 he had an excellent World Series against the Boston Red Sox, hitting .316 with four RBI. In 1950, when injuries shortened his season to 34 games, Garagiola got his wish: he hit .318 for the year.

Garagiola played his last games with the Giants in 1954, and retired with a .257 lifetime batting average.

Dave Winfield's aggressive play and colorful Padre uniform were made for TV, but the San Diego market proved too small for his talent, so in 1980 he went to the Yankees.

age in pushing for changes to rules and scheduling. TV money created another problem: it tended to make the rich teams richer. Invariably, clubs in giant markets like New York, Chicago, Montreal, Philadelphia and Los Angeles were able to sign lucrative contracts with local stations to televise games. In the late 1970s, the Expos had a $6.3 million agreement with a local TV station. The Royals, by contrast, signed a deal that brought in only $500,000.

In proper democratic fashion, each team received equal amounts from the national networks for the rights to the World Series, league championships, the All-Star Game, and a set number of "Games of the Week"—by 1979, the pot had grown to $1.8 million per team. But the have-nots wanted to do better. They thought the owners should turn more of their games over to the networks in exchange for more money, pointing out that each National Football League team was getting more than $5 million a year. The haves, however, resisted, seeing this as creeping socialism. By maintaining the status quo, they held on to their financial superiority, an edge that some of them used to great advantage in the salary bidding wars that began in the fall of 1976.

Certainly, no one could blame television for the arrival of free agency. That was probably inevitable. But there's no question that TV upped the ante on player salaries, first by giving teams more money to play with, and second by bestowing the aura of celebrity on ballplayers, be they extraordinary athletes or .250 hitters with photogenic hair. With its overpowering need to put on a good show, especially if the game wasn't cooperating, television brought fans closer to the players than they had ever been. It

took them into the dugouts, into the bullpens, into the locker rooms. Its cameras came in tight on players' faces as they blew bubbles and screamed obscenities at umpires. But what players lost in privacy, they more than made up for in fame. Under such scrutiny, it was hard for players to maintain their dignity. After all, how regal would Joe DiMaggio have seemed if fans had seen him spit every ten seconds?

Once a player became a celebrity, his value extended far beyond his ability to handle the hit-and-run or to throw strikeouts. He could demand the salary of an entertainer, someone who "put meat in the seats," as Reggie Jackson liked to say about himself. Jackson, in fact, was the ideal TV celebrity. He was attractive, had dramatic flair, and greeted an approaching camera as eagerly as he did a hanging curveball. Most important, he understood and fully supported television's efforts to project him as larger than life; this, after all, was a man who had once referred to "the magnitude of me." In another era, Jackson might have been too one-dimensional a player to be considered a star. But in the age of television, he was right for the times, and soon passed the true test of celebrity—America knew him on a first-name basis.

The camera had another effect—it changed the way people watched the game. To compensate for a fuzzy, two-dimensional image on a small screen, TV producers placed cameras in every available corner of the ballpark and used technology to repackage action. Fans grew used to the close-up views of the pitcher, catcher and batter the center field camera provided. They came to expect instant replays. They wanted to see plays from other angles and in slow motion. They longed for the magic of split screens. It reached the point that people who actually went to the game felt cheated by what they couldn't see, which explains why so many stadiums ended up installing giant

At 9:07 p.m. on April 8, 1974, Atlanta's Hank Aaron drove a 1–0 fastball from Al Downing of the Dodgers out of Fulton County Stadium and into the history books. Aaron's 715th career home run broke Babe Ruth's record and earned him endless congratulations, the first of which came from Dodger shortstop Bill Russell and second baseman Davey Lopes.

Steve Carlton

When Reds manager Russ Nixon was asked what came to his mind when he heard the name Steve Carlton, his answer was simple: "A loss." Lots of opposing managers probably felt the same way about Carlton, whose awesome slider and will to win cut a wide swath through the NL in the 1970s.

His numbers are stunning: four Cy Young Awards—more than anyone else—six 20-win seasons, five NL strikeout titles. Carlton remains one of the game's most intriguing figures, a man whose temperament was as hard to solve as his pitches. Baseball players—even pitchers, considered the flakiest group in the game—rarely do any of the things Carlton swore by. Few are vegetarians or students of metaphysics or experts on French wine. Even fewer go 10 years without talking to the press, or strengthen their pitching arms by plunging them into huge tubs of rice. But Carlton's idiosyncrasies never would have been news if it hadn't been for the help he got from a night watchman in Arizona.

In 1970 Carlton was suffering through a 10–19 season with St. Louis, when he received a ten-page letter from a fan named Briggs, who wrote that he was tired of seeing a man with such talent lose ballgames. "He couldn't have been more tired of my losing than me," Carlton said. "So I read his letter from beginning to end." Briggs' letter centered on techniques of positive thinking, and it caused a complete reversal in Carlton's outlook and his fortunes. The letters kept coming in 1971, and the 6' 4", 210-pounder went 20–9, but after a bitter contract dispute, he was traded to the last-place Phillies. The Phillies finished last again in 1972, but Carlton made history. He went 27–10, was responsible for over 45 percent of his team's wins, and led the NL with a 1.97 ERA, 30 complete games, 346⅓ innings pitched and 310 strikeouts. He was unhittable, and he became the first pitcher ever to win the Cy Young Award while pitching for a last-place team.

But the incredible work load took its toll, and in 1973 he was a 20-game loser. Carlton suffered through two more mediocre seasons before turning to the martial arts and a rigorous physical conditioning regimen that made him once again the NL's most dominant pitcher. "Unbelievable concentration," said the Cubs' Keith Moreland of Carlton. "I honestly believe half the time he doesn't know who's up there hitting against him."

From 1976 through 1982, Carlton used a blazing fastball, a sharp-breaking curve and baseball's best slider to win 20 or more games four times and the Cy Young Award three times. He also stopped speaking to the press. Quotes about Carlton were plentiful; quotes from Carlton were nonexistent. "He just doesn't think it's anybody's business what he does or thinks off the mound," said teammate Mike Schmidt.

In 1982, at 37, Carlton led the NL in wins, innings pitched, complete games, strikeouts and shutouts. On September 23, 1983, Carlton beat his former team, St. Louis, for his 300th career win. On August 5, 1986, he became the first left-hander to strike out 4,000 batters.

Carlton often got more attention for his idiosyncratic behavior than for his talent. He was different, but more than anything he was what baseball values most—a winner. "He is one of the few players who thinks he can win every game he pitches," said outfielder Gary Matthews. "And the freaky thing about it is, he can."

Carlton (above) was a bulldog on the mound, and once he sensed a win, he was all but unhittable. "If you don't get to Steve by the fifth inning, you might as well put your bats away," said four-time batting champ Bill Madlock.

Carlton (below) quickly made the Cardinals regret having traded him to Philadelphia in 1972. He beat his old team four times that season, allowing a total of just two runs.

STEVE CARLTON

Left-Handed Pitcher
St. Louis Cardinals 1965–1971
Philadelphia Phillies 1972–1986
San Francisco Giants 1986
Chicago White Sox 1986
Cleveland Indians 1987
Minnesota Twins 1987–1988

GAMES	**741**
INNINGS	
Career *(8th all time)*	5,217
Season High	346
WINS	
Career *(9th all time)*	329
Season High	27
LOSSES	
Career	244
Season High	20
WINNING PERCENTAGE	
Career	.574
Season High	.765
ERA	
Career	3.22
Season Low	1.97
GAMES STARTED	
Career *(4th all time)*	709
Season High	41
COMPLETE GAMES	
Career	254
Season High	30
SHUTOUTS	
Career	55
Season High	8
STRIKEOUTS	
Career *(2nd all time)*	4,136
Season High	310
WALKS	
Career *(2nd all time)*	1,833
Season High	136
WORLD SERIES	1967–1968, 1980, 1983
CY YOUNG AWARD	1972, 1977, 1980, 1982

6' 1" 220 lbs.   b 11/22/1950
BR TR

GREG LUZINSKI
Outfield, DH

In the early years of free agency and million-dollar contracts, selfishness and greed became synonymous with All-Star players. But Greg Luzinski was a notable exception. The burly Phillie slugger spent $20,000 every year to buy seats at Veterans Stadium for underprivileged kids.

Nicknamed "the Bull," Luzinski started at first base with the Phils, and then was moved to left field in 1972, his first full season. He hit 18 homers, knocked in 68 runs, batted .281 and was so aggressive in the field that it was suggested he wear a bell so shortstop Larry Bowa could hear him charging in after pop flies. "Everybody knew he could hit. I don't think anybody knew he could play the outfield," Bowa said. "Now that I know him, I think he cares more than anybody on the club. Nobody works any harder."

The Bull averaged 32 home runs and 109 RBI for the divisional champions of 1976, 1977 and 1978. He and the Phillies slumped in 1979; Luzinski "only" hit 18 homers and knocked in 81 runs as the team fell into fourth place. In 1980, the Phillies rebounded to win their first World Series ever, but Luzinski didn't regain his mid-career form. He played in 106 games that year, slugged 19 home runs, 56 RBI and averaged .228.

Luzinski took his bat, but not his glove, to the Chicago White Sox in 1981. As a designated hitter, he hit 32 home runs with 95 RBI to lead the Sox to the AL West pennant in 1983. The Bull retired after the 1984 season.

Uniforms went multicolored in the 1970s, and Gaylord Perry had a varied wardrobe. Perry pitched for four teams in the decade, and in 1978 went 21–6 for the Padres (above).

television screens in their scoreboards. Traditionalists worried that television was recasting baseball into a different game than the one that was seen at the stadium, one that was less evocative but probably more entertaining. They warned that the new generation of fans was being spoiled by televised baseball and was starting to believe that the best place to watch a game was from the couch, not the bleachers. Attendance was bound to plummet, they insisted.

In fact, just the opposite happened. Beginning in 1975, when just under 30 million fans turned out for games, major league attendance rose every year through the rest of the decade, topping 40 million in 1979. Some experts traced the surge back to Fisk's wonderfully telegenic home run in the 1975 Series, a scene so exhilarating that it created legions of baseball converts. That may be overstating the case, but an estimated 13 million more viewers did tune in to watch the deciding game the following night, no doubt hooked by repeated replays of Fisk's moment of glory. The total audience for Game 7 was close to 75 million, meaning that almost four out of every ten TV sets in the country were tuned to the game.

Even to skeptics, it became clear that television was boosting the audience for live baseball, not shrinking it. Ironically, TV and inflated player salaries—the two elements most often cursed for perverting the game—probably did more than anything else to swell baseball's popularity in the late 1970s, mainly by transforming it into mass entertainment provided by rich celebrities.

Other forces were at work, of course, although they too were usually based on the notion that the game itself was not enough to keep the customers satisfied. Teams gave away everything imaginable to bring people

Some promotional ideas backfired in the 1970s, but none quite so loudly as Ten-Cent Beer Night at Cleveland Stadium on June 4, 1974. The game was forfeited to visiting Texas, when drunken fans stormed the field, then showered Ranger players with cheap suds as they left the field. Texas manager Billy Martin (left) broke a bat warding off hometown fans on top of the visitors' dugout.

Orioles' BALL GIRLS

The bat boy had been a baseball institution for years. TV needed something more in the 1970s, so on came ball girls, ostensibly to shag slow rollers in foul territory. The Orioles put theirs (above) on a promotional card.

into the park—bats and hats, no-nonsense ski caps in Montreal and Toronto, halter tops in Philadelphia emblazoned with the slogan "All the Good Things Wrapped Up in One." They staged special events—some spectacular, like "Kiteman," titillating Philadelphia fans by soaring over the Veterans Stadium outfield—some bizarre—"Wedlock and Headlock Day" in Atlanta featured weddings at home plate for 15 couples before the game and five professional wrestling matches afterwards—and others—a 10-cent-beer night in Cleveland in 1974 that resulted in a riot by fans and a forfeit for the home team.

In San Diego that same year, a man showed up for a Padres game dressed as a chicken and became as instant a legend as Pete and Reggie. The San Diego Chicken, a.k.a. Ted Giannoulas, grew so popular that according to one survey, 11 percent of the Padres' fans said they came to games just to see him. Other owners didn't ponder the meaning of this; they just wanted a chicken of their own. Soon, strangely dressed men were dancing on dugouts all over the league—a giant parrot at Pirates games, a giant Oriole in Baltimore, a giant unidentifiable green creature called the Phanatic in Philadelphia.

A mascot wasn't crucial, however. The LA Dodgers didn't have one and no team attracted more fans during the decade. In 1978 they became the first major league team to draw more than three million paying customers in one season. They didn't need a mascot because they already had a gigantic market, ideal weather, a consistently good team, and one of the most inviting stadiums in baseball. They also had Vin Scully. The team's broadcaster dating back to its days in Brooklyn, Scully was as much a part of Dodger baseball as the eternal Walter Alston. Knowledgeable, witty, and original in his descriptions of the action on the field, Scully was ideally

Grooming the pitcher's mound with his
hand and talking to baseballs were just
two of the antics that made Detroit pitcher
Mark Fidrych one of the most colorful
characters of the 1970s. Rookie of the Year
in 1976, with a 19–9 mark and a league-
leading 2.34 ERA and 24 complete games,
Fidrych suffered a severe knee injury during
spring training in 1977 and won just ten
games over the next four years, before
retiring at 26.

suited for radio broadcasts, where his insights and graceful language nur-
tured the listener's imagination. But as televised games multiplied, he adjusted to the visual medium so well that by the late 1970s he was a regular
on NBC's national broadcasts.

Scully, however, was a happy aberration. More often, broadcast
booths were crowded with former ballplayers launching second careers as TV talkers. In theory, they brought with them an insider's
perspective on the game. In reality, they brought an instant following. If celebrity players could draw fans to the games, why not celebrity announcers?
Ex-player Tim McCarver joined ex-player Richie Ashburn in the booth at
Phillies games. Ken Harrelson and Rico Petrocelli teamed up to cover the
Red Sox. Brooks Robinson became an announcer in Baltimore; Al Kaline, in
Detroit; Bill White, in New York.

The networks followed suit as ABC hired Don Drysdale, Bob Gibson,
Bob Uecker and Norm Cash. It even brought in Tom Seaver and Reggie Jackson, who both were still playing, to add authority to the loose-lipped duo of
Cosell and Keith Jackson. NBC also turned to ex-jocks, pairing retired shortstop Tony Kubek with retired catcher Joe Garagiola—by the end of the decade they were the most familiar baseball play-by-play crew in the country. It
was a trend that disturbed old-time broadcast announcers who saw their pro-
fession being taken over by men who could not turn a phrase as well as they
could a double play. "I tell young people who want to get ahead in sportscasting that the only way to make it to the top is to hit .315 or win 20 games," said
Red Barber, who had set the standard for radio broadcasts. In one watershed
year, beginning in 1975, 17 local sportscasters were fired by their teams.

The radio announcer who used colorful and sometimes corny language to bring a game to life was suddenly out of date. Who needed an announcer who could vividly describe action if the fans could see what was happening? Much more valuable was someone who could spin a funny tale between pitches, preferably someone who could do it as one of the boys, and who could speak from experience, even if it hadn't been such a good experience. Joe Garagiola was perfect for the role—a good-talk, no-hit catcher who was much better at telling stories about baseball than he was at playing it. Garagiola became court jester at NBC to challenge Cosell's pompous pseudo-intellectual image on ABC. While their styles were dramatically different, they succeeded for the same reason: they were as big as the game. They were TV personalities, which meant that sometimes they told stories that seemed to have little to do with the action on the field, and sometimes they seemed to be as enthusiastic in promoting an upcoming network sitcom as they were when describing a play. Fans screamed and cursed, but in the end, they kept watching. These men were entertainers, and baseball, after all, had become just part of the show. ◗

Pittsburgh pitcher Bruce Kison didn't exactly dazzle the television audience of 60 million with his slide to break up a double play against Baltimore's Davey Johnson in Game 4 of the 1971 World Series. Still, TV executives and fans who worked during the day were excited by the fact that this was the first Series game scheduled in prime time.

Mr. October

Reggie Jackson doesn't fit neatly into any of baseball's accepted categories. Baseball likes its heroes confident but not cocky, outspoken but not outrageous. Yet here was Jackson, the self-proclaimed superstar with an uncanny sense of drama, making headlines as few players had.

His credentials are spotty. Though he ranks sixth on the all-time career home run list, he trails such forgettable names as Gus Zernial and Gorman Thomas in home-run frequency. He had just one .300 season in a 21-year career and only once led the league in RBI. He is, and likely will always be, baseball's all-time strikeout king. What made Jackson great was not so much what he did, but when he did it and how. He provided baseball with some of its most memorable images of the 1970s—crowning moments of October glory and some of the game's lustiest failures. Few players could make the highlight reel by striking out, but Reggie's twisting, knees-to-the-ground version was every bit as familiar to fans as his home run trot.

Jackson alternately charmed and antagonized his teammates, fans and the press with a combination of talent, intelligence, arrogance and ego that left few people neutral about the man who eventually had a candy bar named after him. "Reggie Jackson is at least three different people," said former A's teammate Rick Monday, whose association with Jackson dates back to 1965, when they were both students at Arizona State University. "One of them I have always liked and admired and respected very much. The other two I can't stand. The trouble with being with Reggie is you never know which one of him you get."

The fifth of six children, Jackson grew up in the predominantly white Philadelphia suburb of Cheltenham and was a four-sport star in high school. From his many football scholarship offers, he chose Arizona State because it was the only school willing to let him play both football and baseball. After he was forced to switch from running back to cornerback on the football team, Jackson began to devote his full energies to baseball. It paid off, and in his sophomore year he set an ASU record with 15 home runs. Two years later, Jackson hit the major leagues with Charlie Finley's Kansas City A's. Former A's manager Eddie Lopat got his first glimpse of Jackson at an A's training camp shortly after the young slugger had left college. "He took a few swings, and you fell in love with him," Lopat said. "Only a handful can swing the bat like that. He also had that incredible speed. He had to be the fastest big man I ever saw. And that arm!"

Jackson liked big-league pitching immediately, and in 1969, at 23, he had the finest season of his entire career. He established career highs with 47 home runs, 123 runs scored, 118 RBI and a .608 slugging average. Always a streaky hitter, Jackson drove in ten runs in a single game that season. But his personality was streaky, too, and his relationship with Finley remained stormy throughout Jackson's eight-year tenure in Oakland.

Traded to Baltimore in 1976, Jackson quickly earned the respect of one of baseball's toughest man-

With or without a bat in his hand, whether on the cover of Sports Illustrated *(above)* or admiring his third home run in Game 6 of the 1977 World Series *(bottom left),* Reggie Jackson was the most reliable attention grabber of the 1970s.

Jackson's best seasons came with the A's in the early 1970s, notably 1973, when he captured two-thirds of baseball's elusive Triple Crown and was named the AL's Most Valuable Player.

agers, Earl Weaver. By this time, Jackson was widely perceived as a first-rate hot dog whose overblown ego blunted his value as a slugger. Weaver saw him differently. "Reggie's not a difficult player to manage, because he's what you call a hard player," Weaver said. "He hustles, runs everything out, hates to embarrass himself. Most important, he can reach a special level of concentration in the key situations that win games. And when the score's 9–2 either way, his concentration lapses and he gives away at-bats or makes a meaningless error. That may hurt his batting average or his fielding average, but it don't hurt his team none."

The bright lights of the big city came calling the following year and, as a free agent, Jackson signed with the Yankees and their high-profile owner, George Steinbrenner. The Yankee stage was already filled with stars when Reggie arrived in 1977, but he quickly gave himself top billing—and justified it with a team-high 110 RBI and a World Series performance few will ever forget. He hit a record five home runs, including a stunning three in a row on three swings against three different pitchers in the final game against the Dodgers.

Reggie held the spotlight for the 1978 Series rematch, as he lost a battle but won the war against rookie pitching sensation Bob Welch. Welch fanned Jackson to end Game 2, but Reggie got revenge in Game 6, as his two-run homer off Welch in the seventh sealed the Yankees' Series-clinching 7–2 win.

Jackson's term in the Bronx Zoo had other high points, like after his first homer of 1978, when fans showered the field with the free "Reggie!" candy bars they'd been given as a promotional gimmick. But eventually, the pressure of stardom in New York took its toll. "I never guessed how tough this town was," Jackson said. "It's a city that loves visiting celebrities and treats them great. If they see you two days a year, you're royalty. If they see you every day, you're a bum."

In 1982 Jackson opted for the sunshine and relaxed atmosphere of Southern California, and averaged 25 homers in five seasons with the Angels, including his 500th career homer on September 17, 1984, exactly 17 years after his first major league home run. The Angels took division titles in 1982 and 1986, bringing Jackson's career total to a record 11 league championship series. He finished his career back in Oakland in 1987.

Reggie was a prime-time player for a prime-time era. He often spoke of himself in larger than life terms. "I think Reggie Jackson on your ball club is a part of a show of force. It's a show of power," he said. "I help to intimidate the opposition, just because I'm here." More than anything, he was the best combination player-press agent the game has ever seen. Former A's teammate Catfish Hunter saw him this way: "Reggie's really a good guy, I really like him. He'd give you the shirt off his back. Of course, he'd call a press conference to announce it."

Jackson's high-profile, crowd-pleasing play made Yankee fans stand up and cheer (above), while his quick tongue was less popular with umpires like Jim McKean (left).

REGGIE JACKSON

Outfield, Designated Hitter
Kansas City Athletics 1967
Oakland Athletics 1968–1975, 1987
Baltimore Orioles 1976
New York Yankees 1977–1981
California Angels 1982–1986

GAMES	**2,820**
AT-BATS	**9,864**
BATTING AVERAGE	
Career	**.262**
Season High	**.300**
SLUGGING AVERAGE	
Career	**.490**
Season High	**.608**
HITS	
Career	**2,584**
Season High	**158**
DOUBLES	
Career	**463**
Season High	**39**
TRIPLES	
Career	**49**
Season High	**6**
HOME RUNS	
Career *(6th all time)*	**563**
Season High	**47**
TOTAL BASES	**4,834**
EXTRA-BASE HITS	**1,075**
RUNS BATTED IN	
Career	**1,702**
Season High	**118**
RUNS	
Career	**1,551**
Season High	**123**
WORLD SERIES	**1973–1974, 1977–1978, 1981**
MOST VALUABLE PLAYER	**1973**

The Artificial Game

n his second full season in the majors, Joe Morgan met Astroturf. Like most other Astros, he didn't know what to make of it, except that it made a strange ballpark even stranger. He did know that it wasn't going to go away. Houston owner Roy Hofheinz had tried growing real grass in the Astrodome's first season, 1965, but when the roof panels had to be painted to cut glare, the lack of sunlight turned the field into a sub-urbanite's nightmare. Hofheinz wasn't about to have unsightly brown spots all over his "Eighth Wonder of the World," so the rug was rolled in. Morgan adjusted, assuming that one day the weird green carpet would be just one of the Astrodome's unique quirks, like the Green Monster in Fenway Park or the missing lights in Wrigley Field.

"I couldn't imagine anyone using it anywhere else," he said years later. "I couldn't see that it would change the game completely."

Morgan wasn't alone. Who could have imagined a major league team building its offense around the ability to pound balls into the ground? Or a shortstop perfecting his one-bounce throw to first? Or infielders losing high hops in the lights? By the late 1970s, all of those things were part of baseball.

By then, six other NL stadiums—Riverfront in Cincinnati, Three Rivers in Pittsburgh, Veterans in Philadelphia, Olympic in Montreal, Busch in St. Louis, and Candlestick in San Francisco—and three AL fields—Royals Stadium in Kansas City, Comiskey Park in Chicago, and the Kingdome in Seattle—had opted for the grass that wouldn't die. Artificial turf was seen as

All that was green was not necessarily grass in baseball stadiums in the 1970s, as sheets of artificial turf gave a plastic cast to a pastoral game. In 1977 St. Louis' Busch Stadium (opposite) was among seven artificial NL fields.

Waterlogged outfields became a thing of the past in the new artificial turf stadiums of the 1970s. The Reds' other Big Red Machine (above) was used to vacuum up excess water on the turf at Riverfront Stadium, making for fewer rainouts and happier fans.

a particularly wise investment in smaller markets like Cincinnati and Kansas City, where a large percentage of the fans drove from faraway to see games. If too many people arrived at the ballpark to find the game rained out, they might think twice about making the long journey again. Artificial turf also allowed ground crews to vacuum the rainwater away; by Reds general manager Bob Howsam's estimate, that fact saved Cincinnati at least 27 rainouts one year.

Players were less enthusiastic, and some were offended. "If horses don't eat it, I don't want to play on it," announced hard-to-please Richie Allen in 1972. Allen sufficiently overcame his objections to hit 37 homers and 113 RBI for the White Sox that year and to win an MVP award. Dodger infielder Jim Lefebvre spoke of defilement: "When I think of a stadium, it's like a temple. It's religious. Artificial turf is a desecration. It violates the temple."

But as much as players groused, they adapted, and in time, the playing surface affected everything they did, including chewing tobacco—it's not polite, after all, to spit on the carpet. All major league players, whether their home fields were covered with real or plastic grass, learned to hit differently, pitch differently, field differently, throw differently, run differently when they played on artificial turf. The changes revolved around one thing: speed. Balls that slowed down for fielders on natural grass bounded through artificial infields for base hits. Shod in sneakers, baserunners didn't have to worry about spinning their wheels in mud or sand or slick grass. "It is great for base-stealing," said Reds manager Sparky Anderson. "You get a good start. You won't slip. The traction is great." Outfielders could cover more ground and could even throw better because their pegs, instead of losing speed when they bounced, skipped over the carpet.

Pittsburgh's Bill Madlock (above) much preferred banging hits off artificial turf himself than snagging shots off the bats of others. But the four-time NL batting champ earned his nickname "Mad Dog" for his willingness to put his body on the line in the field and on the basepaths as well as at the plate.

Fielders adjusted first. Basically, everyone backed up. Since the ball got to them more quickly, infielders could play deeper and try to cover more ground. The same was true of outfielders. On artificial turf, line drives shot through the gaps; if a fielder played deep, at least he could use the better angles to cut off hard-hit line drives. Outfielders also had to guard against a new form of humiliation—fly balls that bounced over their heads and became cheap triples or inside-the-park home runs. "Artificial turf limits my defense," complained Fred Lynn. "I have to play deeper because the ball bounces so much higher and faster, and I can't dive for a ball the way I do on grass because of the danger of getting hurt. When a ball bounces 30 feet over your head, I don't think that's the way baseball was meant to be played."

Infielders did less griping. Balls bounced true on synthetic turf, and when someone went on about the romantic serendipity of bad-hop singles, it was usually a sportswriter, not a shortstop. "On artificial turf, the ball says 'Catch me,'" explained Chicago infielder Greg Pryor. "On grass, it says, 'Look out, sucker.'"

With ground balls so easy to read, a lot of mediocre infielders became good ones; good ones became almost flawless. Sparky Anderson went so far as to say that had Bill Mazeroski, the Pirates' sure-handed second baseman of the 1960s, played on artificial surface, he might never have made an error. Of course Mazeroski, who was hardly fleet of foot, probably wouldn't have been able to get to a lot of turf grounders, which explains why teams in the 1970s began placing a premium on a different type of infielder—someone who was quick enough to dart into the hole and strong-armed enough to make the throw once he got to the ball. Technique became secondary to pure athletic ability, and new players, more cocky about the bounce of

Three Rivers Stadium

For its first ten years, Pittsburgh's Three Rivers Stadium led a charmed life. The Pirates won six division titles, two NL pennants and two world championships in the 1970s, and they weren't even the stadium's most successful tenants. That honor went to the NFL Steelers, who won four Super Bowls in the decade.

Situated where the Allegheny and the Monongahela meet to form the Ohio, Three Rivers Stadium is nearly identical to Riverfront Stadium, 295 miles down the Ohio River, in Cincinnati. Three Rivers is a symmetrical, multipurpose stadium with artificial turf and yellow home run lines painted on the outfield walls—the kind of stadium baseball purists hate. But it's hard to argue with success, and since 1970 the Pirates have made Three Rivers one of baseball's toughest places for opponents to play. Their overall record in the 1970s was outstanding at 916–695 for a .569 winning percentage. At home, they were considerably better than that, going 504–302 for a .625 winning percentage.

In 1970 the Pirates won the NL East title largely on the strength of a 50–32 home record. It was the first of six seasons in which they had the best home record in the division, and four times in the 1970s they had the best home record in the entire league.

The Pirates, one of baseball's oldest franchises, had played at Forbes Field from 1909 until their move to Three Rivers. Willie Stargell christened the new stadium on its opening night, July 16, 1970, with the first Pirate home run there. Stargell then got the Pirates rolling early in 1971, and on April 27 at Three Rivers hit his 11th home run of the season to set a major league record for homers in April. The Pirates rolled past the Giants in the NL Championship Series, then came back from a 2–0 deficit to beat Baltimore in the World Series, including a 4–3 win at home in Game 4, the first World Series night game in history.

On September 30, 1972, at Three Rivers, Hall of Fame right fielder Roberto Clemente got his 3,000th—and last—career hit. Three months later, Clemente was killed in a plane crash. The Pirates won division titles again in 1974 and 1975, but won just one game in two National League Championship Series appearances. Pittsburgh's John Candelaria struck out a record 14 batters in a losing cause against the Reds at Three Rivers in the 1975 NLCS, but he came back in 1976 to hurl the Pirates' first no-hitter at the stadium.

The dirt infield at Three Rivers was covered in 1978, and in 1979 the speed of center fielder Omar Moreno—77 steals—and the power of Stargell and outfielders Dave Parker and Bill Robinson—81 home runs between them—led Pittsburgh to another NL East title. The Pirates, who adopted the theme song, "We Are Family," and were led on and off the field by "Pops" Stargell, swept the Reds in the NLCS but fell behind, 3–1, in a Series rematch with Baltimore. The family pulled together, however, and outscored the Orioles, 15–2, in the next three games, with Stargell pounding out two doubles and a homer in a 4–1 win in Game 7.

In 1982 Three Rivers began a $16 million renovation that included a new Astroturf surface, a new scoreboard, and more than 9,000 additional seats. And Three Rivers is a true multiple-use stadium. It has hosted the state high school football playoffs, truck and tractor pulls, circuses, rock concerts, and religious conventions.

The 84-acre Three Rivers Stadium complex includes 27 acres for the stadium, 33 acres of parking, and 24 acres for Roberto Clemente Memorial Park and a Vietnam veterans memorial.

Three Rivers Stadium

Juncture of the Ohio,
 Allegheny and Monongahela
 rivers
Pittsburgh, Pennsylvania

Built 1970

Pittsburgh Pirates, NL
 1970-present

Seating Capacity
58,729

Style
Multipurpose, symmetrical,
 artificial surface

Height of outfield fences
10 feet

Dugouts
Home: 1st base
Visitors: 3rd base

Bullpens
Foul territory
Home: 1st base
Visitors: 3rd base

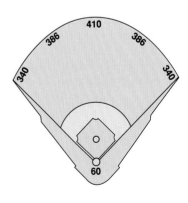

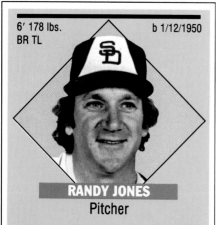

6' 178 lbs.   b 1/12/1950
BR TL

RANDY JONES
Pitcher

Since the Elias Sports Bureau began keeping track of such things in 1975, no starting pitcher has recorded a higher percentage of his outs on ground balls than San Diego's Randy Jones. He started with the Padres in 1973, and made his mark with a sinking fastball that registered just 73 miles per hour on the radar gun, a dozen digits below the major league average. Batters hit Jones' low, slow offering almost at will, but they rarely hit one hard. In 1978 Jones allowed only six home runs in 253 innings—one homer every 42 innings. It's tough to ground one over the wall.

Hitters remained unimpressed. Phillie Mike Schmidt said, "If I were a pitcher, I'd be embarrassed to go out to the mound with stuff like that." But San Diego fans loved their lefty with the Harpo Marx hairdo whose below-average stuff produced extraordinary results.

In 1975 Jones went 20–12 for a 71–91 Padres squad, posting the NL's best ERA, 2.24, and finishing second to Tom Seaver in the Cy Young voting. The Padres didn't improve much in 1976, but Jones did. He went 22–14, leading the league in victories, complete games and innings pitched, and he clinched the Cy Young Award. From May 17 through June 22, Jones hurled 68 straight innings without issuing a walk, tying the NL record Christy Mathewson set in 1913.

In 1977 Jones was plagued by a recurring nerve ailment in his pitching arm that eventually required surgery, and he retired after the 1982 season.

George Brett knew only one speed to play baseball—overdrive. Aggressive at bat, on the basepaths and in the field, in 1979 the Royals' third baseman became the second AL player ever to get at least 20 doubles, 20 triples and 20 home runs in a season.

the ball, began turning in acrobatic plays that made their predecessors look fossilized.

The Reds' Dave Concepcion was really the first infielder to learn the tricks of turf fielding and shape them into a style. He discovered that a ball's bounce varied depending on whether the surface was shaded and cool or baking in the sun or slick with rain—and he adapted his technique accordingly. He also discovered the beauty of the one-hop throw, a toss he learned to aim about four feet short of first base so it would bounce waist-high into Tony Perez' glove. Concepcion first saw it done out of necessity by Brooks Robinson on a play in the 1970 Series. When Concepcion developed a sore arm the following spring, he tried it himself. Soon it became part of his repertoire, usually combined with a fluid cross-step to grab a hit in the hole.

There were those who claim that the Reds were the first to master artificial turf. Like Concepcion, outfielders Cesar Geronimo and Ken Griffey seemed ideally suited for the speed game created by the carpet, and undoubtedly Joe Morgan would have caused less anxiety among pitchers if he had been running on dirt. But Cincinnati had so much talent in those years that as veteran third baseman Buddy Bell once said, "They could have won on Mars." Artificial turf simply gave them another dimension, another means of demoralizing opponents.

The Kansas City Royals were another story—a team fashioned with artificial turf in mind. The Royals always had runners—Amos Otis led the league in stolen bases in 1971—but when Dorrel "Whitey" Herzog took over as manager partway through the 1975 season, it had the effect of a starter's pistol going off. Herzog's motto became, "If we don't

When Busch Stadium covered its dirt infield with artificial turf in 1974, Cardinal outfielder Lou Brock celebrated by shattering Maury Wills's major league record for most steals in a season. Brock's 105th steal on September 10 (left) broke the record, but he went on to steal 13 more. Oakland's Rickey Henderson surpassed Brock with 130 in 1982.

Shortstop Freddie Patek typified the slap-hitting, base-stealing Kansas City Royals in the 1970s. Known as "The Flea," the 5' 5", 148-pound Patek averaged 39 steals from 1972 through 1978 and led AL shortstops in double plays three times.

run, we'll lose," and in 1976, his first full season in charge, his players were in constant motion. Led by shortstop Freddie Patek and his 51 steals, the Royals had six players with at least 20 stolen bases—Otis 26, Al Cowens 23, Hal McRae 22, Jim Wohlford 22, George Brett 21, and Frank White 20. Altogether, the team stole 218 bases, about 60 more than the year before. With so much running, the team did lose less often, finishing 90–72 to take the first of three straight Western Division titles. Only a stunning ninth-inning homer by the Yankees' Chris Chambliss in Game 5 of the League Championship Series kept them out of the World Series.

Away from the fast track of Royals Stadium, Kansas City was just plain ordinary, winning only one more game than it lost. At home, the Royals were carpet wizards, their field an evil fun house. "It's like playing marbles in a bathtub," said White Sox pitcher Dave Lemonds, capturing the frustration of countless Royals opponents who expected to play a nice, quiet game of baseball. As much as its sprinters rattled opponents, the Royals' specially trained hitters did the most damage. Herzog and his batting coach Charlie Lau knew that it made no sense for the Royals to swing for the fences—in Kansas City, the fences were too far away. Better to play the angles, or in this case, the caroms. Lau drilled his pupils not to pull the ball and uppercut it, but to spray line drives all over the field, get the ball bouncing, and let the carpet do the rest. They were taught to beat the ball straight down into the turf and see what happened. More often than not it hopped high over the head of a stupefied infielder. Because they excelled at making singles from ground balls, the Royals took away one of a pitcher's most effective weapons—the low strike. They also made pitchers stop throwing change-ups—even if a Kansas City batter was fooled, he could chop his way to a hit.

Building Boom

Expansion of both leagues in 1969 spurred stadium construction throughout the 1970s. The new stadiums were different—bigger than the ones they replaced and, in most cases, designed for football, too. They could also house rock concerts, rodeos and even old-fashioned tent revivals. A Billy Graham Crusade attracted a record 74,000 to Seattle's Kingdome, while Bruce Springsteen and Pink Floyd rocked Three Rivers in Pittsburgh. Below is information on the eight stadiums completed in the 1970s.

Stadium	Three Rivers	Riverfront	Veterans	Arlington
City	Pittsburgh	Cincinnati	Philadelphia	Arlington, Texas
Completed	1970	1970	1971	1972
Capacity	58,729	52,392	62,382	43,508
Tenants	Pirates, Steelers, NFL	Reds, Bengals, NFL	Phillies, Eagles, NFL	Rangers
Previous Major Stadium	Forbes Field	Crosley Field	Shibe Park	
Capacity	35,000	29,488	33,608	
Stadium	Royals	Kingdome	Exhibition	Olympic
City	Kansas City	Seattle	Toronto	Montreal
Completed	1973	1977	1977	1977
Capacity	40,625	58,850	43,737	59,893
Tenants	Royals	Mariners, Seahawks, NFL, Supersonics, NBA	Blue Jays, Argonauts, CFL	Expos, 1976 Summer Olympics
Previous Major Stadium	Municipal	Sick's		Jarry Park
Capacity	35,020	25,420		28,000

No one learned Lau's lessons better than George Brett. He had first come to the coach for help in 1974, and while Lau didn't promise Brett that he could make him a star, he did say he could make him a .300 hitter. In 1975 Brett hit .308, and the following year he won his first batting title with a .333 average. Talking of Charlie Lau's magic, Brett said, "He made hitting seem like the easiest thing in the world." If Brett could have played all his games in Royals Stadium, he might very well have been the majors' first .400 hitter since Ted Williams; his batting average was consistently higher on artificial turf than on grass, and in 1980 he batted .390.

Another of Lau's students was Hal McRae, the Royals' designated hitter. When he came up to the majors and flailed after curveballs, Lau moved him off the plate and had him cut down on his swing. In 1976 McRae battled Brett for the batting crown, ending up one percentage point behind at .332. When asked what Charlie Lau meant to a hitter, McRae replied, "One hundred grand."

The crowning accomplishment of the Royals' school for wayward batters was Willie Wilson. In 1978, his first full season, Wilson was far from a major league hitter, but he had legs that covered the distance between first and second base in the time it took a pitcher to gulp. Royals coach Steve Boros called him the "fastest person I have seen a in baseball uniform." Wilson had averaged 75 steals his two previous seasons in the minors, which so excited Herzog that he made Wilson his starting left fielder. Some Royals fans questioned the wisdom of this, acknowledging Wilson's speed but pointing out that the rules still did not allow a man to steal first. Herzog was firm. "If I have Willie here and don't play him, he'll never become a hitter," he said. "If he can't hit, he can't run. If he can't run, he can't help us."

It didn't really matter whether the surface was grass or turf when Minnesota's Rod Carew was at bat. Carew's incredible bat control earned him six AL batting titles from 1972 through 1978, and his intelligence and class earned him respect throughout baseball. "Many players are pleasant to manage," said Gene Mauch, "but managing Rodney is a privilege."

That year Wilson didn't hit much—his average was a dismal .217—but when he did, he always ran—he led the team with 46 stolen bases. By 1979 he had mastered Lau's stroke, batting .315—the first of four straight years he batted over .300—and led the AL with 83 steals. In 1980 the man who people joked would have to steal his way to first led the league with 230 hits.

Throughout the leagues, players who spent most of their time on artificial surface focused on hitting for average rather than hitting for power. In 1973 and 1977, the five NL players with the highest batting averages all played for teams with synthetic surface stadiums; in seven seasons during the decade, at least three of the top five NL hitters played for turf teams.

Still it would be wrong to assume that artificial turf gave home teams an unfair advantage. The Royals were a case in point—even though they dominated their division in the late 1970s, they couldn't run past the Yankees. Three times they lost to them in the playoffs, and when they finally did beat them in 1980 to get into their first World Series, they stole only three bases. Nor did every turf team fill its squad with relay runners. The Pittsburgh Pirates of the early 1970s were a prime example. They were a slow team before they moved into Three Rivers Stadium in 1970 and they were a slow team afterward. With players like Willie Stargell, Richie Zisk, Richie Hebner and Bob Robertson, for whom lumbering was top speed, the Pirates stole an average of 51 bases a year in the six seasons between 1970 and 1975, a paltry 23 in 1973. The Cardinals' Lou Brock stole three times as many bases that year all by himself. On top of that, the Pirates were no better than an average defensive team. Yet they were clearly the champs of the NL East, winning the division title five of those six seasons and knocking off the mighty Baltimore Orioles in the 1971 World Series. The Pirates won the old-fashioned

The more Royals outfielder Willie Wilson ran in 1979, the less likely anyone was to catch him. Wilson led the AL with 83 stolen bases that season and was caught just six times. He paced the Royals to a league-high 207 steals.

Mascot Mania

Long the undisputed king of the American sports scene, baseball found itself struggling to maintain its popularity in the 1970s. Pro football, with its dancing cheerleaders, was gaining momentum, and baseball mascots were seen as a new way of attracting America's entertainment dollar back to the national pastime. In San Diego, Ted Giannoulas gave the game a boost when he turned a radio station's promotional gimmick into a ballpark phenomenon made for TV. Other teams followed suit. "Even Elvis had his imitators," the Chicken said. "Now there are geese, kangaroos, beavers—I guess I've really started something."

Until his son Dave became the Philly Phanatic, Tubby Raymond was best known as head football coach at the University of Delaware. "Now I'm known as the father of a green transvestite."

Something of a cross between the Cookie Monster and Dumbo, White Sox mascot Ribbie (right) didn't work alone. He had a small companion, Roobarb.

While the Pirate Parrot (above) and Philly Phanatic (right) were good, all mascots bowed to the undisputed king, Ted Giannoulas' San Diego Chicken (below). But even with all his popularity, it wasn't all gravy. "Some days I wish I wasn't a Chicken," he said.

Sinkerball pitchers—like Cleveland's Dennis Eckersley (right)—are always better off on grass than on turf, since the ground balls their sinkers generate are slowed down by the natural surface. On May 30, 1977, nothing got through against Eckersley, as he walked one and struck out 12 in a 1–0 no-hitter against the Angels.

Playing deep became the norm for shortstops on artificial turf, even great ones like Philadelphia's Larry Bowa (above). Bowa's great range, quickness and throwing arm earned him Gold Glove Awards in 1972 and 1978.

way: they pummeled pitchers. They usually led the division in runs scored and the team batting average was always around .270. More than any other club, they showed that a team did not have to rebuild itself around runners to win consistently on the artificial surface. Once a ball hit the carpet in the gap, even Willie Stargell could make second.

It took Bill Veeck, the eternal iconoclast, to slow the turf revolution. One of his first acts after taking over the White Sox in mid-decade was to rip out the rug and bring natural grass back to Comiskey Park. "Ball parks should be happy places," he said. "They should always smell like freshly-cut grass." The owners of Candlestick Park in San Francisco followed suit in 1979, restoring the real thing in response to complaints from the San Francisco 49ers football team that imitation grass was causing too many injuries.

Baseball players also began to notice the physical toll turf was taking. A diving outfielder could end up with second-degree rug burns on his face to show for his hustle. The surface also absorbed heat, which could turn day games in places like Kansas City and St. Louis into weight-loss sessions. George Brett said it wasn't unusual for a player to sweat off ten pounds in a game. To soothe their scorched feet, the Royals kept a bucket of ice water in the dugout for between-inning dips.

What bothered players even more were the long-term effects of running on the surface every day. Older players said that by the end of a season, they felt soreness in their ankles and lower backs and worried that after they left baseball, the aches would remain.

"Turf shows all your natural ability—your quickness, your leg strength, your range. But most of all it tests your durability, because it does wear you

down," said Royals second baseman Frank White. "You also find out that when you're planting your foot to make the throw to first you almost have to take an extra little jab-step on turf. It grabs your leg so quick you'll lose your balance without that, and that's hard on your legs, too. My biggest complaint about turf is the pounding you take."

So for all the speed and excitement it brought to baseball, the artificial surface began to lose its luster. After an initial flurry in the early 1970s, when it seemed that natural grass was going the way of spitballs and flannel uniforms, the swing to turf slowed dramatically. Since then, in fact, only two other clubs have switched to carpeted fields, the Minnesota Twins and the Toronto Blue Jays, and both of them moved into domed stadiums. The fact that plastic grass has not encroached on more baseball stadiums is a victory for purists who feel that baseball on carpet had moved too far from its roots. Some fans, such as former Senator Eugene McCarthy, have gone so far as to suggest that statistics for grass and artificial surfaces be kept in separate record books. That won't happen, but neither does it seem that carpet will become the field surface of choice.

Today, as always, the grass is greener. ◑

The playing surface at Candlestick Park (above) has shifted back and forth with the prevailing baseball winds. It opened in 1960 with natural grass, went to an artificial surface in 1971 amid the turf boom, then changed back to grass in 1979.

Fire the Manager

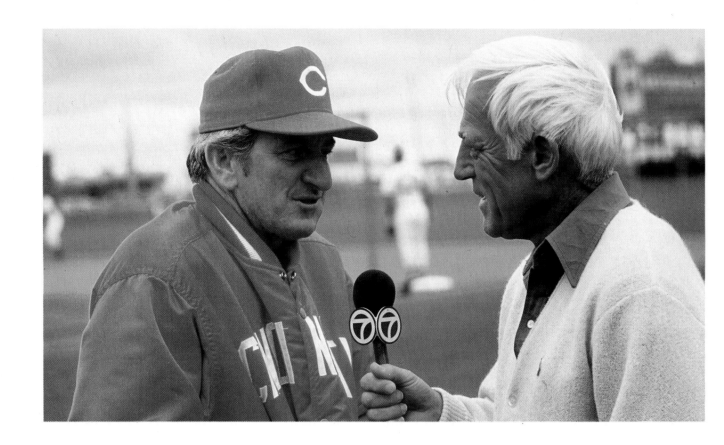

In 1979 the helm of the Cincinnati Reds was passed from Sparky Anderson (right) to John McNamara (left). In his short hiatus from the dugout, Anderson turned sportscaster, but on June 14 he was back—with a six-figure salary—as manager of the Detroit Tigers.

If there was one manager that American League umpires wanted to see fired, it was Baltimore's Earl Weaver (preceding page, arguing with umpire John Rice). Weaver wouldn't cooperate, however, securing his job with five AL East titles, three pennants and one World Series win in the 1970s.

Earl Weaver did many impressive things as manager of the Baltimore Orioles during the 1970s. He won five Eastern Division crowns, three American League pennants, and one World Series. His teams averaged 94 victories a year and won at least 90 games eight times. He managed to get nose to nose with countless umpires much taller than he. But one other accomplishment was more remarkable: he survived.

Not once in ten years was he fired, and for a major league manager at that time, that was a great feat. Only Sparky Anderson came close to matching Weaver's longevity: he almost made it through the decade with the Big Red Machine but was cut loose when his team turned merely human. Success was no guarantee of security. Royals manager Whitey Herzog and the Phillies' Danny Ozark both led their teams to division titles three consecutive years, but when they couldn't get them into the World Series in 1979, they were dumped. National League managers led their teams an average of 2½ years; in the American League, the average stay was less than two. A typical team went through five managers during the decade, but some were more charitable about giving as many people as possible a chance. The club that began the decade as the Washington Senators under Ted Williams and ended it as the Texas Rangers under Pat Corrales tried nine men in the job, four during one stressful week in 1977. The White Sox used eight; the Braves, Tigers, A's, and Angels each tried seven. Altogether, in both leagues in the 1970s, 86 men played the part.

It was a fluid fraternity. The better managers moved from team to team, discarded by one club only to become a savior for another. Billy Martin followed the cycle of damnation and redemption with three teams. So

did Dick Williams and Chuck Tanner. So did Alvin Dark, Dave Bristol, Bob Lemon, Bill Virdon and John McNamara. "I think they recycle more managers than cans," said Oakland's Bill North. Red Sox manager Don Zimmer offered a different perspective. When asked why he had showed up six hours early for a night game in 1977, he replied, "I want to make sure nobody's in my uniform."

Rocky Bridges, a minor league manager for many years, summarized the plight of the modern-day manager. "There are three things the average man thinks he can do better than anyone else," he said. "Build a fire, run a hotel, and manage a baseball team." Fans have always considered it their God-given right to second-guess managers and howl at them when a team struggles. In the 1970s team owners joined the chorus. Few were as churlish as the A's Charlie Finley and the Yankees' George Steinbrenner, but the newer owners tended to be more outspoken than their predecessors, more likely to criticize a manager in the press and, with the media fanning the flames, relationships could burn out quickly. The new owners were also impatient. Many of them were millionaire entrepreneurs who didn't see themselves as just winners in business; they saw themselves as winners in life. Owning a loser did not fit the image. Owning a loser also did not mean big crowds, high TV ratings or acceptable profits. So they were not reluctant to take what they saw as bold actions to create a winner, whether it was to pay millions of dollars for a free agent or to fire the manager of a tumbling team. More than ever, the manager became the easy scapegoat, as writer Thomas Boswell put it, "a sort of human sandbag to be heaved over the side when more altitude was needed."

Billy Martin (far right) had a well-earned reputation for getting into fistfights with his players, but it was his former coach with the Rangers, Frank Lucchesi (near right), who wound up in the hospital after a one-sided scrap in 1977, after Ranger infielder Lenny Randle took exception to Lucchesi's decision to replace him at second base with rookie Bump Wills.

On May 11, 1977, the major league managerial circus reached its climax, as Braves owner Ted Turner left the board room for a one-day stint as the team's manager. He retired with an 0–1 record, a bit less dignity, and the Braves' losing streak reached 17 games.

Braves owner Ted Turner went a step further. In May, 1977, after his team had lost 16 games in a row, he took owner meddling to its logical conclusion and put on a uniform. He sent manager Dave Bristol on a scouting mission and took over, figuring he couldn't do much worse. Not surprisingly, he didn't do any better—the Braves lost number 17 to the Pirates, 2–1. Invoking a league rule that prohibits a manager from owning a team, NL President Chub Feeney ended Turner's dugout fantasy after one game. Turner was disappointed. "Managing isn't all that difficult," he said after the game. "All you have to do is score more runs than the other guy."

Domineering owners were just one side of the shrinking box in which managers found themselves. They also had to contend with a new breed of players—young men with college educations, who, as Leo Durocher complained, didn't want to know *how* to do something but *why* they had to do it. For old-timers like Durocher, who had managed his first team in 1939, it was a bitter adjustment. When he took his last managing job with the Houston Astros in 1972, he vowed to become a sensitive man, or at least as sensitive as "Leo the Lip" could be. He would play cards with players, even listen to their stories. The new Leo lasted a season and a half. Afterwards, he wrote: "The battle cry of today's player is 'I don't have to.' " Even Sparky Anderson, who managed the Reds to championships amid little turmoil, griped that only rookies responded to discipline. "And after three seasons, they're prima donnas."

Power gained by the Players' Association was power lost by both owners and managers. There were now limits on how severely a player could be disciplined. When Luis Tiant threw a tantrum at being yanked from a game and fired the ball into the ground and his glove into the stands, Yankee man-

Bad-boy slugger Dick Allen (left) flourished in 1972 under the patient leadership of White Sox manager Chuck Tanner. Allen's MVP year included league highs in home runs, RBI, slugging percentage and walks. But even Tanner's patience wore thin two years later, when Allen took the final month of the season off to tend to his prize horses.

In 1978 Pittsburgh slugger Dave Parker wore a face mask to protect a broken cheekbone he suffered in a collision with Mets catcher John Stearns. In 1979 he helped the Pirates win a world title under manager Chuck Tanner, but Tanner's loose management style came under fire when Parker and other Pirates were the focus of a cocaine scandal in the early 1980s.

ager Dick Howser could fine him no more than $500, which, given Tiant's salary, was but a blip in his bank account. Free agency shriveled a manager's authority even more. What player with a multi-year contract was going to listen to someone with a one-year contract who made half as much money? And what owner, if he or she had spent hundreds of thousands of dollars to sign a player, would unload him just because he had bad-mouthed his boss? As early as 1972, Billy Martin began lobbying owners to follow pro football's example of paying coaches more than players and giving them long-term contracts. But baseball owners didn't think much of the idea; Martin subsequently was fired four times in eight years, twice by Steinbrenner.

With so much leverage, players became bolder. Many now had incentive clauses in their contracts that gave them bonuses when their statistics reached certain levels, and some were not shy about asking their managers to keep them in mind when deciding who would hit or pitch and how often. When annoyed, they sniped at their managers in the press. Sometimes the feuds turned nasty, like the open revolt by Houston players that drove disciplinarian Harry "The Hat" Walker from his job. Occasionally, they turned violent.

The ugliest incident occurred in spring training of 1977, when Texas Rangers manager Frank Lucchesi and infielder Lenny Randle got into a scrap before an exhibition game. Randle was fined $10,000, suspended without pay for a month, and soon shipped off to the Mets. Lucchesi had plastic surgery for a fractured cheekbone but had lost control of the team and was fired. Eddie Stanky, the onetime Dodger and Giant star, and Connie Ryan served as interim managers until Orioles third-base coach Billy Hunter took the job. Hunter did well enough—the Rangers finished second in their division, but in 1979 he was gone and the Rangers finished third.

Willie Stargell

There were times when Willie Stargell seemed too strong for the game. He stood at the plate, sweeping his bat in a wide arc, spinning it around as if it were a cardboard cutout. Then he strode into a pitch and sent it rising, like a tee shot, to a spot far beyond where baseballs usually landed. Seven times he hit home runs over the 86-foot-high right field stands at Forbes Field in Pittsburgh—something that was done only 18 times in the ballpark's history. In 1969 he hit an Alan Foster curveball well over 500 feet. It was the first homer ever to land outside Dodger Stadium.

"I never saw anything like it," said Don Sutton, another Dodger pitcher. "He doesn't just hit pitchers. He takes away their dignity."

Throughout his 21-year career with the Pirates, Stargell was one of the game's classic sluggers: a bulky man with an oversized swing. For 13 straight seasons he hit at least 20 home runs. Statistically, his best seasons were 1971 and 1973, when he led the league with 48 and 44 homers, respectively. But Stargell is best remembered for 1979, the year the sports world came to know him as "Pops," the head of the Pirates' self-proclaimed "family."

Soft-spoken and unassuming, he was a reluctant leader. For the first half of his career, the leadership role on the Pirates had been carried by other players, primarily the team's superstar, Roberto Clemente. But when Clemente died in a plane crash after the 1972 season, the team looked to Stargell for direction. He led the Pirates to division championships in 1974 and 1975, but then endured two years of misery. During the 1976 season, his wife, Dolores, had brain surgery to remove a blood clot. The following year he pinched a nerve in his elbow

trying to break up a fight, and his season ended in mid-July. He would never fully recover, the experts predicted; he was too old, too battered, too slow to regain his intimidating power. In response, Stargell batted .295, hit 28 homers and knocked in 97 runs to become the NL's Comeback Player of the Year in 1978.

The Pirates had closed fast that year and almost caught the division-winning Phillies. In 1979 they were primed to reclaim the NL East crown. With players like Dave Parker and Bill Madlock, the team was a talky and rambunctious group—one that dressed and undressed to loud disco music in the clubhouse. In the middle of all the noise was Stargell the stabilizer. After most games, he would reward top performances by handing out little cloth stars, which the players had sewn on their caps. There was no doubt as to who was setting the team's standards. He led on the field, too, hitting 32 homers and making only three errors at first base. After the season, his contribution was recognized when he was selected, along with the Cardinals' Keith Hernandez, as the league's MVP. At 38, he was the oldest player ever to win the honor.

When the Pirates swept the Reds in the playoffs that year, Stargell was the catalyst: two homers, six RBI and a .455 average. In the World Series against the Orioles, he was even better. He had three home runs, seven RBI and a record 25 total bases. In Game 7, with his team behind 1–0, he came to bat in the sixth inning with a runner on base, and he lifted a high fly for a homer that gave the Bucs the lead and ultimately the championship.

Once again, in the way he knew best, Pops had spoken.

Whether exploding into a pitch (left) or leaping for joy after a World Series win (below), Willie Stargell played the game with an enthusiasm few could match. "When I lose the desire to go out there every day, then I'll let some other excited youngster enjoy it," Stargell said at 38.

WILLIE STARGELL

Outfield, First Base
Pittsburgh Pirates 1962–1982
Hall of Fame 1988

GAMES	**2,360**
AT-BATS	**7,927**
BATTING AVERAGE	
Career	**.282**
Season High	**.315**
SLUGGING AVERAGE	
Career	**.529**
Season High	**.646**
HITS	
Career	**2,232**
Season High	**160**
DOUBLES	
Career	**423**
Season High	**43**
TRIPLES	
Career	**55**
Season High	**8**
HOME RUNS	
Career	**475**
Season High	**48**
TOTAL BASES	**4,190**
EXTRA-BASE HITS	**953**
RUNS BATTED IN	
Career	**1,540**
Season High	**125**
RUNS	
Career	**1,195**
Season High	**106**
WORLD SERIES	**1971, 1979**
MOST VALUABLE PLAYER	**1979**

The Durable Half-Dozen

Volatile team owners and millionaire players combined to make managers a team's most dispensable commodity. Six hardy souls did manage to last for at least eight years in the decade, most notably Gene Mauch, who lasted all ten seasons without a single division title.

Sparky Anderson				Gene Mauch				Earl Weaver			
Year	Team	W-L	Standing	Year	Team	W-L	Standing	Year	Team	W-L	Standing
1970	CIN NL	102–60	1st*	1970	MON NL	73–89	6th	1970	BAL AL	108–54	1st†
1971		79–83	4th	1971		71–90	5th	1971		101–57	1st*
1972		95–59	1st*	1972		70–86	5th	1972		80–74	3rd
1973		99–63	1st	1973		79–83	4th	1973		97–65	1st
1974		98–64	2nd	1974		79–82	4th	1974		91–71	1st
1975		108–54	1st†	1975		75–87	5th	1975		90–69	2nd
1976		102–60	1st†	1976	MIN AL	85–77	3rd	1976		88–74	2nd
1977		88–74	2nd	1977		84–77	4th	1977		97–64	2nd
1978		92–69	2nd	1978		73–89	4th	1978		90–71	4th
1979	DET AL	56–49	5th§	1979		82–80	4th	1979		102–57	1st*

Billy Martin				Chuck Tanner				Dick Williams			
Year	Team	W-L	Standing	Year	Team	W-L	Standing	Year	Team	W-L	Standing
1971	DET AL	91–71	2nd	1970	CHI AL	3–13	6th§	1971	OAK AL	101–60	1st
1972		86–70	1st	1971		79–83	3rd	1972		93–62	1st†
1973		76–67	3rd§	1972		87–67	2nd	1973		94–68	1st†
1974	TEX AL	84–76	2nd	1973		77–85	5th	1974	CAL AL	36–48	6th§
1975		44–51	3rd§	1974		80–80	4th	1975		72–89	6th
1975	NY AL	30–26	3rd§	1975		75–86	5th	1976		39–57	4th§
1976		97–62	1st*	1976	OAK AL	87–74	2nd	1977	MON NL	75–87	5th
1977		100–62	1st†	1977	PIT NL	96–66	2nd	1978		76–86	4th
1978		52–42	1st†§	1978		88–73	2nd	1979		95–65	2nd
1979		55–41	4th§	1979		98–64	1st†				

* Pennant winner   † World champion   § Partial season

When Whitey Herzog took over as manager of the Royals midway through the 1975 season, the team was 50–46. Under Herzog, the Royals went 41–25, then in 1976 began a string of three straight AL West titles.

Sometimes a manager lost his job simply because someone with a bigger name came along. That happened to poor Les Moss in 1979. After more than 20 years of laboring with raw talent and enduring bus rides from hell in the minors, he had been given his big chance with the Tigers. He hadn't turned the young team into champs, but neither were they chumps, playing at a .500 pace about a third of the way through the season. They had even gone on a hot streak, winning 11 of 16 games, when Moss was called into general manager Jim Campbell's office. Campbell got right to the point. He told Moss that Sparky Anderson, who had been axed the previous winter by the Reds, had let it be known that he was ready to get back into baseball. Given the choice between Anderson, who had won two World Series and four NL pennants, and Moss, who had won 27 games, there was no choice. Moss was offered another position in the organization; he never got another chance to manage. "It's part of the business," Moss lamented. "I always said there's no sympathy in baseball."

Four years earlier, Bill Virdon had been dropped by the Yankees for the same reason. A top-notch center fielder with the Pirates throughout the 1960s, he was hired by the Yankees in 1973 after being replaced as the Pirates' manager by Danny Murtaugh, whom he had replaced two years earlier. In 1974, under Virdon, the Yankees jumped from fourth to second place, finishing only two games behind the Orioles. In 1975 they struggled again but were hanging on to third place two-thirds of the way through the season, when fate intervened. Billy Martin and George Steinbrenner found each other. Martin had become available when he was fired by Texas three weeks into July, with the Rangers in fourth place. Martin said he was unloaded because Texas owner Brad Corbett "wanted a yes man," which, Martin re-

minded everyone, he definitely was not. Steinbrenner was enchanted. He had his general manager, Gabe Paul, offer Virdon's job to Martin. Not that Virdon was out of work long. Three weeks later, on the day they were officially eliminated from the race, the Houston Astros hired him to replace Preston Gomez.

That 1975 season, in fact, provided a fairly typical rendition of the manager shuffle. Martin was the first thrown overboard and the ill-fated Frank Lucchesi took his place. Three days later, Jack McKeon was canned by the Kansas City Royals; Whitey Herzog was called in to try his hand. Hardly a week passed before Martin was making his grand entrance into New York. Five days later, one of his old Yankees teammates headed in the other direction—Yogi Berra, the second manager to win pennants in both leagues, was let go by the Mets. Gracious to the end, Yogi offered to pray for his old team. Under Roy McMillan, they still finished third. Within two weeks, Virdon was with his new team, the Astros. Eleven days later, the Braves, 31½ games out of first, cut Clyde King adrift. Connie Ryan was brought in to mop up. On the last day of the regular season, Del Crandall was dumped by the Brewers and replaced by Pirates third-base coach Alex Grammas. Meanwhile, in Minneapolis, Frank Quilici, at 36 the youngest manager in baseball, was, after 3½ years, deemed "too fine a guy" by Twins owner Calvin Griffith, who wanted someone with more experience. Three days later, he found his man, when the Montreal Expos unloaded Gene Mauch, who despite his reputation as a cagey tactician, had not been able to get the expansion Expos over .500 in seven years.

In the off-season, the revolving door kept spinning. A's manager Alvin Dark helped bring about his own demise, from a church pulpit, of all places.

In 1973 Yogi Berra (above, left) managed the Mets to an 82–79 record, which happened to be good enough to win the NL East. In 1975 a 56–53 record got Berra fired by general manager Joe McDonald (right), and replaced by former Mets shortstop Roy McMillan (center).

6' 2" 195 lbs.   b 12/1/1911
                   d 10/1/1984

WALTER ALSTON
Manager

Soft-spoken and stoical, Dodger manager Walter Alston seemed to be as unmysterious a figure as small-town America has ever produced. Yet during his 23-year career with the Dodgers, which gave players and fans ample time to study the man, no one was able to determine whether he was a fool, a genius, or just lucky.

Brooklyn Dodgers' owner Walter O'Malley chose Alston to pilot his team in 1954. Alston's only managing experience had been in the minors, and his major league playing experience consisted of a single game in 1936. The players saw him as weak and lacking in baseball knowledge. But Alston led the Dodgers to their first ever World Series victory in 1955, and to an NL pennant again the following year.

In no time, Alston discovered the miraculous effect that winning had on a manager's reputation. His quiet ignorance became reticent wisdom; his laissez-faire demeanor, the mark of a brilliant handler of men. And after the Dodgers moved to Los Angeles in 1958, Alston lived up to his new image. He won five pennants, three World Series, and finished second seven times.

Until he retired in 1976, Alston was the epitome of the organization man. He respected O'Malley wishes, proving that an accommodating nature does not have to be a liability in baseball. As for the secret to his success, even Walter himself may have scratched his head and resorted to one of his favorite phrases, "Danged if I know."

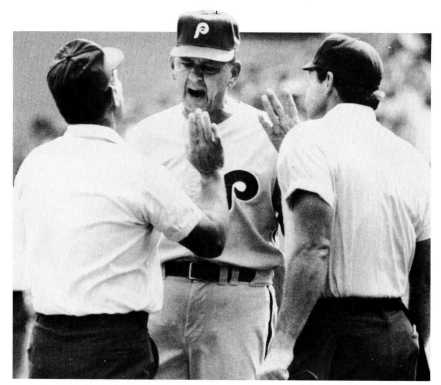

With Danny Ozark (above, center) at the helm, the Phillies won three straight NL East titles and averaged 97 wins from 1976 through 1978. But when it really counted—in the postseason—they won just two of 11 games.

Speaking as a lay preacher, he announced, "To God, Charlie Finley is just a little bitty thing. And if he doesn't accept Jesus Christ as his personal savior, he's going to hell." Finley did not appreciate Dark's concern for his soul and fired him immediately. A month later, the Giants, under new ownership, dismissed Wes Westrum and brought back Bill Rigney, who had run the team in the late fifties. Finally, in December, the White Sox, also under new ownership, decided to start fresh without Chuck Tanner. Within 24 hours, Charlie Finley was on the phone, offering Tanner a job.

For all his traveling—Chicago, Oakland, Pittsburgh—Tanner was one of the decade's more successful managers. Credit his personality. He was no master strategist. Nor was he a dynamic clubhouse leader. What he was was a nice guy. It was a quality that would not have won many games in earlier times when drill sergeants ruled the dugouts. And it was a quality that brought him under fire in the early 1980s when the Pirates developed a reputation as a team on which players overindulged in the cravings of their choice—for some it was food, for others, cocaine. But Tanner was right for the 1970s. He was the player's friend, never scolding or reproachful, always the smiling optimist. At the beginning of the season, each player was going to have his best year ever, according to Tanner. If at the end of the season, each player had had his worst season ever, he would point out that things could only get better.

His positive thinking did get results, though. With the White Sox in 1971, he convinced relief pitcher and knuckleball specialist Wilbur Wood that he could be a starter. Wood responded by winning at least 20 games each of the next four years, his best season coming in 1972, when he went 24–17.

Walter Alston (far left) had a reputation for being extremely patient with his players, but occasionally the placid manager built up enough steam to get tossed out of a game, as here in 1972 by umpire Dick Stello.

After surviving the frantic 1978 season, nothing fazed Boston manager Don Zimmer (above). The Red Sox saw a seven-game lead over the Yankees evaporate, then won their last eight games to earn a tie for the AL East title, then lost it in a one-game playoff. After the Red Sox slipped to fourth in 1980, Zimmer lost his seat in the dugout.

That season Tanner also coaxed a career year out of Richie Allen, mainly by letting Richie be Richie. Allen had long been a disciplinarian's bad dream, a talented player who figured that management should just worry about the number of home runs he hit, and not the number of team meetings he missed.

If Tanner disagreed, he didn't make an issue of it. Allen, loose and liberated, delivered an MVP season and the White Sox were the surprise team of baseball, chasing the much stronger A's all year. That raised expectations the White Sox couldn't deliver in seasons to come, so three years later, Tanner was on his way to Finleyland. His one year there is hard to judge. On one hand, the A's failed to win their division for the first time in six years and had their worst record in eight years. On the other hand, they were a team on which most of the regulars were soon-to-be free agents counting the days until they could escape Charlie Finley. But the Pirates must have been impressed because they agreed to give up $100,000 and Manny Sanguillen, their first-string catcher, for Tanner. Finley, for whom a manager was a throwaway item, was certainly not above trading one.

In Pittsburgh, Tanner was replacing an icon, the chair-rocking, milk-sipping Danny Murtaugh, whom the Pirates kept re-hiring when his replacements couldn't live up to his legend. Tanner was also getting a team that had slipped a bit in 1976, failing to win the National League East for only the second time in six years. The Pirates did have a few holdovers from the Clemente years, namely Willie Stargell and Al Oliver, but overall, they were a younger and much faster team than the one that had slugged and lumbered its way to division titles in the earlier seventies. The best of the new crew was right fielder Dave Parker, a tight end posing as a .300 hitter. He didn't make anyone forget Clemente, but he could remind people of him. In 1977, with

A New Breed of Owner

wners of baseball teams are like mimes—good ones should be seen but not heard. And until the 1970s, with a few notable exceptions, most baseball owners followed this simple homily and stayed in the background, content to let their players do the headline grabbing.

But in the 1970s an array of high-profile owners dotted the baseball landscape, as free agency, television and competition from pro football put the spotlight on the business end of the game. Some brought their celebrity with them, such as Gene Autry, America's singing cowboy, and Ray Kroc, the hamburger king. Others just brought money, like shipbuilder George Steinbrenner and plastics king Brad Corbett, whose fondness for free spending and meddling in on-field decision making earned them celebrity status.

The new owners were big businessmen who assumed the purchase of high-priced free agents guaranteed the success of their teams. They quickly learned that baseball was different from corporate wheeling and dealing. Of the owners who jumped into the free agent market with both feet, only Steinbrenner has had any success, and even that is mixed. His Yankees won back-to-back world titles in 1977 and 1978, but haven't won one since.

The new owners basically split into two camps —the benign and the meddlesome. While the meddlesome went as far as Atlanta's Ted Turner deciding to manage the team in 1977, benign owners like Autry kept a hands-off policy. A lifelong fan, he bought the expansion Los Angeles Angels in 1960 and did everything he could to make the team a winner. He paid millions of dollars for free agents like Bobby Grich, Don Baylor and Joe Rudi and offered $100,000 bonuses to untried rookies. Nothing worked. His Angels didn't win an AL West title until 1979 and through the 1980s still hadn't made it to a World Series. Some said Autry was just too nice, too devoted to his players and managers to make tough, winning decisions.

In 1974 Ray Kroc, the man who made McDonald's a national institution, bought the San Diego Padres, who had made last place in the NL West their home since becoming an expansion team in 1969. "I just wanted a hobby," Kroc said. Kroc brought stars like Rollie Fingers, Gene Tenace and Steve Garvey to the team, but they failed to win anything until 1984, when the Padres went to the World Series but lost to the Tigers. Kroc's enthusiasm failed to inspire his players, but did wonders for attendance, which almost doubled in his first year as owner. His ploys to attract fans included the announcement that after each Padre victory, ticket stubs could be redeemed for free Big Macs.

Texas's Brad Corbett spent as much as anyone, buying names like Bert Campaneris, Richie Zisk and Doyle Alexander, but the best his teams could do was second place. Corbett tried to apply the techniques he used in the plastics industry to the running of his club. Players were shuttled in and out like pieces of equipment, and general managers had to be light on their feet. "Brad became successful by selling one plant here and then buying another one over there," said Ranger general manager Danny O'Brien. "It means I have to be, shall we say, very flexible."

Gene Autry wasn't the only movie star-team owner in the 1970s. Danny Kaye (above, left) was one of six partners who purchased the expansion Seattle Mariners, earning him a seat alongside Commissioner Bowie Kuhn for the Mariners' first game in 1977.

Ray Kroc was all smiles before his Padres took the field in their 1974 home opener, but by the eighth inning, he expressed his displeasure over the public address system. "This is the most stupid ballplaying I've ever seen," he told 39,000 fans.

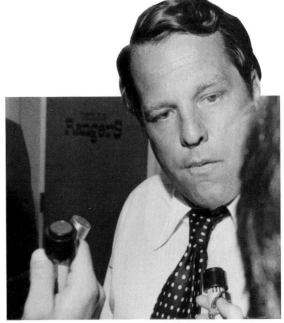

Brad Corbett (above) was an ex-minor leaguer who hit it big in plastics, but his free-spending policy never got his Texas Rangers any higher than second place.

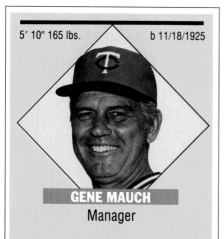

5' 10" 165 lbs. **b 11/18/1925**

GENE MAUCH
Manager

In an informal 1980 poll, sportswriters picked Gene Mauch as one of the best managers in baseball. But in his 26 years of service he won no pennants, lost 2,037 games to place third on the all-time losing managers list, and presided over the longest losing streak of the 20th century, when the pathetic 1961 Philadelphia Phillies dropped 23 in a row.

Mauch had the misfortune of being assigned to lead miserable teams to mediocrity. He started with the Phils in 1960, one of the worst teams ever, moved on to the horrendous expansion Montreal Expos in 1969, and arrived in Minnesota in 1976, just in time to wave good-bye to the most talented members of the Twins as they set out for the greener pastures of free agency.

Mauch became one of the great tinkering managers, revising his lineups night by night and using pinch hitters so often that his teams threw locker room celebrations for any player who lasted the full nine innings.

In 1981 Mauch finally got a decent team in the California Angels. But after winning two division titles without a pennant, he was replaced before the 1988 season. But Rod Carew, who played for Mauch in both Minnesota and California said, "I have tremendous respect for Gene. I can't think of anyone who has ever played for him who can say he hasn't learned from him."

Danny Murtaugh (above) loved milk and the Pittsburgh Pirates, but not necessarily in that order. Murtaugh had four stints with the Pirates covering 15 seasons from 1957 through 1976, and won four NL East and two world titles.

Stargell injured, Parker, with a league-leading .338 average and 21 home runs, first baseman Bill Robinson, with 26 homers and 104 RBI, and left-hander John Candelaria, with a 20–5 record, carried the team to its best record in five years, but the Pirates couldn't catch their cross-state rivals, the Phillies. Parker was even better the following year, again winning the batting title, but this time hitting 30 homers and knocking in 117 runs. Once more, though, the Phillies prevailed, taking the division by a game and a half.

In 1979 the Pirates made two key moves. Two weeks into the season they picked up shortstop Tim Foli from the Mets, and in late June they closed a deal with the Giants for third baseman Bill Madlock. Neither would ever win a good-citizenship award; Foli had a reputation as a hothead, Madlock as a malcontent. But for Tanner, it was like Richie Allen all over. Why rant when he could root? With Foli and Madlock as major contributors, Tanner handing out good cheer, and Stargell passing out stars for jobs well done, the Pirates merrily rolled into first place. From the large selection of disco hits that boomed through the clubhouse, the Pirates selected "We Are Family" as their theme song. Sports teams can get carried away with the "family" imagery, but in this case it probably was apt. Stargell, nicknamed "Pops," was the classic locker room father figure, and Tanner was everyone's favorite uncle. After holding off a late charge by the Expos in their division, the Pirates swept the Reds in the playoffs and then, after falling behind three games to one in the World Series, bounced back to tie the Orioles. In the seventh game, Stargell hit the go-ahead home run and the Pirates went on to win the championship, just like Tanner always said they would.

If Tanner had a soul mate in the managers' ranks, it was the Dodgers' Tommy Lasorda. He too was one nice guy and a man rabid with rah-rah.

Lasorda also replaced a legend, the stoic and silent Walter Alston, who had finally retired as the Dodgers' manager in 1976, after 23 years. Lasorda was a backslapping, loud-laughing buddy who bordered on caricature. There were nights when he actually had a better lineup than Johnny Carson, as one celebrity after another paraded through the Dodgers' clubhouse—Frank Sinatra one night, Gene Kelly another, Don Rickles for comic relief a third. With each, Lasorda would share some wine, twirl some linguini, tell some jokes. But mainly, he went on about Dodger Blue. "Cut my veins," he told them, "and Dodger Blue will flow." If it had, at least it wouldn't have stained the carpet; it too was Dodger Blue. Lasorda also made frequent references to "the Big Dodger in the Sky," who apparently was always looking out for Tommy and his boys.

Whether it was the help from above or just the bear hugs and platitudes, the Dodgers were an inspired team under their rookie manager in 1977. With third baseman Ron Cey batting .425, with nine homers and a record 29 RBI in April, the team sprinted ahead of the competition, winning 17 of its first 20 games. By the end of May, it was 13 games ahead of the Reds and cruising to a pennant. With Lasorda as cruise director, the Dodgers belted 191 homers, the most they had hit since moving to L.A. 20 years earlier. Four players had at least 30 homers—a major league record: Steve Garvey, 33; Reggie Smith, 32; Ron Cey, 30; and Dusty Baker, 30. Baker, who added 86 RBI and hit .291—37 points higher than his average the past three years—had his best season. So did Tommy John, who, at 34, and with a reconstructed left arm, had a 2.78 ERA and won 20 games for the first time in his career.

If a player had a problem, Lasorda was there with a comforting compliment. Shortstop Bill Russell, with 29 errors, was the weak link of the

Manager Tommy Lasorda (above, center) was baseball's ultimate company man, and his company was the Los Angeles Dodgers. A Dodger player and coach since 1950, Lasorda was elated when named manager in 1976. "It's like inheriting the Hope Diamond," he said. Better than diamonds, Lasorda had All-American All-Star first baseman Steve Garvey (below), who hit six home runs in three NL Championship Series in the 1970s.

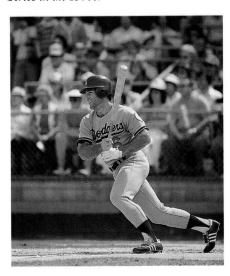

As manager Chuck Tanner (right) amply demonstrated in the 1970s, nice guys don't always finish last. After eight years of frustration, including four second-place finishes, Tanner grabbed the brass ring with his 1979 world champion Pittsburgh Pirates. Gene Mauch (opposite) wasn't so lucky. Mauch began the decade with Montreal and ended it with Minnesota and without even a division title after 20 years as a big league manager.

Leo Durocher began his managing career in 1939. By the 1970s, he had trouble dealing with pampered, high-priced players and eroding managerial authority. He also couldn't bring the Cubs a pennant, and was fired midway through the 1972 season.

Dodgers perpetual infield that included Cey at third, Garvey at first and Davey Lopes at second base. But Lasorda announced, "I wouldn't trade Bill Russell for any shortstop in baseball," and Russell settled down. Lasorda's cheerleading worked best, though, with Reggie Smith. Smith had come to the Dodgers part way through the 1976 season. He was no Richie Allen but had a reputation as a malingerer who could make the most of any injury. A dose of Lasorda sunshine took care of that. Smith stayed healthy and was the team's most productive player.

In the playoffs the Dodgers lost the opener, but knocked off the Phillies in the next three games, highlighted by a two-out, three-run, ninth-inning rally in Game 3. But Lasorda's *bonhomie* couldn't overcome Reggie Jackson's October magic in the Series against the Yankees, and Los Angeles lost in six. To show that the 1977 pennant hadn't been beginner's luck, Lasorda led the Dodgers to another division title the following season, although this time, they had to overcome the Reds and the Giants. They also had to overcome some bad Dodger Blue blood between Garvey and pitcher Don Sutton that culminated in an eye-gouging wrestling match on the locker room floor. But peace and happiness were restored, and again the Dodgers met the Phillies in the playoffs, and again they beat them. Once more they fell short against the Yankees in the Series.

Still, Lasorda had proved his point: a major league manager could win with love. "Our team is a big family," he told reporters during the Series. "My players have got manners, they've got morals. They're outstanding human beings. I love my players."

Somewhere, Leo Durocher cringed. ❿

The Earl and The Prince

Physically, they couldn't have been more different. At 6′ 3″ and 190 pounds, Jim Palmer was a regal, handsome, all-around athlete whose natural ability was enhanced by a passion for fitness. Earl Weaver was 5′ 7″ and 160 pounds, a fireplug of a man whose limited athletic gifts kept him in the minor leagues for all of his playing career.

But that's where the differences ended. Emotionally, Palmer and Weaver were near mirror images. Both were perfectionists who were driven to succeed. Neither ever missed a chance to say what was on his mind. And from 1969 to 1982, Palmer the pitcher and Weaver the manager played out their intriguing love-hate relationship as prime characters in one of baseball's longest, most successful runs—that of the Baltimore Orioles.

Palmer won 268 games in his career; all but 28 came with Weaver as his manager. Weaver won six AL East titles; Palmer won at least 20 games in three of those seasons, and was 7–3 in postseason play under Weaver. Their relationship was dotted with high-volume, high-energy disputes, both at the mound and in the dugout. At low points, Palmer saw Weaver as irrational, illogical and unsympathetic, while Weaver saw Palmer as a childish, hypercritical hypochondriac. During one visit to the mound, Weaver challenged Palmer to a fistfight. In another mound debate, Palmer handed his glove to Weaver and said, "Here, you can pitch if you think you can do it better."

Their battles were well publicized, but what rarely made the papers was the respect, admiration, and even affinity each had for the other. "Earl and Palmer are like father and son," said Oriole pitching coach Ray Miller. "Their fights are bizarre, the conversations hard to follow. During the game, Palmer will ask Earl about certain strategies and other things. Earl enjoys it. He often says Jim would make a good manager."

Weaver should know. The son of a St. Louis dry cleaner, Weaver was a minor league second baseman for eight years before getting a shot as a player-manager with a Class AA team in Montgomery, Alabama, in 1956. In 1961, at the tender age of 30, he was put in charge of the Orioles' minor league spring training camp, where he designed a comprehensive instructional program for all levels of play below major league. He made unprecedented use of computers and scouting reports, poring over information to come up with matchups that seemed to go against the percentages, but only because no one had ever calculated individual matchups as precisely as Weaver. Some criticized Weaver early in his career as a "push-button manager," to which Oriole general manager Harry Dalton replied, "Push-button manager? Earl built the machine and installed all the buttons."

Weaver became manager of the Orioles in 1968. He went on to post five 100-win seasons—second only to Joe McCarthy's six—and win four AL pennants and one World Series. He is an intelligent man who understood the role of manager as few have. "You have to keep your distance from your players no matter how much you like them," he once said.

Oriole pitcher Jim Palmer (above, left) and manager
Earl Weaver (above, right) did share some smiles in their
14 years together, but more often than not their
discussions ended loudly. "Instead of having my parents
scream at me, I now have Earl Weaver," Palmer said.
Weaver also liked to scream at umpires (left), so much so
that he was ejected 91 times in his 17-year career.

Palmer (right, on pitcher's mound) practiced his patented look of disgust while Weaver (4), Oriole catcher Elrod Hendricks (center) and first baseman Boog Powell registered displeasure with home plate umpire Larry Napp in Game 3 of the 1969 World Series against the Mets. They lost the argument, the game, and the Series.

"You're the one who has to pinch hit for them, bench them, trade them, fire them. You know the day will come when you've got to look every one of them in the eye—these guys who have given their all for you—and tell them: 'I'm sorry. You can't do the job anymore.' It rips your heart, but it goes with the manager's office. You can't help loving them, yet you can't afford to."

Palmer was probably Weaver's toughest case. A high school all-state selection in football, basketball and baseball, in 1966 he became the youngest pitcher ever to record a World Series shutout. Arm trouble sent him back to the minors, where he had his first—and probably his favorite—run-in with Weaver. Palmer was struggling in a game for Class AAA Rochester, and walked the bases full. Weaver, who was managing Rochester at the time, came out and said, "Ah, throw this hamburger a strike. This guy won't hit it. Throw it down the middle." So Palmer did as he was told, and a hamburger named Johnny Bench tagged him for a grand slam.

Palmer returned to the majors in 1969 and went on a decade-long tear, winning 20 or more games eight times in nine years. He had great stuff—a rising fastball and an outstanding curve—great control, and a great mind for the game. "When Palmer is on a roll," said teammate Mike Flanagan, "the innings go so fast they're a blur. We can call every pitch he throws. Maybe once a game he crosses us up. When he gets back to the dugout he'll tell us why before we

can ask. Usually it's 'cause he's thinking three batters ahead."

But Palmer's strong personality and philosophy often collided with Weaver's. "I have to move my outfielders ten steps to the right, so that after Palmer moves them back five steps to the left, they'll end up in the right place," Weaver said. The real friction between Palmer and Weaver came after 1979, when Palmer started missing starts because of what Weaver considered questionable injuries, and it usually peaked when Palmer wanted to come out of a game and Weaver wanted him to keep pitching. "I'll tell Earl my arm is stiff and he tells me I am a Cy Young Award winner," Palmer said. "What kind of dumb remark is that. He doesn't listen to me." Weaver countered: "His problem is he won't listen to anybody. When I want him, I'll just send Ray Miller to drag him back by his diaper."

Weaver left the Orioles in 1982, and by the time he was persuaded to return in 1985, Palmer had retired. They shared a broadcast booth for a short time with ABC, and they shared fond, if turbulent, memories of their 14 years together. "See this head of gray hair? Every one of them belongs to Jim Palmer," Weaver said. But once when he was asked how Palmer played golf, Weaver replied: "Like he does everything else. Perfectly." Even Palmer managed a compliment in a 1979 interview. "Earl's a great manager," he said. "The only thing is, I don't know why."

JIM PALMER

Right-Handed Pitcher
Baltimore Orioles 1965–1967,
1969–1984

GAMES	**558**
INNINGS	
Career	**3,948**
Season High	**323**
WINS	
Career	**268**
Season High	**23**
LOSSES	
Career	**152**
Season High	**13**
WINNING PERCENTAGE	
Career	**.638**
Season High	**.800**
ERA	
Career	**2.86**
Season Low	**2.07**
GAMES STARTED	
Career	**521**
Season High	**40**
COMPLETE GAMES	
Career	**211**
Season High	**25**
SHUTOUTS	
Career	**53**
Season High	**10**
STRIKEOUTS	
Career	**2,212**
Season High	**199**
WALKS	
Career	**1,311**
Season High	**113**
NO-HITTERS	**1969**
WORLD SERIES	**1966,**
1969–1971, 1979, 1983	
CY YOUNG AWARD	**1973, 1975,**
	1976

The Specialists

Bullpens got a lot of attention in the 1970s, as managers and fans kept their eyes peeled for the next great relief specialist. The Reds (preceding page) had some of the best, including Pedro Borbon (34)—who shared space with starter Tom Seaver (left of Borbon), pitching coach Larry Shepard (4) and outfielder Cesar Geronimo (right of Borbon). First-base coach Russ Nixon (2) is at the far right.

A lot of strange and intense men came striding out of the bullpens of America in the 1970s, a decade when relief pitchers became the country's oddest millionaires. They were baseball's new heroes, one-inning wonders who used trick pitches or simple fierceness to break the will of opponents mounting a final charge. By the end of the decade, every team had to have a bullpen ace—a pitcher who, above all, knew how to get the last out.

Not that there hadn't been star relievers before. As far back as 1924, Firpo Marberry was a short-relief specialist, probably baseball's first, and in the process, helped the Washington Senators win their only world championship. The 1927 Yankees scared everyone with their bats, but Wilcy Moore won 19 games for the team that year, 13 of them out of the bullpen. Jim Konstanty became the idol of relievers everywhere when he won the National League's Most Valuable Player Award on the strength of 16 wins and 22 saves for the 1950 Phillies. A few years later, the Yankees' Ryne Duren terrified batters with the combination of his thick glasses and his fiery fastball. In 1959 Elroy Face, the Pirates' forkball-throwing relief whiz, won an amazing 17 games in a row. Time after time in the 1960s, Dick Radatz used his bulk and his fastball to get the Red Sox out of trouble. And by the time he retired in 1972, Hoyt Wilhelm—the man who made kids all over the world try to throw a knuckleball—had managed to get the last out 651 times.

But in those days, relief pitchers were used as a last resort, exceptions to the rule of letting the starter finish all but the most critical games. In the 1970s relievers became part of the normal game plan. Even with his team ahead, a relief ace might still have started warming up in the late innings, preparing for his inevitable entrance. He was no longer used simply as a reaction

to trouble; now he was almost an offensive weapon brought into games to stop rallies before they could start. More than ever before, pitching became a group effort. Starters were told that six or seven strong innings was a job well done; relievers would take over from there. Complete games became increasingly rare; in 1979 NL pitchers threw over 100 fewer complete games than they had in 1970. Complete games in the AL actually increased, but the reason was another innovation unique to that league, the designated hitter, as well as having two more teams than the NL.

Many top teams, in fact, didn't rely on just one closer in the bullpen; usually, they built a squad of relievers, each member having his own special role. Unlike most things done by committee, it usually worked. Consider the 1972 Oakland A's. Even with its daunting starting rotation of Catfish Hunter, Ken Holtzman, Vida Blue and Blue Moon Odom, the team's bullpen of Rollie Fingers, Darold Knowles and Bob Locker made the A's champions, according to manager Dick Williams. Fingers, the right-handed short reliever, saved 21 games and was 11–9. Knowles, the left-handed short reliever usually brought in to face left-handed batters, saved 11 games and was 5–1. Locker, a right-hander who usually was first out of the pen and expected to keep the game close, saved ten games and finished 6–1.

Reds manager Sparky Anderson had a full supporting cast in his bullpen of Rawley Eastwick, Will McEnaney, Clay Carroll and Pedro Borbon, and he often used all four in tight games. To his way of thinking, it was easier to find four pitchers who could throw one or two good innings every other day than it was to find four who could pitch nine good innings every fourth or fifth day. "I think baseball's reached the point where, for most clubs, relief pitching may be the most important part of the pitching staff," said Anderson. It was no

Darold Knowles pitched in 765 games in his 16-year career, all but eight in relief. A member of the talented Oakland bullpens of the early 1970s, Knowles went 5–1 with 11 saves and a microscopic 1.36 ERA in 1972, the A's first world championship season.

Phillies relief ace Tug McGraw (above, left) threw his famed screwball only about 30 percent of the time, but the threat of it was enough. "You can set a guy up for it, and then not give it to him," McGraw said. "I still have enough velocity to throw a fastball by a hitter if he's looking for the scroogie." Detroit's John Hiller (above, right) called on the natural tenacity of a relief pitcher after suffering a heart attack in 1971. He capped his 1972 comeback season with 3⅓ innings of scoreless relief in the ALCS against Oakland.

accident that Eastwick was not just another failed starter who found his muse in the bullpen; from the time the Reds signed him at age 20, he was groomed to be a reliever.

Another 1970s team that liked to call on its bullpen early and often was the Philadelphia Phillies. In 1976, when the Phillies won the first of three straight NL East titles, the trio of Ron Reed, Tug McGraw and Gene Garber accounted for 36 saves and each of them got into at least 58 games. The next year, the save total rose to 43; Garber pitched in 64 games, Reed, in 60. But that threesome was easily outdone by the Pittsburgh Pirates' bullpen during the team's world championship season of 1979. That year, stringy submarine reliever Kent Tekulve led the league in games pitched with 94. Second place went to his bullpen buddy Enrique Romero, who pitched 84 times. Third place went to Grant Jackson, also a Pirates reliever. He got into 72 games.

Even when a team used its relievers in swarms, one hurler usually stood out. He was the recognized closer, the one whose entrance announced the game's last act. For most closers, finesse was considered an unnecessary complication. Usually they relied on one pitch—Sparky Lyle, his slider; Goose Gossage, his fastball; Tug McGraw, his screwball; Bruce Sutter, his split-finger fastball—and threw it over and over, taunting batters with the predictability of it all. They were seen as baseball's lone warriors, not pitching to hitters so much as confronting them, paring competition to its most basic level—"If I get you out, we win; if you get a hit, we lose."

Not everyone was meant to pitch on that edge. "Anyone can start a ballgame," said Reds pitching coach Larry Shepard, "but a pitcher must have a very special temperament to relieve. He's got to be high-strung and yet he's

After struggling as a starter in the 1960s, Dave Giusti (left) found the bullpen much more to his liking. He pitched 5⅓ scoreless innings and earned saves in all three Pirate wins in the 1971 NLCS against the Giants. Knuckleball relief pitchers like Charlie Hough (below) made catchers pretty nervous with runners on base and the game on the line. Still, Hough had 12 wins and 18 saves for the Dodgers in 1976. Unlike most relievers, he later became a starter—with Texas in the early 1980s.

got to combine this with great poise and self-control—after all, he's coming into an inning which has been damaged." Former relief pitcher and pitching coach Tom Ferrick put it more bluntly: "A perfect reliever is a guy with no imagination and his brains beat out. All he wants is to get the ball and throw strikes. Of course, he is absolutely fearless." Once a closer showed he could dance with disaster day after day, he had the job until he lost it. Some lasted a month, some a season or two, but not many hung on for the entire decade. In 1971 Ken "Daffy" Sanders pitched in 83 games for the Milwaukee Brewers, saved 31 and had an ERA of 1.92. The next year, his saves dropped to 17 and his record to 2–9. The next four years, he bounced around on five different teams, each one hoping he would re-create his year of glory.

When a closer had staying power, he could mean as much to his team as a .300 hitter or a 20-game winner. The Pirates had only an average starting rotation and, without Dave Giusti, probably would not have ruled the NL East through the early 1970s. Tug McGraw, pitching in Tom Seaver's near-perfect shadow, was the spark of the Mets' bullpen for five years. In their wondrous stretch drive to a division title in 1973, he was virtually unhittable, posting an ERA of 0.88 from August 8 through October 1. Then there was the Tigers' John Hiller; relief pitching would not seem to be the best therapy for a man with a heart condition, but somehow it worked for Hiller. After four years as a left-handed spot starter and fill-in reliever, Hiller, only 27, had a heart attack in 1971. Two years later, he was the best reliever in baseball, setting a record with 38 saves, pitching in a league-leading 65 games, and registering an ERA of 1.44. He never quite matched that year again, but for the next five seasons he was a Sinatra on a team of saloon singers.

6' 2" 210 lbs.   b 9/17/1937
BR TR

ORLANDO CEPEDA
First Base, DH

Puerto Rican Orlando Cepeda approached the plate with a 43-ounce bat and a plan: "If ball in strike zone, I swing. If I hit it, she go." Thanks to the designated hitter rule, Cepeda kept going, finishing his 17-year career in 1974 with 379 home runs, 1,365 RBI and a .297 average.

In 1955 the Giants signed the 17-year-old Cepeda out of a tryout camp for a $500 bonus and airfare to Florida. Cepeda came up in 1958 and hit his first major league homer during the Giants' opener in San Francisco. He batted .312 for the season with 25 homers and 96 RBI to become NL Rookie of the Year.

Shuttled between first base and left field with Willie McCovey, Cepeda set a historic pace at the plate with 222 homers plus 747 RBI and a .309 average during his first seven seasons—the last two on a bandaged right knee.

After knee surgery in 1965, Cepeda was traded to the Cardinals in May 1966, where he emerged as a team leader, capturing 1967 MVP honors as his NL-best 111 RBI powered St. Louis to the flag. After a poor 1968, he was traded to Atlanta, where he helped the Braves to their first NL West title in 1969. Virtually immobilized by further knee surgery in 1971, Cepeda was traded to Oakland and released in 1972 after playing just three games.

The new DH rule prompted the Red Sox to offer him a contract for 1973. Cepeda popped 20 homers and won the AL's first Outstanding Designated Hitter Award.

In the 1970s no pitch had a more devastating break than Bruce Sutter's split-finger fastball. "When it's working, I'll throw it 90 percent of the time," he said. In 1977 it was good for 31 saves.

No other relievers in the 1970s, though, were so good for so long as Mike Marshall, Sparky Lyle and Rollie Fingers. That each was also a bit out of the ordinary may have been coincidental. Marshall, with his long sideburns and his doctorate in physiology, was a bullpen workhorse, first in Montreal, then in L.A., and later in Minnesota. He elevated the role of relief pitcher to new heights in 1974, winning the Cy Young Award—the first bullpen artist to do so—and pacing the Dodgers to the NL pennant, then pitching in each of the five World Series games. No pitcher had ever done that before either.

The MVP of that Series was another reliever—the A's Rollie Fingers, he of the heavily waxed handlebar moustache, who won one game and saved three. Facial hair was about all he and Marshall had in common. Marshall was short and chunky, Fingers, tall and slender. Marshall was an academic, Fingers a fan of W.C. Fields and Saturday-morning cartoons. Marshall liked to analyze games; Fingers was at his best if he didn't think too much. He said he usually wouldn't pay much attention to a game until the sixth or seventh inning. For a guy who saved 209 games in the decade, averaging 21 a season, that was enough.

The only pitcher to come close was Sparky Lyle, who, over the same period, recorded 190 saves. Lyle was built like Marshall, but like Fingers, was not a man who thought deep thoughts. He was best known in the Yankees' clubhouse for sitting naked on birthday cakes. He liked to do things naked. Once he popped out of a coffin naked. That happened late in the 1975 season, when Yankees manager Bill Virdon called a locker room meeting, and noticing that Lyle was missing, yelled, "Where's Sparky?" Behind him was a coffin that one of the players wanted to convert into a bar for his van. Slowly its lid began to creak open and from inside a voice bellowed, "You raaang,

Whether Al Hrabosky (left) was called "the Mad Hungarian" because he seemed either crazy or angry didn't matter much to hitters, because facing him was unpleasant in any case. He peaked in 1975 with 13 wins, 22 saves and a 1.67 ERA for St. Louis, then closed out the decade with the Royals.

All great relief pitchers in the 1970s had something that made them distinctive, and for Pittsburgh's Kent Tekulve, it was his slingshot delivery. Tekulve baffled the Orioles in the 1979 World Series, saving Games 2, 6 and 7.

skipper?" There, in repose, lay Sparky, wearing only the charcoal he had smeared under his eyes.

On the mound, Lyle was not only more properly dressed, but also more predictable. Every right-handed batter who faced him knew what was coming: a hard slider on the fists, a pitch that according to one player was "like hitting a sliding bowling ball." That's all southpaw Sparky threw. That's all he needed to throw. He had been a good reliever with Boston in the early 1970s but became a master after his trade to the Yankees in 1972. He saved 35 games that first year in New York and had an ERA of 1.91. For the next five years, Lyle was the one constant on a Yankee pitching staff that otherwise changed as often as a Manhattan traffic light. He was most impressive, though, in the last half of the 1977 season, when after getting out of manager Billy Martin's doghouse, he buoyed the Yankees as they climbed over the Red Sox into first place. As the team surged in late August and early September, he won four games and saved seven others in 13 appearances. He finished 60 of the 72 games in which he pitched, went 13–5, had 26 saves and a 2.17 ERA. For his efforts, he won the AL Cy Young Award and a $35,000 bonus from Yankees owner George Steinbrenner. Unfortunately, Steinbrenner didn't stop there. Impressed by what one relief ace could do, he went out during the off-season and bought two more, Rich "Goose" Gossage and Rawley Eastwick. Gossage was paid $333,000 a year and Eastwick, $156,000 a year. This disturbed Lyle, who was paid $140,000 a year. He asked to be traded and, a year later, his wish was granted. He was shipped off to Texas and although he pitched in 67 games and saved 13 in 1979, the downslide had begun. By 1983, after short stints with the Phillies and the White Sox, Lyle was out of baseball.

Mike Marshall

Mike Marshall said he considered baseball his hobby. "Other than the actual playing of the game, I find the whole of professional baseball extremely boring and mind-dulling." Fortunately for Marshall, he played the game a lot. His record for most innings pitched by a reliever in a single season—208—has stood since 1974. That same year he became the first reliever in history to win the Cy Young Award.

Marshall came to the mound with an uncompromising nature, an unshakable belief that he knew at least as much about pitching as anyone else, and a doctorate in exercise physiology. It seemed obvious to him that he should be allowed to prepare his own training regimen and to decide which pitches to throw. Unfortunately, this philosophy did not sit well with some of the managers he played for early in his career. From the moment he arrived in the majors with Detroit in 1967, the two things he practiced most were his future money-pitch, the screwball, and how to pack and unpack a suitcase. It wasn't until 1970, when he was traded to the Montreal Expos, that Marshall met a manager he could work with— "a man," Marshall claimed, "who approached baseball the way it should be approached." The manager was Gene Mauch.

It wasn't only managers who had experienced the rub of Mike Marshall's rough edges. Throughout the 1970s he was never kinder to reporters than when he refused to say anything at all. He also never signed autographs, telling kids he would comply only if they could show him the autographs of their teachers. "As an athlete, I am no one to be idolized," he

explained. "I will not perpetuate that hoax." Even without his cooperation, the fans idolized him.

By the time he joined the Expos, partway through the 1970 season, Marshall was a full-time reliever. For the next three years he was the stopper of choice, culminating in 92 appearances—with 31 saves and 14 wins—in 1973. But that just loosened up his arm for what followed. The Dodgers picked up Marshall in the off-season, and in 1974 he barely sat down. His jog from the bullpen to the mound was almost a daily event. At one point, he pitched in 13 consecutive games, a major league record. By year's end Marshall had appeared in a record 106 games— winning 15, saving 21, and getting the last out 83 times—and the Dodgers were in the World Series. Naturally, he pitched in all five games of the Series, but he couldn't make up for his teammates' anemic hitting, and the A's became the world champions.

Over the next several years, Marshall suffered a rash of injuries, and by the winter of 1977 he considered himself a retiree. But in May 1978, Gene Mauch, who at that time was piloting the Twins, asked him to return. In one of the great comebacks in baseball history, Marshall went on to save 53 games and win 20 over the next two years. He remained with Minnesota in 1980, and then donned a Mets uniform in 1981, his final season. He appeared in 20 games, and wound up with a 2.61 ERA.

Shortly after his return to baseball, Marshall was overheard chastising himself for returning to the game he once described as mind-dulling. "Oh, it's a shame I love this game so." No doubt a lot of hitters in both leagues felt the same way.

Rubber-armed reliever Mike Marshall made his 100th appearance of the 1974 season on September 22, and at the time, it probably seemed that this was the beginning of a trend. But Marshall's 106 appearances are still an all-time record, and he is still the only pitcher ever to reach three digits.

MIKE
MARSHALL

Right-Handed Pitcher
Detroit Tigers 1967
Seattle Pilots 1969
Houston Astros 1970
Montreal Expos 1970–1973
Los Angeles Dodgers 1974–1976
Atlanta Braves 1976–1977
Texas Rangers 1977
Minnesota Twins 1978–1980
New York Mets 1981

GAMES	723
INNINGS	
Career	1,386
Season High	208
WINS	
Career	97
Season High	15
LOSSES	
Career	112
Season High	15
WINNING PERCENTAGE	
Career	.464
Season High	.636
ERA	
Career	3.14
Season Low	1.78
SAVES	
Career	188
Season High	32
STRIKEOUTS	
Career	880
Season High	143
WALKS	
Career	514
Season High	75
WORLD SERIES	1974
CY YOUNG AWARD	1974

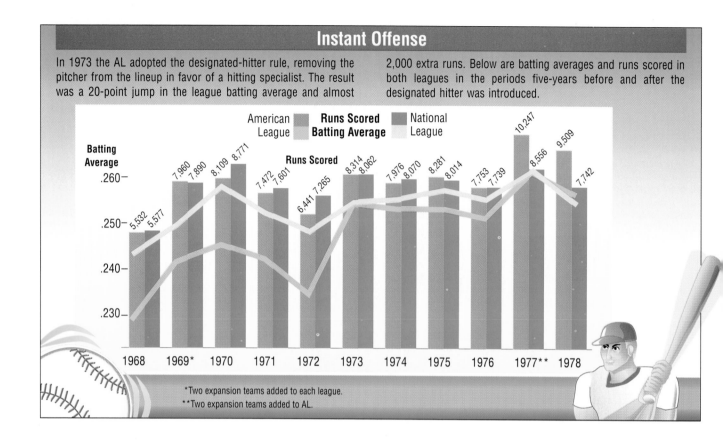

Instant Offense

In 1973 the AL adopted the designated-hitter rule, removing the pitcher from the lineup in favor of a hitting specialist. The result was a 20-point jump in the league batting average and almost 2,000 extra runs. Below are batting averages and runs scored in both leagues in the periods five-years before and after the designated hitter was introduced.

American League — Runs Scored / Batting Average — National League

Batting Average

Runs Scored

.260
.250
.240
.230

5,532 5,577
7,960 7,890
8,109 8,771
7,472 7,601
6,441 7,265
8,314 8,062
7,976 8,070
8,281 8,014
7,753 7,739
10,247 8,556
9,509 7,742

1968 1969* 1970 1971 1972 1973 1974 1975 1976 1977** 1978

*Two expansion teams added to each league.
**Two expansion teams added to AL.

Gossage slid right into Lyle's spot in the Yankees' bullpen in 1978, saving 27 games. He was strictly a power pitcher, a hulking man with long arms, who stared down batters, then reared back and threw as hard as he could, which was frighteningly hard. His fastball was clocked at 99 mph, and the fact that it sometimes sailed out of control was enough to make batters wonder about the effectiveness of batting helmets. Catfish Hunter once said that Gossage was the one pitcher he would refuse to bat against because he was sure the Goose didn't know where his pitches were going. With fear as his ally, Gossage never had fewer than 18 saves with the White Sox, Pirates, and Yankees from 1975 through 1980, with the exception of 1976, when White Sox manager Paul Richards tried to make him a starter. Robbed of his concentrated fury, Gossage lost 17 games.

Al Hrabosky was another reliever who won through intimidation. The Mad Hungarian's ploy was to make it seem that he was always in need of a sedative. His back to the plate, Hrabosky stalked around behind the mound, talking to himself and slamming his fist into his glove. When he returned to the rubber, he glowered at the hitter, a Fu Manchu moustache framing his scowl. His scare tactics worked best in 1975, when he won 13 games and saved 22 for the Cards, and in 1978, when he saved 20 and helped the Royals win the AL West.

The premier reliever of the late 1970s used aerodynamics, not fright, to overpower batters. Bruce Sutter joined the Cubs' minor league organization in 1972 and promptly suffered an elbow injury. After surgery, his fastball was no more, so Sutter mastered the split-finger fastball. Held between the fingers like a forkball but thrown like a fastball, the

pitch approached the plate sluggishly but, just as the batter's eyes began to widen, dropped straight down, far below his swing. Dick Williams pronounced it "unhittable" and "worse than a knuckleball." By 1977, Sutter, then in his second season with the Chicago Cubs, was throwing it incessantly, and no one had any idea how to hit it. He had 22 saves by the first week of July, a record pace, but a muscle strain slowed him down. Still, he ended up with 31 saves and a 1.35 ERA. Two years later, with the Cubs struggling as usual, Sutter still managed to tie the NL record with 37 saves. It was enough to win him the NL Cy Young Award, the third reliever to be chosen for the prestigious award in the seventies, proving once and for all that the bullpen was a place where stars could be born.

Another kind of specialist evolved during the seventies, the consummate good-hit, no-field man, otherwise known as the designated hitter. No change upset purists more. The point was to try to get more hitting into the game, to make it a better show. Not surprisingly, A's owner and dedicated huckster Charlie Finley was one of those pushing hardest for the idea. Fans—especially TV viewers—craved excitement and fast action, he argued, so why waste an at-bat with a weak-hitting pitcher? At a time when strong pitching tended to shackle hitters anyway, why not replace him in the lineup with an offensive specialist who could knock in runs, get on base and just keep things moving? After a four-year tryout in the minors, the American League took the plunge in 1973. For nine straight years they had seen their batters outhit by the National League's; this was one way to make theirs the hitters' league once more. They voted to use the DH on a trial basis.

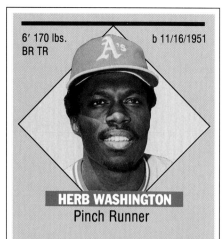

HERB WASHINGTON
Pinch Runner

6' 170 lbs.
BR TR

b 11/16/1951

In the spring of 1974, Charlie Finley was determined to get a sure base stealer for his A's, and he set his sights on sprinter Herb Washington. A former world-record holder in the indoor 50- and 60-yard dashes who hadn't played organized baseball since high school, Washington agreed to trade in his track shoes for a life of crime on the basepaths.

The A's brought base-running great Maury Wills to Oakland to teach "Hurricane Herb" the mysteries of reading pitchers, getting a lead and sliding. Unfortunately, Washington soon found that a crash course is no substitute for experience when it comes to making the split-second decisions required of a baserunner. Although he had 28 steals in 45 attempts and scored 29 runs his first year, he was a frequent pick-off victim, and he tended to come up short of the base on his slides.

Washington had another problem. Because his only job was base stealing —he never came to bat—he had about as much of an element of surprise as sunshine. Opposing pitchers and catchers began planning his demise from the moment he trotted out of the dugout.

Early in 1975, after appearing in only 13 games and stealing two bases, Herb was given his walking papers. Reaction among his teammates was mixed.

"I'd feel sorry for him," said A's captain Sal Bando, "if he were a player."

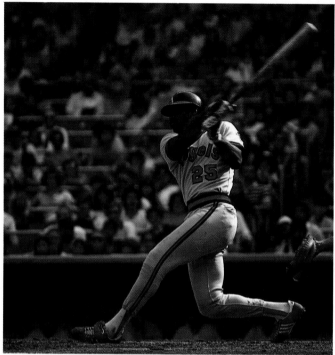

Despite his limited role as designated hitter, Don Baylor was a team leader wherever he played. In his 19-year career, Baylor played on five teams for seven division-winning seasons.

Traditionalists were appalled. This was not baseball, they moaned. If managers no longer had to worry about their pitchers' batting, what would happen to the strategy of pinch hitting? If pitchers no longer batted, the bunt would surely die. And with managers making fewer strategic decisions, opportunities for second-guessing them would disappear. Was nothing sacred?

Nonetheless, on April 6, 1973, Ron Blomberg of the Yankees became the major leagues' first official designated hitter. Facing the Red Sox' Luis Tiant with the bases loaded in the first inning, he was presented with an opportunity to christen the concept with dramatic flair. Instead, he walked. Cynics pointed out that it was nothing a pitcher couldn't have done. In that season, the Yankees also tried aging veterans Johnny Callison and Ron Swoboda at the job, until settling on Jim Ray Hart. Hart, after a long career with the Giants, had been sold to the Yankees at the beginning of the season. He was thrilled. "I have three gloves in my locker and I hope they fall apart before I get a chance to use them," he said. "I might just get a rocking chair for the dugout like old Satch Paige had."

Most teams followed the same strategy. Since no one was trained as a designated-hitting specialist, anyone who could hit well was qualified, even if he had stone hands and lead feet. Suddenly, a dozen fading careers were back on track. Orlando Cepeda was a classic example. A feared hitter for almost 15 years, his knees were so battered that he retired in 1972 after only 31 games with Atlanta and Oakland. The Red Sox, however, found him on a beach in Puerto Rico and offered him a new life as a hitting machine. Cepeda threw himself into the job—between at-bats he went into the Red Sox clubhouse and rode a stationary bike to keep his knees loose. He swung and rode, swung and rode, and by season's end had 20 homers, 86 RBI and a .289 aver-

Rico Carty (above, left) was among the many aging NL sluggers who switched leagues in order to take advantage of the DH rule. Carty topped the .300 mark in his first three years with the Indians, 1974 through 1976.

age. Other reclamation projects were just as successful. Deron Johnson seemed through in Philadelphia but, reborn in Oakland, hit 19 homers and helped the A's win their division. Former NL batting champ Tommy Davis did the same for Baltimore, batting .306 with 89 RBI. At 38, Frank Robinson was young again with the California Angels, adding 30 homers and 97 RBI to his totals. In Chicago, Carlos May had 20 homers and 96 RBI; in Minnesota, Tony Oliva, a two-time batting champ in the sixties, came back to life with 92 RBI and a .291 average.

It was like adding chase scenes to a dull movie. The AL cumulative batting average jumped 20 points that year, to .259, compared to the NL's .254. AL teams hit almost 400 more homers than the year before and scored almost 2,000 more runs. But those whom the rule offended saw other effects. For one, the sacrifice bunt was dying fast. In 1973 AL teams averaged only 49 sacrifice bunts for the season—about one every three games—compared to an average of 80 per team in the NL. Also, now that they were no longer getting yanked for pinch hitters, AL starters were pitching until they could pitch no more. Before the DH rule, they had been throwing complete games about once every four starts. With the DH, it increased to once every three starts. In 1973, 22 AL pitchers—a modern-day high—threw at least 250 innings. The next year, 23 did. At that pace, some of the league's best pitchers were bound to wear out their arms, the skeptics warned.

Some pitchers probably did. In the four years after the DH was introduced, for instance, Catfish Hunter pitched an average of 70 more innings a year, which may explain why he was able to give the Yankees only two good years after he signed his huge contract with them. Initially, most managers fell into the bad habit of overworking their starters, but eventually they ad-

Jim Rice (right) was an exception to the outfielder-turned-designated hitter rule. The Boston slugger split his time evenly between left field and DH his first four seasons, then became an almost full-time outfielder. Rusty Staub (below) proved he didn't have to play the field to be an asset to the Tigers in the late 1970s, where he had back-to-back 100-RBI seasons as a full-time DH in 1977 and 1978.

justed, relying more and more on relief specialists to finish. By the end of the decade, the number of complete games had returned to pre-DH levels. In fact, AL managers claimed the rule made the job of handling pitchers harder, not easier. Instead of automatically removing one for a pinch hitter when his team needed a run, a manager now had to make that decision strictly on how the pitcher was throwing. "You have to have the ability as a manager to say, 'This guy has had it,' and then take him out," said Baltimore pitching coach Ray Miller. Managers adapted in other ways, too. Kansas City's Whitey Herzog juggled his batting order so that his two best hitters, George Brett and Hal McRae, were at the top of the lineup and two of his fastest runners, Frank White and Fred Patek, were at the bottom. The idea was to have them on base when Brett and McRae came to bat. That meant more steals, more hit-and-run plays, more anxiety for opposing pitchers.

Unlike most early designated hitters, McRae was no plodding slugger. A player who hit for average and could steal bases, he showed that the position could be used to open up a team's offense, not just produce home runs. More managers began to use their imaginations. Some still saw it as a way to ease stars into retirement. Carl Yastrzemski did that with the Red Sox; Al Kaline, with the Tigers; Lee May, with the Orioles and the Royals. Hank Aaron was able to have his last hurrah as a DH back in Milwaukee, where his career had started 22 years earlier. But more often, the DH slot was used for other purposes. The rule allowed the Orioles to get rookie Eddie Murray into the lineup in 1977, and he responded with 27 homers. The Angels did the same thing with Willie Aikens in 1979. Earlier, they had used Don Baylor, who, like McRae, could be counted on to steal bases along with hitting homers. Boston's Jim Rice was a power swinger who also hit for average; in

1977, when he played DH two-thirds of the time, he batted .320 and hit 39 homers, with 114 RBIs.

But the designated hitter who probably did the most for his team was the Tigers' Rusty Staub. He was never happy about playing DH; although a bit lead-footed, he had been a solid right fielder with the Astros, Expos, and Mets for 13 years. But the Tigers gave him no other choice but DH, and in 1977 and 1978, he did nothing else. The first year, he hit 22 homers and drove in 101 runs; the second year, he homered 24 times and had 121 RBIs. He was a natural, or at least he seemed to be. But Staub insisted that it wasn't an easy adjustment. "The toughest thing about being a DH is being mentally prepared to hit," he said. "I'm a very intense person and if I mess up I need something to take my mind off it. I used to be able to do that by playing defense. Now between at-bats, I go back into the clubhouse and do crossword puzzles."

No doubt about it. Baseball had entered a new age. ◗

A short reliever's job is generally quick, but not always painless. Cleveland's Jim Kern (above, center) wasn't happy to be visited by catcher Dave Duncan and manager Ken Aspromonte. But Kern was a solid closer in the 1970s, peaking in 1979 with a 13–5 record, a 1.57 ERA and 29 saves for Texas.

Rollie Fingers

When baseball fans discuss the greatest relief pitchers, the name Rollie Fingers is sure to come up. With a record 341 saves to his credit and 13 uncannily consistent years of re-solving crises from the mound, Fingers may have been the best reliever in baseball.

Fingers made his big-league debut with Oakland in 1968, but he bombed as a starter, in part because he didn't like waiting—and worrying—four days be-tween starts. He didn't have much stamina, either. But in 1971, someone on the A's staff realized that if you dropped Fingers into a crisis where he could fo-cus on only two or three batters, he was untouch-able. The difference, Rollie explained, was that "in starting I have to kind of pace myself, but as a reliever I go out there and throw as hard as I can for as long as I can." He was such an outstanding control pitcher, with a lifetime strikeout-to-walk ratio of better than 2.5–1, that it is easy to forget he also had a 95-mph fastball that could leave hitters slack-jawed.

In the five years he was a full-time reliever with the A's, his ERA never went above 3.00 and he averaged 21 saves a season. When he became a free agent after the 1976 season, no one seemed sur-prised that San Diego Padres owner Ray Kroc was willing to pay him almost $270,000 a year to jump leagues. Fingers was still pitching in California, but his new team was light-years behind the one he had left. The Padres had George Hendrick, young Dave Winfield, and not much else.

Nothing seemed to disturb Finger's aplomb on the mound, but at the same time his A's teammate Catfish Hunter considered him the all-time leader in "most bitches, career . . . when the sun rose in the east, Rollie bitched, asking, 'What's wrong with the west once in a while?' "

Fingers was a guileful hurler who liked to get ahead in the count and make batters chase bad balls that were low and away, but there were times when it seemed he had left his brain in the locker room. Once, Sal Bando handed him a ball that was coming unstitched, telling him to get one strike before the umpire threw it out of the game. No sooner had Ban-do returned to his position than Rollie called time.

"Ump, ump," he yelled, "I need a new ball. Cover's coming off this one."

That first season in San Diego he led the NL in saves with 35, and in games pitched, with 78. The next year he saved 37 more, and the Padres, with a better supporting cast that included 21-game winner Gaylord Perry and rookie Ozzie Smith, finished above .500 for the first time in the team's ten-year history. Fingers had an off year in 1979, saving only 13 games, and after the 1980 season he was traded to the St. Louis Cardinals, who immediately dealt him to the Milwaukee Brewers. In 1981 he led the AL with 28 saves, racked up a superhuman ERA of 1.04, and became the first reliever to win the Cy Young Award and be selected MVP in the same year. The next year he saved 29 games and then missed the 1983 season because of an elbow injury and subsequent surgery. He came back in 1984 at the age of 37 to record 40 more saves in the next two seasons. Fingers retired after the 1985 season, with a modest view of his ac-complishments: "I'm just a starting pitcher who couldn't get out of the third inning."

Rollie Fingers' overpowering stuff and unflappable nature set the standard for relief pitchers in the 1970s and probably paved his way to Cooperstown. "If they take a reliever to the Hall of Fame," said Reggie Jackson, "he's on his way. The Ice Man cometh."

ROLLIE FINGERS

Right-Handed Pitcher
Oakland Athletics 1968–1976
San Diego Padres 1977–1980
Milwaukee Brewers 1981–1982,
1984–1985

GAMES *(4th all time)*	**944**
INNINGS	
Career	**1,701**
Season High	**148**
WINS	
Career	**114**
Season High	**13**
LOSSES	
Career	**118**
Season High	**13**
WINNING PERCENTAGE	
Career	**.491**
Season High	**.667**
ERA	
Career	**2.90**
Season Low	**1.04**
SAVES	
Career *(1st all time)*	**341**
Season High	**37**
STRIKEOUTS	
Career	**1,299**
Season High	**115**
WALKS	
Career	**492**
Season High	**48**
WORLD SERIES	**1972–1974**
CY YOUNG AWARD	**1981**
MOST VALUABLE PLAYER	**1981**

George, Reggie and Billy

t's hard to pinpoint just when the Steinbrenner Era began. Technically, it started in 1973, when George Steinbrenner and his partners bought the Yankees from CBS for $10 million and George promised a pennant in five years. But it may have been December 31, 1974, when Steinbrenner paid a small fortune for Catfish Hunter, baseball's first unofficial free agent. Or was it August 2, 1975, when Billy Martin, dumped by the Texas Rangers 13 days earlier, put on the pinstripes once again and took over what he thought were *his* Yankees? Or the day after the Yankees were swept by the Reds in the 1976 Series, when Steinbrenner swore that never again would his team be so humiliated? Each event was momentous, yet each in a way was only part of the buildup. The Steinbrenner Era, in all its twisted glory, truly began on November 29, 1976—the day Reggie arrived.

With that, baseball's oddest love-hate triangle was in place. Over the next two years Billy learned to hate Reggie, who learned to love George, who fired Billy, who insulted George, who insulted Reggie, who reconciled with Billy, who spurned Reggie, who through it all, still loved Reggie.

The irony is that in the beginning, neither George Steinbrenner nor Billy Martin wanted Reggie Jackson. Jackson may have been the biggest name in baseball's first class of free agents, but he wasn't the Yankees' first choice. That was Don Gullett, the Reds' dazzling left-hander who had beaten them in Game 1 of the Series. Jackson wasn't even the second choice. That was Bobby Grich, the Orioles' multitalented second baseman. The Yankees

Yankee oufielder Reggie Jackson (opposite, center) and manager Billy Martin (right) argued with each other almost constantly in the late 1970s, but once in a while they turned their hostility on an umpire. The victim here is Bill Haller (left).

The Yankee locker room (above) was pretty quiet in the spring of 1972. The team went on to finish fourth in the AL East, and sported few of the colorful personalities that enlivened the locker room later in the decade.

After a stormy year and a half, Reggie Jackson got Billy Martin off his back midway through the 1978 season. When Bob Lemon replaced Martin, Jackson said, "I felt like I'd won the lottery."

almost landed him, except that Steinbrenner, pushing to close the deal, began bad-mouthing Harry Dalton, the Angels' general manager, who had signed Grich to his first contract. Grich rejected the offer, so Steinbrenner insisted that he had really wanted Reggie all along. Within a week, Reggie became a Yankee, welcomed with a \$2.9 million five-year contract. Montreal and San Diego had offered more, but as Reggie saw it, he and New York were meant for each other.

His new teammates were not filled with jubilation. They knew about Jackson's home runs. They also knew about his fielding lapses. And they knew about his mouth. Catfish Hunter told Yankee friends to expect Reggie to talk a lot, mainly about himself and mainly in front of the media. But the Yankee players, who had not gone through the minors with Reggie as his Oakland teammates had, weren't likely to be as forgiving. Besides, the Yanks had won the American League pennant without him in 1976 and had been a happy team doing it. Mickey Rivers, the team's top hitter at .312, or Willie Randolph would get on base and invariably be driven in by Chris Chambliss, 96 RBI; Graig Nettles, 93 RBI and a league-leading 32 homers; or the AL's Most Valuable Player, Thurman Munson, 105 RBI. Ed Figueroa won 19 games, Hunter and Dock Ellis each won 17, and Sparky Lyle recorded 23 saves. They had run away from the Orioles; then, in the playoffs with the Royals, the score tied in the ninth inning of the deciding game, Chambliss lifted the first pitch of the inning over the right center field fence, just beyond reach of the leaping Hal McRae, to give the Yankees their first pennant in 12 years. All without Reggie Jackson.

Then there was Jackson's money. It bothered almost everyone in the Yankees' clubhouse, particularly Nettles and Munson—Nettles, because his

Catcher Thurman Munson (above) was the captain and the heart of the Yankees in their world championship seasons, 1977 and 1978. "Thurman was a battler," said Oriole catcher Rick Dempsey. "What every fan thinks is thrilling about the game, Thurman was a part of, some way—a ninth-inning hit to win the ball game, a slide in to beat somebody up. Thurman was always in the middle of it."

contract gave him about a quarter of what Jackson signed for, and Munson, because Steinbrenner had told him that no other Yankee would make more than he did, except Hunter, who was a special case. Once the season started, Jackson did little to win new friends. He was quoted in the papers about how "I didn't come to New York to be a star. I brought my star with me." He also had a cute habit of counting rolls of $100 bills in front of the other players.

Martin had his own problems with Reggie, and not just because he thought he was an overrated player. Reggie had been seen dining in fancy restaurants with Steinbrenner; Billy had never been invited to sup privately with George. This only fed Martin's paranoia, which had a ravenous appetite. Reggie also symbolized Steinbrenner's obsession with running the team —something that infuriated Martin, who insisted that when the players were on the field *he* was in absolute control. Martin and Steinbrenner kicked off the 1977 exhibition season with a clubhouse screaming match over lineups and Martin's reprobate personal habits. It ended with Billy calling the boss "fat man" and knocking a pan of ice water on him. For this, Billy was fired and replaced by Yogi Berra. By the next morning, Steinbrenner had calmed down and changed his mind.

The Yankees staggered through April, losing eight of their first ten games. Thurman Munson, the team captain, tried to thaw relations between Reggie and the rest of the Yankees, but just before their first game of the season against arch-rival Red Sox, a time bomb that had been ticking since spring training exploded. Back in March, Jackson had told writer Robert Ward that on the Yankees, he was "the straw that stirs the drink." In the same *Sport* magazine interview, published in May, 1977, Reggie was quoted as saying, "Munson thinks he can be the straw that stirs the drink but he can

Manager Billy Martin took Reggie Jackson out of the game for what he considered lazy play on June 18, 1977, against Boston. A nationwide TV audience watched as Martin had to be physically restrained from attacking Jackson during a heated verbal exchange. To add insult to injury, the Yankees lost the game, 10–4.

only stir it bad." Someone suggested that Jackson had been quoted out of context. "For three pages?" bellowed Munson. That night, Reggie, as he often did, made matters worse. With the Yankees down by a run, he hit a long homer to tie the game. As he approached the dugout where his teammates stood to congratulate him, Jackson strolled past their outstretched hands to the empty part of the bench—as public a snub as a ballplayer can make.

The tension eased a bit several days later, when Jackson walked from locker to locker offering apologies. The team even started to win and, by mid-June, in Boston for another series with the Red Sox, it was in first place. The Red Sox won the Friday-night opener, and the next day's game was featured as NBC's Game of the Week. That turned out to be a gross understatement. The Yankees were losing, 7–4, in the sixth inning when Jim Rice hit a check-swing pop-up to right. Jackson started slowly after the ball, fielded it on the bounce and made a half-hearted throw to the infield, allowing Rice to reach second. Billy immediately sent Paul Blair out to right to replace Jackson, who couldn't believe this was happening to him—getting yanked in the middle of an inning and on national TV, yet. When he reached the dugout, Jackson raised his arms in the universal gesture of "What gives?"

Billy was ready with an answer. "You're not hustling, that's what," he snarled, jumping off the bench.

"You don't know what you're doing, old man," Jackson spat back. "You showed me up in front of 50 million people."

Martin may not have heard the second comment because, at the words "old man," he responded much as Steinbrenner had when Billy called him "fat man." He went crazy. He tried to climb over coaches and players to get at Jackson and probably would have started slugging if Yogi Berra hadn't

grabbed him in a bear hug. Jackson had overestimated the audience for the ugly scene—only 30 million were watching—but one very important person was among them. Within minutes, a long-distance call came into the Fenway Park press box: George Steinbrenner wanted to talk to general manager Gabe Paul. In George's mind, Billy had just dived headfirst into quicksand; nothing could save him. Well, almost nothing. Paul made a convincing case that bouncing Martin would make it seem that Jackson was running the team. Billy hung on again.

But he never left the precipice. Within a month, Steinbrenner, with Paul's approval this time, was ready to push Billy over the edge. The clubhouse had become so tense, the sniping among players, manager and owner so spiteful, that only firing Billy, it seemed, could clear the air. Steinbrenner and Paul agreed on a replacement—third base coach Dick Howser. On July 23, Paul called Howard Cosell and told him to hold a spot open on ABC's "Wide World of Sports" for an announcement. Howser, unfortunately, didn't cooperate. No one could do a better job with the club than Billy Martin, he insisted. "The problem isn't the manager, it's the players," he added. Martin survived again.

Howser had a point. Munson was clearly unhappy and wanted to be traded to Cleveland to be nearer his family in Ohio. Nettles, frustrated because he had missed out on the free agency bonanza by signing a contract, felt underappreciated, as did Figueroa, one of the few Yankee starters who wasn't injured or ineffective. Bucky Dent, the team's new shortstop, whom Steinbrenner had managed to get from the White Sox, almost bolted because Martin kept pinch-hitting for him. And Reggie told a writer that he had to make himself go to the ballpark every day. "Color me gone," he warned.

The Yankee lineup packed a serious wallop in 1977. Third baseman Graig Nettles (above, left) led the team with 37 homers and was one of three Yankees with at least 100 RBI, while outfielder and designated hitter Lou Piniella (right) hammered AL pitching for a team-high .330 average.

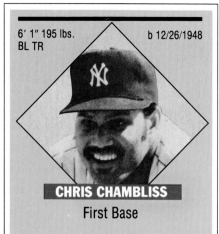

6' 1" 195 lbs.
BL TR
b 12/26/1948

CHRIS CHAMBLISS
First Base

In a decade filled with historic homers, Chris Chambliss's 1976 pennant-winning blast often gets overlooked. That's altogether fitting, since the rock-solid first baseman was overlooked for most of his 16-year career.

Cleveland made Chambliss baseball's number one draft pick in January 1970. He joined the Indians after a year of Class AAA ball, hit .275, and was voted AL Rookie of the Year. In April 1974 a seven-player trade made Chambliss a Yankee. New York veterans criticized the deal, since Chambliss hit just .243 with 43 RBI that season.

During the next five years, Chambliss was a model of quiet consistency, batting between .274 and .304, getting at least 90 RBI in three straight seasons, plus a Gold Glove in 1978. Chambliss's teammates got the headlines—especially "Mr. October," Reggie Jackson—but manager Billy Martin said, "I'll take Chris Chambliss. He's Mr. Season."

Chambliss had his own memorable October in 1976, as the Yankees met the Kansas City Royals for the AL pennant series. In Game 3, Chambliss's two-run homer and three RBI powered a 5–3 comeback win. In the decisive fifth game, the score was 6–6 when Chambliss led off the bottom of the ninth. He launched reliever Mark Littell's first pitch over the right center field wall, sending the Yankees to their first World Series since 1964 and setting off a mob scene in the Bronx. "Now I think I know how Bobby Thomson felt," Chambliss beamed.

In Game 6 of the 1977 World Series, Jackson homered on three straight pitches. Even the Dodgers' Steve Garvey was awed. "I must admit, when Reggie hit his third home run and I was sure nobody was looking, I applauded in my glove."

Tension like that takes its toll and, by late June, the Yanks were in danger of falling six games behind Boston. Facing Red Sox bullpen ace Bill Campbell in a game they were losing, 5–3, with two out in the ninth, Willie Randolph hit a fly ball that Carl Yastrzemski misjudged. It rolled to the wall for a triple. Roy White followed with a homer to tie the game. An inning later, Jackson knocked in the winning run with a pinch-hit double. The Yanks took two more from the Sox and moved to within two games of the lead. A month later, they were struggling again, losing a pair of sloppy games to the lowly Brewers. The next week, they were soaring, coming from behind in the ninth to tie the league-leading Orioles on a two-run pinch-hit homer by Cliff Johnson, whom Steinbrenner had picked up from the Astros, and then winning in the tenth on another Reggie showstopper—a lead-off homer. Just when consistency threatened, in early August the team took another plunge, losing four of five games—including two to the expansion Seattle Mariners—and dropping five games out of first.

On August 10, Martin made the lineup change that Steinbrenner had been nagging him to make since spring training. Reggie Jackson became cleanup hitter. It's what Jackson felt his status had merited all along. For all his swaggering, Reggie needed constant stroking. By batting him sixth in the lineup, Martin had been sending Jackson a message that he was just one of nine starters. Billy also felt that Jackson struck out too often and wouldn't be able to protect the Yankees' base stealers at the top of the lineup. But worn down and anxious about a late-season fade, Billy finally gave in.

Reggie was reborn. In the final two months of the season, he hit 13 homers and drove in 40 runs. Suddenly "the best team that money can buy" was living up to its billing. The Yankees won 39 of the next 49 games and, for

A low-profile slugger, first baseman Chris Chambliss (left) outshone his headline-grabbing teammates in the 1976 AL Championship Series against Kansas City. Chambliss hit .524 with eight RBI, including the pennant-clinching homer in the ninth inning of Game 5.

the first time since 1963, had 100 season victories. Jackson ended up with 110 RBI, the most by a Yankee since Mickey Mantle's 111 in 1964. Nettles had 37 homers and 107 RBI, and Munson got 100 RBI, while Chambliss added 90 more. Lou Piniella, named the team's designated hitter at Steinbrenner's insistence, made the boss happy with his .330 average. Mickey Rivers, the most decrepit speedster in baseball, hit .326. Dent and Randolph had become New York's best double-play combination in at least ten years. Ron Guidry, who pitched so badly as a reliever in spring training that he was almost thrown into the Dent trade, closed the season as the team's top starter with a 16–7 record. Ed Figueroa, Mike Torrez and Don Gullett, when he was healthy, also pitched well, and behind them was Sparky Lyle, the master of the bullpen, whose slider on the fists stifled hitter after numbed hitter and ultimately won him the Cy Young Award.

New York had left the Orioles and Red Sox 2½ games back, and they again faced Kansas City in the playoffs. Like the year before, the series went five games and the Yankees won the deciding game in the ninth, scoring three runs off the Royals' 20-game winner Dennis Leonard and relievers Larry Gura and Mark Littell, who had given up Chambliss's championship homer the year before.

Their World Series foes were the Los Angeles Dodgers, who, with their scrubbed looks and unfailing manners, seemed like a boy scout troop next to the Yankees' street gang. Game 1 stayed even until a 12th-inning single by Paul Blair, a defensive replacement for Jackson, won it for New York. But Reggie had his moment. In fact, Reggie had his whole night. In Game 6, New York ahead three games to two, Jackson walked on four pitches in his first at-bat, then homered on the first pitch from Burt Hooton, with Munson

Center fielder Mickey Rivers' hitting and base-stealing ability ignited the Yankee offense, and his quirky personality kept the team loose. Once, when relief ace Goose Gossage was suffering through a slump, Rivers threw himself in front of the bullpen car carrying Gossage onto the field. "No, not him!" Rivers screamed. "Anybody but him!"

IN MEMORY OF
Thurman Munson
1947 1979

Thurman Munson

When George [Steinbrenner] proposed that Thurman be named captain in 1976," said Marty Appel, onetime Yankees public relations man, "I reminded him of Joe McCarthy's pledge that there would never be another captain after Lou Gehrig. It was a pledge McCarthy made at Gehrig's grave site. George said, 'If Joe McCarthy and Lou Gehrig could have known Thurman, they would know this was the time and this was the man.'"

Thurman Munson grew up in Canton, Ohio, where his father was a truck driver. In high school, Munson became an all-around athlete and a dominant player on the football, basketball and baseball teams. But baseball was his favorite sport. He turned down several colleges that offered him football scholarships and chose Kent State, the only school that offered him a baseball scholarship. He started as a middle infielder, then moved behind the plate, where he quickly showed signs of greatness. "The first thing I noticed about Thurman was his speed," remembers former Yankee scout Gene Woodling. "He was very fast for a catcher. And he had a quick arm, the quickest I ever saw."

Munson became a Yankee regular in 1970, after only 99 games in the minors. He promptly hit .302, and became the first catcher to be named AL Rookie of the Year.

In 1971 his .998 fielding percentage—one error in 615 chances—led the majors. Munson had won three Gold Gloves and had been an All-Star seven times by 1976, the year he was named MVP. His 17 homers, 105 RBI, .302 average, and 186 hits led the Yankees to the World Series for the first time in 12 years. Although New York was swept by a potent Reds team, Munson shined. He hit .529, which set a record for a player on a losing team, and he finished the Series with a record-tying six straight hits. The following year, when Munson singled in his first at-bat in the 1977 World Series, he broke the record for most straight hits in Series play—the record he had tied the previous year. He hit .320 in both the 1977 and the 1978 Series, leaving him at .373 overall—the third best Series average ever. And he hit .339 in three AL Championship Series.

But Munson was at his most comfortable—and best—behind the plate. Just ask his batterymates. "He calls the game based on who the batter and pitcher are," Sparky Lyle once said, "not what he might be looking for if he were the hitter."

"Knowing the hitters is what makes a good catcher," Munson said. "It's not how many runners you throw out or how many balls in the dirt you block. Since I play almost every game, I know opposing hitters a lot better than most pitchers. That's why I don't want anyone, including the manager, calling pitches from the bench."

Munson was a leader, and a fitting captain for the Yankees of the late seventies. Even if Reggie Jackson was correct when he said, "I'm the straw that stirs the drink," Munson's tremendous impact on the team became evident when he died at 32 in a plane crash on August 2, 1979. After three straight World Series, the Yankees began to fall apart.

Munson never took the game, or his gifts, for granted. "I love baseball. It's given me everything I have. Look, there are only about six hundred major leaguers in the country. You have to feel special."

Whether at the plate or behind it, Thurman Munson was at his best when it meant the most. In 16 World Series games, Munson hit .373 with 11 runs scored and 12 RBI, threw out 13 runners trying to steal, and committed no errors.

THURMUN MUNSON

Catcher
New York Yankees 1969–1979

GAMES	**1,423**
AT-BATS	**5,344**
BATTING AVERAGE	
Career	.292
Season High	.318
SLUGGING AVERAGE	
Career	.410
Season High	.487
HITS	
Career	1,558
Season High	190
DOUBLES	
Career	229
Season High	29
TRIPLES	
Career	32
Season High	5
HOME RUNS	
Career	113
Season High	20
TOTAL BASES	**2,190**
EXTRA-BASE HITS	**374**
RUNS BATTED IN	
Career	701
Season High	105
RUNS	
Career	696
Season High	85
WORLD SERIES	**1976–1978**
ROOKIE OF THE YEAR	**1970**
MOST VALUABLE PLAYER	**1976**

A hefty World Series share melted away a season of hostility for Billy and Reggie. At the press conference after the Yankees' 1977 World Series win over the Dodgers, Reggie put his arm around Billy and laughed at his jokes, while Billy called Reggie "a super guy."

aboard to give the Yankees a 4–3 lead. An inning later, with another runner on, Jackson nailed the first pitch again, this one a fastball from Elias Sosa, and hit a liner to right that just cleared the fence. In the eighth, he faced knuckleballer Charlie Hough. Later, Jackson said that he had nothing to lose—"They were going to cheer me even if I struck out." Reggie strode into Hough's first pitch and drove a fly that was high, slow and appropriately picturesque before it dropped into the center field stands. As he rounded first, the chant began—"Reg-*gie,* Reg-*gie,* Reg-*gie*"—and by the time he touched third, the two-beat thunderclap had rolled over Yankee Stadium. Three swings, three home runs. The purity of the feat was stunningly heroic, and through it, Reggie was transformed from celebrity to legend. He became "Mr. October."

That week he set World Series records with five home runs, ten runs scored and 25 total bases, a record that broke one held by Billy Martin. "I love this man," Reggie proclaimed in the locker room, his arm around Billy's shoulder. "There's nobody else I'd rather play for. Next year we're gonna be tough. If you mess with Billy Martin, you're in trouble, and if you mess with Reggie Jackson, you're in trouble."

It was about three and a half months into the next season before anyone really messed with Billy Martin again, and as Reggie had said, that person got into trouble. The person, unfortunately, was Reggie. By mid-July, the Yankees were in a free fall to mediocrity—in fourth place, 14 games behind the Red Sox, who seemed destined to coast to an anxiety-free championship. New York had been stripped by injuries—Randolph, Rivers and Dent had all been hurt, as had pitchers Don Gullett and Catfish Hunter.

Munson was so banged up that he had been moved to right field to ease the pounding on his legs. Psyches were also bruised. Sparky Lyle was bitter because, even though he had won the Cy Young Award, Steinbrenner had paid big money for two more relievers, Rich "Goose" Gossage and Rawley Eastwick. Billy was drinking heavily and aging about a year a day. Munson still wanted to move back to Ohio. Reggie was being used as a DH, primarily against right-handed pitchers. Not only had he been replaced in right, but replaced by a catcher with bad legs. Was this any way to treat a man who had just had a candy bar named after him?

Reggie took up the matter with his friend George, who didn't make him feel any better. The owner told him that he wasn't much of a fielder and that he was most useful as a DH. This sent Reggie into a deep funk that lasted through the game that night against the Royals. Batting in the tenth inning, with the score tied and Munson on first, Reggie tried to show what a team player he was by bunting. When he missed the first time, third base coach Dick Howser called time and walked down the line to him.

"Billy wants you to swing the bat," he said.

"I'm gonna bunt," Reggie answered.

"Yeah, but Billy wants you to hit."

"I want to bunt." And with that, Jackson tried to bunt again. And failed. When he tried a third time and fouled off the pitch, he was out. Unlike the year before, Martin did not try to slug Reggie when he got back to the bench —although he said that he had never been angrier in his life; he simply had one of his coaches tell Jackson he was out of the game.

Later, after the Yankees had lost, Billy vented, demanding in a phone call to Steinbrenner that Jackson be suspended for the season. Instead,

While his players were fighting each other in the locker room and winning on the field, Yankee owner George Steinbrenner (above, center) was stirring things up from above. His meddling earned him mostly contempt from his players and managers. Relief ace Sparky Lyle said Steinbrenner "didn't know diddly about baseball, but he could second-guess better than anybody."

Off the field, Martin (below) ran into almost constant trouble, but on it, he was an undeniable success. "The white lines are Billy's arena," said Yankee president Al Rosen. "Between them he becomes the king. Outside of the lines, he is out of character."

Manager Bob Lemon (above) brought much-needed calm to the Yankees. Billy Martin's departure and Lemon's arrival midway through 1978 had a physical effect on shortstop Bucky Dent. "My stomach stopped churning," Dent said.

Reggie's penalty was five days without pay. When he returned—the team had won four straight games in his absence—Reggie was greeted by a swarm of reporters and, instead of taking batting practice, he held a press conference. Among other things, he said that he had tried to bunt because he wasn't hitting well and he didn't see why he should apologize. Reggie also said he didn't know if he and Martin would talk about the incident, adding that "he hasn't talked to me for a year and a half." When he read Jackson's comments, Billy lost what little composure he had. Jackson wouldn't play until he shut up, Martin swore, and if Steinbrenner didn't like it, he could fire him. Billy might have saved his job had he stopped there, but like his two adversaries, he just didn't know when to close his mouth. "The two of them deserve each other," he said of Reggie and George. "One is a born liar and the other's convicted."

Color Billy gone.

Steinbrenner—who had pleaded guilty to making an illegal campaign contribution to Richard Nixon in 1972—didn't actually fire Martin. He allowed him to resign, which let Billy still collect a salary. Steinbrenner brought in Bob Lemon, who had been dumped by the White Sox a few weeks earlier. Compared with Martin, Lemon was comatose—a soft-spoken, witty and unexcitable man whose steady pitching got him into the Hall of Fame. When Martin had taken over in 1975, his first words to the team were: "We're gonna win. We're gonna play ball. And we're gonna do it my way." Lemon's were: "Go have some fun."

Five days after Billy was fired, the annual Old-Timers' Game was held at Yankee Stadium. By tradition, Joe DiMaggio was the last player introduced. This time, however, another player was saved for last. It was Billy Martin. As he ran out onto the field waving his cap, the announcement came that he

would be back as manager of the Yankees in 1980, with Lemon as general manager. The crowd roared its approval. Had George gone crazy? Or even more unthinkable, had he gone soft? No, George just knew that the calls to the Yankees' switchboard had been running about a hundred to one in Billy's favor and he knew that the crosstown Mets were making noises about snatching up Billy, which would have been a public relations disaster for the Yankees. So what if Billy was unstable, belligerent, fanatical and a stone in George's kidney. Business was business.

On the field, the Yankees started to stir. That they made any difference in the 1978 pennant race was due almost solely to Ron Guidry, whose fastball surprised and bedeviled hitters. That year, no one could hit him. "It seemed that everytime I went out there, I just knew I was going to blow people away," he said. Guidry won his first 13 games, finishing at 25–3, with a remarkable ERA of 1.74, and nine shutouts, the most for an AL lefthander since 1916.

In early August, the rest of the team finally began to follow Guidry's lead. Lemon had the effect of a sedative in the locker room water fountain; that and a New York newspaper strike put an end to the clubhouse sniping. For the first time in two years, the place seemed almost relaxed. Lemon also moved Munson back behind the plate, Jackson back out in right, Piniella and White back into the everyday lineup, pointing out matter-of-factly that that team had won the World Series the year before. There was one other crucial development: after his shoulder popped while being manipulated by a doctor, Catfish Hunter's arm came back from the dead. After struggling all season, he went 6–0 in August, with a 1.64 ERA, and the Yankees were 19–8 for the month.

At spring training in 1977, Ron Guidry (above) had a horrendous 10.42 ERA in six appearances, but fortunately for the Yankees, general manager Gabe Paul saw past the numbers to Guidry's live left arm. Steinbrenner suggested trading Guidry. "Over my dead body," Paul replied, and Guidry went 41–10 over the next two seasons.

5′ 11″ 165 lbs.   **b 7/6/1954**
BR TR

WILLIE RANDOLPH
Second Base

Willie Randolph seemed destined to be a Yankee. Like countless other Brooklyn kids, he played stickball, then high school baseball, and he dreamed of a career in the big leagues with the Yankees. But it was the Pirates who signed him in 1972. During spring training in 1975, the Yankees and the Pirates played six games. Impressed with the 20-year-old infielder who swung a good bat, drew walks and stole bases with the best of them, the Yankees negotiated a trade for Randolph. He had come home.

He's never looked back. As a testament to his longevity, it's been calculated that Randolph, the team's longest-lasting second baseman, has played with 31 different shortstops during his 13 years with the Yankees.

"Willie's been the heart and soul of the Yankees," former teammate Catfish Hunter said. "Willie was the type of guy you get on him and he'd accept the challenge: 'I'll show ya. I'll show ya,' is his attitude."

Randolph has played in three World Series, five All-Star games, led the league's second basemen in putouts, assists, and double plays in 1979, and led the league with 119 walks in 1980.

Like the finest of wines and the rarest of baseball players, Randolph seemed to improve with age. He hit over .300 only once—in 1987, his next-to-last year with New York. Indeed, it was Randolph's best-ever season, with a .305 batting average and a .981 fielding percentage.

The great Red Sox-Yankee rivalry hit its postwar peak on Monday, October 2, 1978, as the two teams clashed in a one-game playoff for the AL East title. The Fenway Park crowd of 32,925 witnessed another chapter in Red Sox frustration.

Still, they began September 6½ games behind Boston. But the Red Sox were infirm and teetering, no longer the stout-hearted men who had trampled the rest of the league most of the season. Shortstop Rick Burleson had been out, injured since the All-Star break. Fred Lynn was hobbled, Carlton Fisk had tender ribs, Carl Yastrzemski a bad back, second baseman Jerry Remy a broken wrist. Dwight Evans still had dizzy spells from a recent beaning. Third baseman Butch Hobson's elbow was so damaged that whenever he could, he'd run halfway across the infield before throwing to first. In similar straits earlier in the year, New York had been able to rest its aching regulars because it had a bench strong enough to fill the gaps. Boston had no such second wave.

By the time they faced each other in Fenway on September 7, Boston's lead had shriveled to four games. The Sox had lost five of their last eight; the Yankees had won 12 of their last 14. Their dream season a fast-fading memory, Boston unraveled. They lost, 15–3, 13–2, 7–0, and the finale, 7–4. It was the first Yankee four-game sweep at Fenway in 35 years, and it was hard to imagine a more brutal exhibition. The Yankees outscored Boston 42–9, outhit them 49–16, and outfielded them four errors to eleven. The series was dubbed "The Boston Massacre," a phrase since woven into the dark tapestry of Red Sox angst.

When the Yankees took two of three games in a return series in Yankee Stadium a week later, the collapse seemed complete: Boston had fallen out of first by 2½ games. Of the nightmarish streak in which his team lost 14 of 17 games, batted .192 and made 33 errors, Boston manager Don Zimmer said, "I have never seen a good team do absolutely everything so poorly." Yastrzemski predicted that if the Red Sox expected to win the division, they

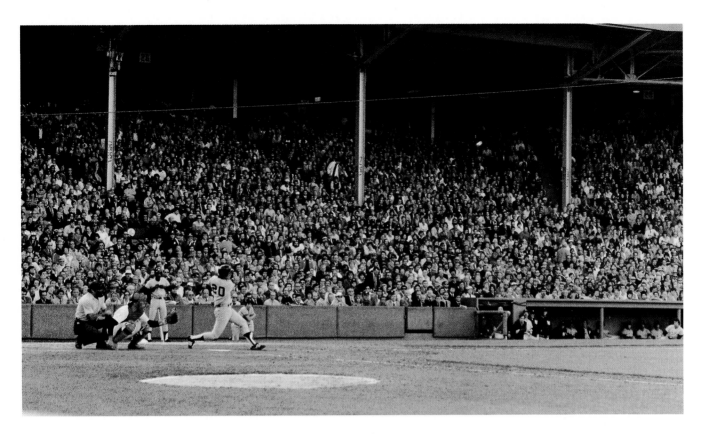

could lose only one game in the final two weeks. They lost two the first week, but with time running out, the team regained its balance. Day after day, each time the Yankees won, the Red Sox matched them with a victory of their own. With one game left, Boston had closed to within a game. That day, the Indians bombed Catfish Hunter, Luis Tiant shut out the Blue Jays, and the AL East race was tied at 99–63. A one-game playoff was required, the first in 30 years, and only the second in American League history.

The next day, in Boston, the weather was appropriately World Series cool. Baseball's most passionate rivalry had been distilled to its purest form, and when Carl Yastrzemski told reporters "today is the biggest ballgame of my life," no one thought he was overselling the show. No one would have made a more fitting hero than the long-suffering Yastrzemski, a point that both he and the Boston fans seemed to appreciate. The crowd saluted him with a standing ovation for his first at-bat, and he responded with a liner off Ron Guidry that cleared the wall just inside the right-field foul pole. Boston moved another run ahead in the sixth when Jim Rice blooped a single that brought home Rick Burleson. It was a stressful lead, but former Yankee Mike Torrez had so far baffled his old teammates. The sun still shone in Boston.

Red Sox followers, always searching for destiny's clues, wondered about "the Mike Factor"—all three of Guidry's infrequent losses during the season had been against pitchers named Mike: Caldwell, Flanagan and Willis. The fans started losing faith in the seventh when, with one out, Roy White and Chris Chambliss singled for the Yankees and Bucky Dent was due up. Dent was no home run threat—he had hit only four all year. Lately, he hadn't been any kind of threat. In the past 20 games, his average was a sickly .140. He took the first pitch from Torrez for a strike, then fouled the next one off

With two on and two out and the Yankees trailing the Red Sox, 2–0, in the AL East playoff game in 1978, Yankee shortstop Bucky Dent fouled a Mike Torrez slider off his ankle. Dent hobbled over to third-base coach Dick Howser and said, "If that son of a bitch comes in there again with that pitch, I'm going to take him into the net." Torrez did, and Dent's drive (above) found the netting above Fenway's "Green Monster" to spark the Yankee victory.

Ron Guidry

In July 1976, Ron Guidry's pitching career was headed south, and he was following along. After a poor relief outing, Yankee owner George Steinbrenner said Guidry had "no guts," and the wiry left-hander sat idle in the Yankee bullpen for 46 straight games. Then he was ordered down to Class AAA Syracuse but decided not to go. With his wife Bonnie, Guidry set out for home—the Louisiana bayou. One hundred miles into the trip, Bonnie persuaded him to reconsider. "You've never quit at anything you thought you could do in your life," she said. "Don't quit on your own."

Guidry turned the car around—a decision AL hitters had reason to regret. In his first outing with Syracuse, Guidry got out of a one-out, bases-loaded jam with two strikeouts, then struck out the side in the ninth. "Not bad for a kid with no guts," someone said to Steinbrenner.

Back in the majors, Guidry learned to throw a slider—to go along with his 95-mph fastball—from Yankee relief ace Sparky Lyle. Guidry got a chance to start a game in late April 1977, and threw 8⅓ shutout innings. He became the ace of the staff and won his last eight decisions as the Yankees came from third place to win the AL East. He wound up with a 16–7 record, 2.82 ERA, and two complete-game wins in post-season play, one in the ALCS and one in the World Series.

In 1978 Guidry parlayed his fastball and biting slider into an incredible season—25–3, with a 1.74 ERA and nine shutouts. He won his first 13 decisions, and during one five-game stretch gave up just four runs and struck out 58 in 43⅓ innings. He beat the Red Sox on three days' rest in the AL East's one-game playoff, then picked up a win in the AL championship and a complete-game victory in the

World Series. At 5' 11" and 161 pounds, Guidry appeared downright skinny, but got his power from a strong leg drive and was able to generate amazing arm speed. In one of his famous malapropisms, broadcaster Jerry Coleman put it best: "Ron Guidry is not very big, maybe 140 pounds, but he has an arm like a lion."

Despite his size, Guidry was one of the best all-around athletes in baseball. In high school he ran the 100 in 9.8 seconds, triple-jumped 45 feet and starred in football and basketball. They called him "Louisiana Lightning" for his fastball, but Guidry's quickness—honed while hunting frogs on the bayou—earned him five Gold Glove Awards as the AL's best fielding pitcher.

"He and Palmer are the two best athletes among pitchers I've ever seen," Reggie Jackson said. "The few times I've seen him swing the bat make me think he could be an everyday player." The fastest Yankee, he was also one of the strongest. Once Catfish Hunter stopped by the Yankee weight room after Guidry had been doing arm curls with the bar set at 75 pounds. "Catfish couldn't budge it," Guidry said. " 'Goddamn!' he said. 'Who's been working out on this?' "

Although he never matched his 1978 season, he remained one of the AL's best pitchers into the 1980s, winning 21 in 1983 and 22 in 1985. In 1988 a rotator-cuff injury ended Guidry's career in the big leagues, but his fluid, rocking-chair pitching motion and quiet, confident manner amid the Yankee turmoil are lasting memories of the 1970s. When Yankee manager Billy Martin was on one of his rampages, Guidry found an unusual way to contribute. "I'd spit tobacco juice on his socks—right on the back of his ankles, where he couldn't see."

RON GUIDRY

Left-Handed Pitcher
New York Yankees 1975–1988

GAMES	**368**
INNINGS	
Career	**2,393**
Season High	**274**
WINS	
Career	**170**
Season High	**25**
LOSSES	
Career	**91**
Season High	**12**
WINNING PERCENTAGE	
Career	**.651**
Season High *(3rd all time)*	**.893**
ERA	
Career	**3.29**
Season Low	**1.74**
GAMES STARTED	
Career	**323**
Season High	**35**
COMPLETE GAMES	
Career	**95**
Season High	**21**
SHUTOUTS	
Career	**26**
Season High	**9**
STRIKEOUTS	
Career	**1,778**
Season High	**248**
WALKS	
Career	**633**
Season High	**80**
WORLD SERIES	**1977–1978, 1981**
CY YOUNG AWARD	**1978**

One hundred and seventy-two tension-packed minutes after the game started, Carl Yastrzemski, who had two RBI on a homer and a single, ended the 1978 AL East playoff game with a pop to third. "I'll always think about that swing," Yaz said.

Two Stellar Seasons

Two young flamethrowers, Vida Blue and Ron Guidry, turned in the best single-season performances of the 1970s. Blue and the A's took the division but lost the ALCS in 1971; Guidry's Yankees became world champions in 1978. Blue won both the Cy Young and MVP awards, and Guidry took the Cy Young Award.

Vida Blue		Ron Guidry
Oakland A's AL 1971		NY Yankees AL 1978
24–8	Won-Lost	**25**–3
.750	Percentage	**.893**
1.82	ERA	**1.74**
312	Innings	273⅔
209	Hits	187
39	Starts	35
24	Complete Games	16
8	Shutouts	**9**
301	Strikeouts	248
88	Walks	72

Boldface indicates league leader.

his foot. Dent hopped from the plate in pain and a Yankee trainer came running out to take a look at him. While Dent limped around, out on the mound Torrez was losing his concentration, as he later conceded. His 0–2 pitch hung over the plate and Dent couldn't pass it up. He lofted it down the left-field line. Even so, both Zimmer in the dugout and Fisk behind the plate thought Torrez had escaped a fat pitch—they expected it to fall gently into Yastrzemski's glove. But the ball floated in the wind as Yaz stared helplessly from below. Seeing him gazing upward, Zimmer and Fisk realized the worst: the ball was going to carry over the wall. In one quick jolt, the Yankees were ahead. A jarred Torrez walked Mickey Rivers, then was replaced by Bob Stanley, who gave up an RBI double to Munson. When Jackson led off the eighth with a soaring homer to center, then stopped off at Steinbrenner's box for a celebratory handslap on his way back to the dugout, the conquest seemed complete.

But in their desperate season-saving drive, Boston had honed itself to be a counterpuncher, and in its half of the eighth struck back with two runs on a double by Remy and singles by Yastrzemski, Fisk and Lynn. The Red Sox were still down by a run and now facing Goose Gossage in relief of Guidry. With one out in the bottom of the ninth, Burleson walked. Remy followed with a liner to right that Lou Piniella immediately lost in the bright sun. As he waited for the ball to land, Piniella fought to hide his panic; he didn't want Burleson to know he was fielding blind. Luckily, the ball dropped in front of him and bounced just to his left, close enough to keep Burleson from trying to reach third. That combination of luck and caution proved critical when Rice flied deep to right. Burleson went to third, but had he already been there, he would have easily scored the tying run. Instead, the Red Sox had two

Led by the high-flying Mickey Rivers (above), the Yankees flew by Carlton Fisk (27) and the Red Sox in a one-game playoff for the AL East title in 1978.

outs with runners at first and third, and the meaning of everything that had happened the previous six months was hanging on one batter. Naturally, it was Yastrzemski.

He took the first fastball from Gossage for a ball. The second one he popped up to third, a foul fly that somehow seemed much too ordinary. When Nettles caught it, Yastrzemski turned to the dugout and never looked back. Later, in the training room, he wept. He was 39, and while he played five more years, he never again came close to the chance for a championship.

The Yankees, though, rolled to another one, beating the Royals in four games, despite three homers by George Brett in Game 3. In the World Series, they did something no team had ever done before—spotting the Dodgers the first two games, they swept the next four. It was the Series in which the rest of the country discovered Graig Nettles. Diving to his right, lunging to his left, he ruled third base, making one spectacular play after another. It was also the Series in which Reggie helped win a game with his hip. In the sixth inning of Game 4, the Dodgers leading, 3–0, Jackson knocked in a run with a single. With Reggie on first and Munson on second, Piniella hit a soft liner that Dodgers shortstop Bill Russell bobbled, then recovered to force Jackson at second and throw to first, finishing the double play. But at the last instant, Reggie, who had stopped between bases because he thought the ball would be caught, cocked his hip into the ball. The contact deflected the ball into foul territory, Munson scoring on the ricochet. The Dodgers protested vigorously, claiming Jackson was guilty of dirty pool. They were more incensed when the Yankees won the game in extra innings. The always-proper Steve Garvey accused Jackson of cheating, or at least a "subcategory" of cheating. "How does that go," he said, "you're only cheat-

Lou Piniella (far left) and Chris Chambliss (10) went crazy when umpire Ron Luciano called Piniella out in Game 3 of the 1978 AL Championship Series against Kansas City. But it was the Royals' George Brett who had cause to be upset, as despite his three home runs, K.C. lost the game, 6–5, and the following day lost the series, its third straight ALCS loss to New York.

ing if you get caught, otherwise it's a heads-up play." To Yankee haters, it was just more proof that George's boys would do anything to win.

But they did win. Since George's promise in 1973 that he would deliver a pennant in five years, the Yankees had won three pennants and two world championships. In that, at least, George Steinbrenner was true to his word.

But in 1979 everything fell apart. The disenchanted Sparky Lyle was traded to Texas. Goose Gossage broke his thumb. Arm trouble ended the careers of Catfish Hunter and Don Gullett and the effectiveness of Ed Figueroa, a 20-game winner in 1978. Guidry, Jackson and Nettles all spent time on the bench nursing ailments. There were other darker, more wrenching problems. Ten days after the Yankees won the 1978 Series, Bob Lemon's son died in an automobile accident; winning a baseball game never meant as much to Lemon again.

The Yankees were bumbling along in fourth place by mid-June, when George brought back Billy, a half-season early. Billy promised that he would get along with Jackson. Reggie was not convinced. "I can't play for that man," he moaned. "He hates me." He also was not happy that Steinbrenner had not consulted him beforehand, to which George replied, "When I think you should have a have a say in who manages the New York Yankees, I'll call you. You better get your head on straight, boy." It was a put-down from which the George-Reggie relationship never recovered. Two years later, when his contract expired, Reggie took his act to the California Angels.

All the misery of the summer of 1979, however, was overshadowed by one tragic moment. On August 2, while practicing takeoffs and landings at the Akron-Canton Airport, Thurman Munson crashed his twin-engine jet. His

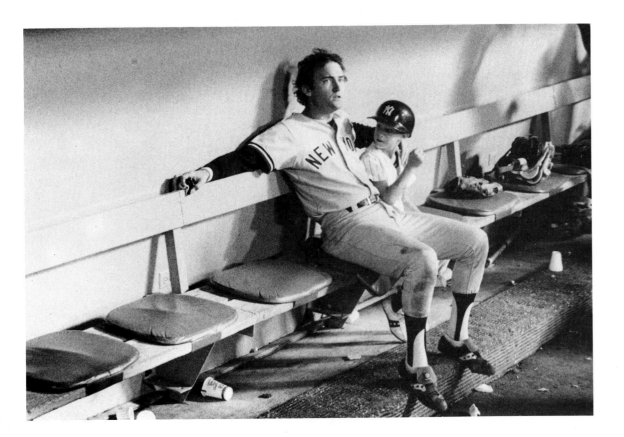

death devastated the team. Sometimes surly and often sarcastic, Munson had been an inspirational player, one whose discipline and dedication matched his talent. Without him, the Yankees played without purpose. "It was the final shot of the season," said Ron Guidry.

Actually, there was one more shot, although it did come after the season ended with the Yankees in fourth place, 13½ games behind Baltimore. On October 28, after Billy had again made headlines by punching out a marshmallow salesman in a Minnesota bar, he was fired. "How much can the Yankees take and still command my respect?" asked Steinbrenner, who already knew the answer. Billy, as was usually the case, answered in kind: "I think the man is sick. I'll be honest with you, I'll only go back if George is gone. I'll never put on a Yankee uniform as long as he is there."

Three years later he was back. ◑

The fielding wizardry of third baseman Graig Nettles (above, with his son Mike) helped win the 1978 World Series for the Yankees, their second straight. Even though the Dodgers took a 2–0 Series lead, Nettles and his mates came back to win four straight. The magic carpet ride ended in 1979, however, as the Yankees finished fourth.

1970s Statistics

1970

American League

East Division

	W	L	PCT	GB
Baltimore	108	54	.667	—
New York	93	69	.574	15
Boston	87	75	.537	21
Detroit	79	83	.488	29
Cleveland	76	86	.469	32
Washington	70	92	.432	38

West Division

	W	L	PCT	GB
Minnesota	98	64	.605	—
Oakland	89	73	.549	9
California	86	76	.531	12
Kansas City	65	97	.401	33
Milwaukee	65	97	.401	33
Chicago	56	106	.346	42

Most Valuable Player	B. Powell, BAL
Cy Young Award	J. Perry, MIN
Rookie of the Year	T. Munson, NY

League Leaders

Batting	A. Johnson, CAL	.329
Runs	C. Yastrzemski, BOS	125
Home Runs	F. Howard, WAS	44
RBI	F. Howard, WAS	126
Steals	B. Campaneris, OAK	42
Wins	D. McNally, BAL	24
Saves	R. Perranoski, MIN	34
ERA	D. Segui, OAK	2.56
Strikeouts	S. McDowell, CLE	304

World Series
Baltimore (AL) def. Cincinnati (NL) 4–1

All-Star Game
July 14 at Cincinnati—NL 5–AL 4

Record Setters
Most strikeouts, season—189, B. Bonds, SF
Most home runs by a team at home, season—133, Cleveland, 81 games
Lowest slugging percentage, 150 or more games—.223, D. Maxvill, StL
Fewest at-bats, 150 or more games—399, D. Maxvill, StL

National League

East Division

	W	L	PCT	GB
Pittsburgh	89	73	.549	—
Chicago	84	78	.519	5
New York	83	79	.512	6
St. Louis	76	86	.469	13
Philadelphia	73	88	.453	15½
Montreal	73	89	.451	16

West Division

	W	L	PCT	GB
Cincinnati	102	60	.630	—
Los Angeles	87	74	.540	14½
San Francisco	86	76	.531	16
Houston	79	83	.488	23
Atlanta	76	86	.469	26
San Diego	63	99	.389	39

Most Valuable Player	J. Bench, CIN
Cy Young Award	B. Gibson, StL
Rookie of the Year	C. Morton, MON

League Leaders

Batting	R. Carty, ATL	.366
Runs	B. Williams, CHI	137
Home Runs	J. Bench, CIN	45
RBI	J. Bench, CIN	148
Steals	B. Tolan, CIN	57
Wins	G. Perry, SF	23
	B. Gibson, StL	23
Saves	W. Granger, CIN	35
ERA	T. Seaver, NY	2.81
Strikeouts	T. Seaver, NY	283

1971

American League

East Division

	W	L	PCT	GB
Baltimore	101	57	.639	—
Detroit	91	71	.562	12
Boston	85	77	.525	18
New York	82	80	.506	21
Washington	63	96	.396	38½
Cleveland	60	102	.370	43

West Division

	W	L	PCT	GB
Oakland	101	60	.627	—
Kansas City	85	76	.528	16
Chicago	79	83	.488	22½
California	76	86	.469	25½
Minnesota	74	86	.463	26½
Milwaukee	69	92	.429	32

Most Valuable Player	V. Blue, OAK
Cy Young Award	V. Blue, OAK
Rookie of the Year	C. Chambliss, CLE

League Leaders

Batting	A. Johnson, CAL	.329
Runs	C. Yastrzemski, BOS	125
Home Runs	F. Howard, WAS	44
RBI	F. Howard, WAS	126
Steals	B. Campaneris, OAK	42
Wins	D. McNally, BAL	24
	M. Cuellar, BAL	24
	J. Perry, MIN	24
Saves	R. Perranoski, MIN	34
ERA	D. Segui, OAK	2.56
Strikeouts	S. McDowell, CLE	304

World Series
Pittsburgh (NL) def. Baltimore (AL) 4–3

All-Star Game
July 13 at Detroit—AL 6–NL 4

Record Setters
Most years with 300 or more total bases—15, H. Aaron, MIL (NL) 1955–1963, 1965; ATL 1966–1969, 1971
Most consecutive years leading the league in strikeouts, AL—4, 1968 through 1971, R. Jackson, OAK
Most times hit by a pitch, season, NL—50, R. Hunt, MON, 152 games
Most grounding into double plays, rookie season, NL—20, G. Foster, SF, CIN, 140 games

National League

East Division

	W	L	PCT	GB
Pittsburgh	97	65	.599	—
St. Louis	90	72	.556	7
Chicago	83	79	.512	14
New York	83	79	.512	14
Montreal	71	90	.441	25½
Philadelphia	67	95	.414	30

West Division

	W	L	PCT	GB
San Francisco	90	72	.556	—
Los Angeles	89	73	.549	1
Atlanta	82	80	.506	8
Cincinnati	79	83	.488	11
Houston	79	83	.488	11
San Diego	61	100	.379	28½

Most Valuable Player	J. Torre, StL
Cy Young Award	F. Jenkins, CHI
Rookie of the Year	E. Williams, ATL

League Leaders

Batting	J. Torre, StL	.363
Runs	L. Brock, StL	126
Home Runs	W. Stargell, PIT	48
RBI	J. Torre, StL	137
Steals	L. Brock, StL	64
Wins	F. Jenkins, CHI	24
Saves	D. Giusti, PIT	30
ERA	T. Seaver, NY	1.76
Strikeouts	T. Seaver, NY	289

Records listed in **Record Setters** still stand as of publication date.

1970s STATISTICS

1972

American League

East Division	W	L	PCT	GB
Detroit	86	70	.551	—
Boston	85	70	.548	½
Baltimore	80	74	.519	5
New York	79	76	.510	6½
Cleveland	72	84	.462	14
Milwaukee	65	91	.417	21
West Division				
Oakland	93	62	.600	—
Chicago	87	67	.565	5½
Minnesota	77	77	.500	15½
Kansas City	76	78	.494	16½
California	75	80	.484	18
Texas	54	100	.351	38½

Most Valuable Player	D. Allen, CHI
Cy Young Award	G. Perry, CLE
Rookie of the Year	C. Fisk, BOS

League Leaders

Batting	R. Carew, MIN	.318
Runs	B. Murcer, NY	102
Home Runs	D. Allen, CHI	37
RBI	D. Allen, CHI	113
Steals	B. Campaneris, OAK	52
Wins	W. Wood, CHI	24
	G. Perry, CLE	24
Saves	S. Lyle, NY	35
ERA	L. Tiant, BOS	1.91
Strikeouts	N. Ryan, CAL	329

World Series
Oakland (AL) def. Cincinnati (NL) 4–3

All-Star Game
July 25 at Atlanta—NL 4–AL 3

Record Setters
Most games pitched—1,070, H. Wilhelm, nine teams, 1952 through 1972, 622 games (AL), 448 games (NL)

Most games won by a left-handed pitcher, season, NL (since 1900)—27, S. Carlton, PHI (tied record by S. Koufax, LA, 1966)

Most consecutive batters retired by a pitcher, season —41, J. Barr, SF

Fewest runs, season, 150 or more games—25, L. Cardenas, CAL

Most total bases in a doubleheader, nine-inning games, NL—22, N. Colbert, SD, August 1

National League

East Division	W	L	PCT	GB
Pittsburgh	96	59	.619	—
Chicago	85	70	.548	11
New York	83	73	.532	13½
St. Louis	75	81	.481	21½
Montreal	70	86	.449	26½
Philadelphia	59	97	.378	37½
West Division				
Cincinnati	95	59	.617	—
Houston	84	69	.549	10½
Los Angeles	85	70	.548	10½
Atlanta	70	84	.455	25
San Francisco	69	86	.445	26½
San Diego	58	95	.379	36½

Most Valuable Player	J. Bench, CIN
Cy Young Award	S. Carlton, PHI
Rookie of the Year	J. Matlack, NY

League Leaders

Batting	B. Williams, CHI	.333
Runs	J. Morgan, CIN	122
Home Runs	J. Bench, CIN	40
RBI	J. Bench, CIN	125
Steals	L. Brock, StL	63
Wins	S. Carlton, PHI	27
Saves	C. Carroll, CIN	37
ERA	S. Carlton, PHI	1.97
Strikeouts	S. Carlton, PHI	310

1973

American League

East Division	W	L	PCT	GB
Baltimore	97	65	.599	—
Boston	89	73	.549	8
Detroit	85	77	.525	12
New York	80	82	.494	17
Milwaukee	74	88	.457	23
Cleveland	71	91	.438	26
West Division				
Oakland	94	68	.580	—
Kansas City	88	74	.543	6
Minnesota	81	81	.500	13
California	79	83	.488	15
Chicago	77	85	.475	17
Texas	57	105	.352	37

Most Valuable Player	R. Jackson, OAK
Cy Young Award	J. Palmer, BAL
Rookie of the Year	A. Bumbry, BAL

League Leaders

Batting	R. Carew, MIN	.350
Runs	R. Jackson, OAK	99
Home Runs	R. Jackson, OAK	32
RBI	R. Jackson, OAK	117
Steals	T. Harper, BOS	54
Wins	W. Wood, CHI	24
Saves	J. Hiller, DET	38
ERA	J. Palmer, BAL	2.40
Strikeouts	N. Ryan, CAL	383

World Series
Oakland (AL) def. New York (NL) 4–3

All-Star Game
July 24 at Kansas City—NL 7–AL 1

Record Setters
Most strikeouts pitched, season, AL—383, N. Ryan, CAL

Most hits by a switch-hitter, season, NL—230, P. Rose, CIN

Most home runs by a leadoff batter, season, NL—11, B. Bonds, SF

Most years with 40 or more home runs, NL—8, H. Aaron, MIL, 1957, 1960, 1962, 1963; ATL, 1966, 1969, 1971, 1973

National League

East Division	W	L	PCT	GB
New York	82	79	.509	—
St. Louis	81	81	.500	1½
Pittsburgh	80	82	.494	2½
Montreal	79	83	.488	3½
Chicago	77	84	.478	5
Philadelphia	71	91	.438	11½
West Division				
Cincinnati	99	63	.611	—
Los Angeles	95	66	.590	3½
San Francisco	88	74	.543	11
Houston	82	80	.506	17
Atlanta	76	85	.472	22½
San Diego	60	102	.370	39

Most Valuable Player	P. Rose, CIN
Cy Young Award	T. Seaver, NY
Rookie of the Year	G. Matthews, SF

League Leaders

Batting	P. Rose, CIN	.338
Runs	B. Bonds, SF	131
Home Runs	W. Stargell, PIT	44
RBI	W. Stargell, PIT	119
Steals	L. Brock, StL	70
Wins	R. Bryant, SF	24
Saves	M. Marshall, MON	31
ERA	T. Seaver, NY	2.08
Strikeouts	T. Seaver, NY	251

Records listed in **Record Setters** still stand as of publication date.

1970s Statistics

1974

American League

East Division

	W	L	PCT	GB
Baltimore	91	71	.562	—
New York	89	73	.549	2
Boston	84	78	.519	7
Cleveland	77	85	.475	14
Milwaukee	76	86	.469	15
Detroit	72	90	.444	19

West Division

	W	L	PCT	GB
Oakland	90	72	.556	—
Texas	84	76	.525	5
Minnesota	82	80	.506	8
Chicago	80	80	.500	9
Kansas City	77	85	.475	13
California	68	94	.420	22

Most Valuable Player	J. Burroughs, TEX
Cy Young Award	C. Hunter, OAK
Rookie of the Year	M. Hargrove, TEX

League Leaders

Batting	R. Carew, MIN	.364
Runs	C. Yastrzemski, BOS	93
Home Runs	D. Allen, CHI	32
RBI	J. Burroughs, TEX	118
Steals	B. North, OAK	54
Wins	C. Hunter, OAK	25
	F. Jenkins, TEX	25
Saves	T. Forster, CHI	24
ERA	C. Hunter, OAK	2.49
Strikeouts	N. Ryan, CAL	367

1974 Center

World Series
Oakland (AL) def. Los Angeles (NL) 4–1

All-Star Game
July 23 at Pittsburgh—NL 7–AL 2

Record Setters

Most stolen bases, season, NL—118, L. Brock, StL

Most plate appearances, season, NL—771, P. Rose, CIN

Most singles by a switch-hitter, season, NL—181, P. Rose, CIN

Most years with 20 or more home runs, NL—20, H. Aaron, MIL 1955–1965, ATL 1966–1974

Most years playing 150 or more games, AL—14, B. Robinson, BAL, 1960–1964, 1966–1974

Most games finished by a relief pitcher, season, NL—83, M. Marshall, LA

National League

East Division

	W	L	PCT	GB
Pittsburgh	88	74	.543	—
St. Louis	86	75	.534	1½
Philadelphia	80	82	.494	8
Montreal	79	82	.491	8½
New York	71	91	.438	17
Chicago	66	96	.407	22

West Division

	W	L	PCT	GB
Los Angeles	102	60	.630	—
Cincinnati	98	64	.605	4
Atlanta	88	74	.543	14
Houston	81	81	.500	21
San Francisco	72	90	.444	30
San Diego	60	102	.370	42

Most Valuable Player	S. Garvey, LA
Cy Young Award	M. Marshall, LA
Rookie of the Year	B. McBride, StL

League Leaders

Batting	R. Garr, ATL	.353
Runs	P. Rose, CIN	110
Home Runs	M. Schmidt, PHI	36
RBI	J. Bench, CIN	129
Steals	L. Brock, StL	118
Wins	P. Niekro, ATL	20
	A. Messersmith, LA	20
Saves	M. Marshall, LA	21
ERA	B. Capra, ATL	2.28
Strikeouts	S. Carlton, PHI	240

1975

American League

East Division

	W	L	PCT	GB
Boston	95	65	.594	—
Baltimore	90	69	.566	4½
New York	83	77	.519	12
Cleveland	79	80	.497	15½
Milwaukee	68	94	.420	28
Detroit	57	102	.358	37½

West Division

	W	L	PCT	GB
Oakland	98	64	.605	—
Kansas City	91	71	.562	7
Texas	79	83	.488	19
Minnesota	76	83	.478	20½
Chicago	75	86	.466	22½
California	72	89	.447	25½

Most Valuable Player	F. Lynn, BOS
Cy Young Award	J. Palmer, BAL
Rookie of the Year	F. Lynn, BOS

League Leaders

Batting	R. Carew, MIN	.359
Runs	F. Lynn, BOS	103
Home Runs	G. Scott, MIL	36
	R. Jackson, OAK	36
RBI	G. Scott, MIL	109
Steals	M. Rivers, CAL	70
Wins	J. Palmer, BAL	23
	C. Hunter, NY	23
Saves	G. Gossage, CHI	26
ERA	J. Palmer, BAL	2.09
Strikeouts	F. Tanana, CAL	269

1975 Center

World Series
Cincinnati (NL) def. Boston (AL) 4–3

All-Star Game
July 15 at Milwaukee—NL 6–AL 3

Record Setters

Most hits in a nine-inning game—7, R. Stennett, PIT (NL), September 16 (tied record by W. Robinson, BAL [NL], June 10, 1892)

Most doubles by a rookie, season, AL—47, F. Lynn, BOS

Most hits by a pinch hitter, AL—107, G. Brown, DET, 1963–1975, 525 games

Most no-hit games pitched, AL—4, N. Ryan, CAL, 1973 (2), 1974, 1975

Most players used by both clubs in a nine-inning game, AL—42, Oakland, 24, vs. Kansas City, 18, September 20

Fewest players used, season, NL—29, Cincinnati

National League

East Division

	W	L	PCT	GB
Pittsburgh	92	69	.571	—
Philadelphia	86	76	.531	6½
New York	82	80	.506	10½
St. Louis	82	80	.506	10½
Chicago	75	87	.463	17½
Montreal	75	87	.463	17½

West Division

	W	L	PCT	GB
Cincinnati	108	54	.667	—
Los Angeles	88	74	.543	20
San Francisco	80	81	.497	27½
San Diego	71	91	.438	37
Atlanta	67	94	.416	40½
Houston	64	97	.398	43½

Most Valuable Player	J. Morgan, CIN
Cy Young Award	T. Seaver, NY
Rookie of the Year	J. Montefusco, SF

League Leaders

Batting	B. Madlock, CHI	.354
Runs	P. Rose, CIN	112
Home Runs	M. Schmidt, PHI	38
RBI	G. Luzinski, PHI	120
Steals	D. Lopes, LA	77
Wins	T. Seaver, NY	22
Saves	R. Eastwick, CIN	22
	A. Hrabosky, StL	22
ERA	R. Jones, SD	2.24
Strikeouts	T. Seaver, NY	243

Records listed in **Record Setters** still stand as of publication date.

1970s Statistics

1976

American League

East Division	W	L	PCT	GB
New York	97	62	.610	—
Baltimore	88	74	.543	10½
Boston	83	79	.512	15½
Cleveland	81	78	.509	16
Detroit	74	87	.460	24
Milwaukee	66	95	.410	32
West Division				
Kansas City	90	72	.556	—
Oakland	87	74	.540	2½
Minnesota	85	77	.525	5
California	76	86	.469	14
Texas	76	86	.469	14
Chicago	64	97	.398	25½

Most Valuable Player — T. Munson, NY
Cy Young Award — J. Palmer, BAL
Rookie of the Year — M. Fidrych, DET

League Leaders

Batting	G. Brett, KC	.333
Runs	R. White, NY	104
Home Runs	G. Nettles, NY	32
RBI	L. May, BAL	109
Steals	B. North, OAK	75
Wins	J. Palmer, BAL	22
Saves	S. Lyle, NY	23
ERA	M. Fidrych, DET	2.34
Strikeouts	N. Ryan, CAL	327

World Series
Cincinnati (NL) def. New York (AL) 4–0

All-Star Game
July 13 at Philadelphia—NL 7–AL 1

Record Setters
Most home runs, career—755, H. Aaron, MIL (NL) 1954–1965, ATL (NL) 1966–1974, MIL (AL) 1975–1976
Most RBI, career—2,297, H. Aaron, MIL (NL) 1954–1965, ATL (NL) 1966–1974, MIL (AL) 1975–1976
Most total bases, career—6,856, H. Aaron, MIL (NL) 1954–1965, ATL (NL) 1966–1974, MIL (AL) 1975–1976
Most hits by a pinch hitter, season—25, J. Morales, MON
Most consecutive innings pitched with no bases on balls, season, NL—68, R. Jones, SD (tied record by C. Mathewson, NY, 1913)
Most stolen bases by a team, season, AL—341, OAK

National League

East Division	W	L	PCT	GB
Philadelphia	101	61	.623	—
Pittsburgh	92	70	.568	9
New York	86	76	.531	15
Chicago	75	87	.463	26
St. Louis	72	90	.444	29
Montreal	55	107	.340	46
West Division				
Cincinnati	102	60	.630	—
Los Angeles	92	70	.568	10
Houston	80	82	.494	22
San Francisco	74	88	.457	28
San Diego	73	89	.451	29
Atlanta	70	92	.432	32

Most Valuable Player — J. Morgan, CIN
Cy Young Award — R. Jones, SD
Rookie of the Year — P. Zachry, CIN
B. Metzger, SD

League Leaders

Batting	B. Madlock, CHI	.339
Runs	P. Rose, CIN	130
Home Runs	M. Schmidt, PHI	38
RBI	G. Foster, CIN	121
Steals	D. Lopes, LA	63
Wins	R. Jones, SD	22
Saves	R. Eastwick, CIN	26
ERA	J. Denny, StL	2.52
Strikeouts	T. Seaver, NY	235

1977

American League

East Division	W	L	PCT	GB
New York	100	62	.617	—
Baltimore	97	64	.602	2½
Boston	97	64	.602	2½
Detroit	74	88	.457	26
Cleveland	71	90	.441	28½
Milwaukee	67	95	.414	33
Toronto	54	107	.335	45½
West Division				
Kansas City	102	60	.630	—
Texas	94	68	.580	8
Chicago	90	72	.556	12
Minnesota	84	77	.522	17½
California	74	88	.457	28
Seattle	64	98	.395	38
Oakland	63	98	.391	38½

Most Valuable Player — R. Carew, MIN
Cy Young Award — S. Lyle, NY
Rookie of the Year — E. Murray, BAL

League Leaders

Batting	R. Carew, MIN	.388
Runs	R. Carew, MIN	128
Home Runs	J. Rice, BOS	39
RBI	L. Hisle, MIN	119
Steals	F. Patek, KC	53
Wins	J. Palmer, BAL–D. Goltz, MIN	20
	D. Leonard, KC	20
Saves	B. Campbell, BOS	31
ERA	F. Tanana, CAL	2.54
Strikeouts	N. Ryan, CAL	341

World Series
New York (AL) def. Los Angeles (NL) 4–2

All-Star Game
July 16 at New York—NL 7–AL 5

Record Setters
Longest career with a single team—23 years, Brooks Robinson, BAL, 1955–1977 (tied by C. Yastrzemski, BOS, 1961–1983)
Most home runs on the road, season, NL—31, G. Foster, CIN
Most consecutive hits, start of career—6, T. Cox, BOS, September 18 and 19
Most runs in a six-game World Series—10, R. Jackson, NY (AL)
Most home runs in a six-game World Series—5, Reggie Jackson, NY (AL)

National League

East Division	W	L	PCT	GB
Philadelphia	101	61	.623	—
Pittsburgh	96	66	.593	5
St. Louis	83	79	.512	18
Chicago	81	81	.500	20
Montreal	75	87	.463	26
New York	64	98	.395	37
West Division				
Los Angeles	98	64	.605	—
Cincinnati	88	74	.543	10
Houston	81	81	.500	17
San Francisco	75	87	.463	23
San Diego	69	93	.426	29
Atlanta	61	101	.377	37

Most Valuable Player — G. Foster, CIN
Cy Young Award — S. Carlton, PHI
Rookie of the Year — A. Dawson, MON

League Leaders

Batting	D. Parker, PIT	.338
Runs	G. Foster, CIN	124
Home Runs	G. Foster, CIN	52
RBI	G. Foster, CIN	149
Steals	F. Taveras, PIT	70
Wins	S. Carlton, PHI	23
Saves	R. Fingers, SD	35
ERA	J. Candelaria, PIT	2.34
Strikeouts	P. Niekro, ATL	262

1970s Statistics

1978

American League

East Division

	W	L	PCT	GB
New York	100	63	.613	—
Boston	99	64	.607	1
Milwaukee	93	69	.574	6½
Baltimore	90	71	.559	9
Detroit	86	76	.531	13½
Cleveland	69	90	.434	29
Toronto	59	102	.366	40

West Division

	W	L	PCT	GB
Kansas City	92	70	.568	—
California	87	75	.537	5
Texas	87	75	.537	5
Minnesota	73	89	.451	19
Chicago	71	90	.441	20½
Oakland	69	93	.426	23
Seattle	56	104	.350	35

Most Valuable Player — J. Rice, BOS
Cy Young Award — R. Guidry, NY
Rookie of the Year — L. Whitaker, DET

League Leaders

Batting	R. Carew, MIN	.333
Runs	R. LeFlore, DET	126
Home Runs	J. Rice, BOS	46
RBI	J. Rice, BOS	139
Steals	R. LeFlore, DET	68
Wins	R. Guidry, NY	25
Saves	G. Gossage, NY	27
ERA	R. Guidry, NY	1.74
Strikeouts	N. Ryan, CAL	260

World Series

New York (AL) def. Los Angeles (NL) 4–2

All-Star Game

July 11 at San Diego—NL 7–AL 3

Record Setters

Longest consecutive-game hitting streak, NL—44 games, P. Rose, CIN (tied record by W. Keeler, BAL, 1897)

Most grand slams by a pinch hitter, season—2, D.Johnson, PHI, April 30, June 3; M. Ivie, SF, May 28, June 30

Most players used by both clubs in a nine-inning game, NL—45, Chicago, 24, vs. Montreal, 21, September 5

Most home runs in two consecutive World Series—7, R. Jackson, NY (AL), 1977, 5; 1978, 2

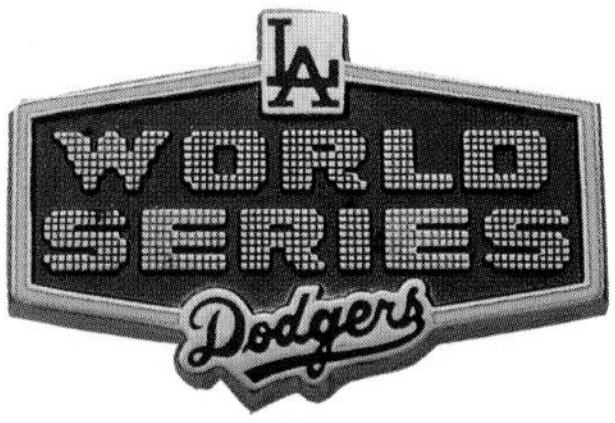

National League

East Division

	W	L	PCT	GB
Philadelphia	90	72	.556	—
Pittsburgh	88	73	.547	1½
Chicago	79	83	.488	11
Montreal	76	86	.469	14
St. Louis	69	93	.426	21
New York	66	96	.407	24

West Division

	W	L	PCT	GB
Los Angeles	95	67	.586	—
Cincinnati	92	69	.571	2½
San Francisco	89	73	.549	6
San Diego	84	78	.519	11
Houston	74	88	.457	21
Atlanta	69	93	.426	26

Most Valuable Player — D. Parker, PIT
Cy Young Award — G. Perry, SD
Rookie of the Year — B. Horner, ATL

League Leaders

Batting	D. Parker, PIT	.334
Runs	I. DeJesus, CHI	104
Home Runs	G. Foster, CIN	40
RBI	G. Foster, CIN	120
Steals	O. Moreno, PIT	71
Wins	G. Perry, SD	21
Saves	R. Fingers, SD	37
ERA	C. Swan, NY	2.43
Strikeouts	J. Richard, HOU	303

1979

American League

East Division

	W	L	PCT	GB
Baltimore	102	57	.642	—
Milwaukee	95	66	.590	8
Boston	91	69	.569	11½
New York	89	71	.556	13½
Detroit	85	76	.528	18
Cleveland	81	80	.503	22
Toronto	53	109	.327	50½

West Division

	W	L	PCT	GB
California	88	74	.543	—
Kansas City	85	77	.525	3
Texas	83	79	.512	5
Minnesota	82	80	.506	6
Chicago	73	87	.456	14
Seattle	67	95	.414	21
Oakland	54	108	.333	34

Most Valuable Player — D. Baylor, CAL
Cy Young Award — M. Flanagan, BAL
Rookie of the Year — A. Griffin, TOR
                     J. Castino, MIN

League Leaders

Batting	F. Lynn, BOS	.333
Runs	D. Baylor, CAL	120
Home Runs	G. Thomas, MIL	45
RBI	D. Baylor, CAL	139
Steals	W. Wilson, KC	83
Wins	M. Flanagan, BAL	23
Saves	M. Marshall, MIN	32
ERA	R. Guidry, NY	2.78
Strikeouts	N. Ryan, CAL	223

World Series

Pittsburgh (NL) def. Baltimore (AL) 4–3

All-Star Game

July 17 at Seattle—NL 7–AL 6

Record Setters

Most stolen bases, career—938, L. Brock, StL

Most years with 200 or more hits—10, P. Rose CIN, 1965–1966, 1968–1970, 1973, 1975–1977, PHI, 1979

Most triples by a switch-hitter, season, NL (since 1900)—19, G. Templeton, StL (tied record by M. Carey, PIT, 1923)

Most consecutive years leading the league in triples, NL (since 1900)—3, G. Templeton, StL, 1977 through 1979

Most games finished by a relief pitcher, season, AL—84, M. Marshall, MIN

Fewest strikeouts in a World Series—0, T. Foli, PIT, 30 at-bats in 7 games

National League

East Division

	W	L	PCT	GB
Pittsburgh	98	64	.605	—
Montreal	95	65	.594	2
St. Louis	86	76	.531	12
Philadelphia	84	78	.519	14
Chicago	80	82	.494	18
New York	63	99	.389	35

West Division

	W	L	PCT	GB
Cincinnati	90	71	.559	—
Houston	89	73	.549	1½
Los Angeles	79	83	.488	11½
San Francisco	71	91	.438	19½
San Diego	68	93	.422	22
Atlanta	66	94	.413	23½

Most Valuable Player — K. Hernandez, StL
                       W. Stargell, PIT
Cy Young Award — B. Sutter, CHI
Rookie of the Year — R. Sutcliffe, LA

League Leaders

Batting	K. Hernandez, StL	344
Runs	K. Hernandez, StL	116
Home Runs	D. Kingman, CHI	48
RBI	D. Winfield, SD	118
Steals	O. Moreno, PIT	77
Wins	P. Niekro, ATL	21
	J. Niekro, HOU	21
Saves	B. Sutter, CHI	37
ERA	J. Richard, HOU	2.71
Strikeouts	J. Richard, HOU	313

Records listed in **Record Setters** still stand as of publication date.

INDEX

Aaron, Henry "Hank", 43, 78, **95,** 156
Abbott, Glenn, 30
Aikens, Willie, 156
Alexander, Doyle, 132
Allen, Mel, 89
Allen, Richie, 44, 108, **125,** 131, 134
Alou, Jesus, 33
Alou, Matty, 25
Alston, Walter, 55, 130, **131,** 134-135
Anderson, George "Sparky", **10,** 13, 16, 29, 50, **65,** 67-68, 69, 70, 72-73, 74-75, **80, 83,** 86, 108, **122,** 124, 145
Andrews, Mike, 33-35
Angell, Roger; on Bernie Carbo, 11; on 1975 World Series, 16, 17; on World Series, 93
Appel, Marty, 168
Armbrister, Ed, 8-9, 69
Arrigo, Jerry, 84
Ashburn, Richie, 100
Aspromonte, Ken, 157
Autry, Gene, 50, **56,** 57, 132, 133

Baker, Dusty, 135
Bando, Chris, 34
Bando, Sal, 21, **22,** 23, 25, **28,** 30, **33,** 34, **35,** 36, 38, 52, 158
Barber, Red, 89, 100
Barnett, Larry, 9
Bauer, Hank, 34
Baylor, Don, 37, 38, 57, 58, 59, 132, **154,** 156
Belinsky, Bo, 54
Bell, Buddy, 112
Bench, Johnny, 9, 10-11, 12, 16, **17,** 32, 40, 50-51, **64-65,** 66, 67, 68, 69, **72,** 73, 75, 76, 80, 81, 84-87
Berra, Yogi, 74, **129,** 163, 164-165
Billingham, Jack, 16, **69,** 73, 74
Bird, Doug, 32
Blackmun, Harry, 47
Blair, Paul, 164, 167
Blass, Steve, 24, 48, 73
Blomberg, Ron, 154
Blue, Vida, 23, 24-25, 28-29, 30, 32, 33, 34, **35,** 36, 37, 40-**41,** 145, 178
Blyleven, Bert, 57
Borbon, Pedro, 10, 73, 74, 77-80, **142-143,** 145
Boros, Steve, 114
Bostock, Lyman Jr., **56,** 57, 59
Boswell, Thomas, 123
Bouton, Jim (*Ball Four*), 54
Bowa, Larry, 98, **118**
Brett, George, 60, **112,** 113, 114, 118, 156, 179, 180
Bridges, Rocky, 123
Briles, Nelson, 73
Bristol, Dave, 8, 84, 123, 124
Brock, Lou, **113,** 115
Buckner, Bill, 36
Burleson, Rick, 10, 12, 16, 174-175, 178
Burton, Jim, 16
Busch, August "Gussie", 43, 50
Busch Memorial Stadium, **106,** 107

Caldwell, Mike, 175
Callison, Johnny, 154
Campaneris, Dagoberto "Bert", **21,** 23, 25, 28, **32,** 34, **35,** 38, 132
Campanis, Al, 49
Campbell, Bill, **55,** 57, 59, 166
Campbell, Jim, 128
Candelaria, John, 110, 131-134
Candlestick Park, 107, 118, **119**
Capra, Buzz, 74
Caray, Harry, 22
Carbo, Bernie, 9, 10, **11,** 68
Carew, Rod, 26, 57, **115,** 134
Carlton, Steve, 81, 96-**97**
Carroll, Clay, 16, 72, 73, 77-80, 80, 145
Carty, Rico, **155**
Cash, Norm, 100
Cepeda, Orlando, 25, 40, 148, **153,** 154
Cey, Ron, 135-136
Chambliss, Chris, 113, 162, 166, **167,** 175, **180**
Chaney, Darrel, 76
Clemente, Roberto, 43, 48-**49,** 73, 110, 126
Cobb, Ty, **44**
Coleman, Jerry, 176
Collins, Bud, 13
Comiskey Park, 107, 118
Concepcion, Dave, 13, 67, **68,** 72, 75, 76, 112
Corbett, Brad, 128-129, 132, **133**
Corrales, Pat, 122
Cosell, Howard, 90-**91,** 100, 101
Cowens, Al, 113
Coyle, Harry, 89
Crandall, Del, 129
Cuellar, Mike, 24-25

Dalton, Harry, 84, 161-162
Darcy, Pat, 13, 15
Dark, Alvin, **35,** 123, 129-130
Davalillo, Vic, 33
Davis, Tommy, 155
Dempsey, Rick, 163
Dent, Bucky, 165, 167, 170, **175**-178
Designated hitter rule, 91, 153-157
Devine, Bing, 44
DiMaggio, Joe, 21, 172
Dobson, Pat, 24-25
Doyle, Denny, 11, **12,** 16
Drago, Dick, 12
Driessen, Dan, 76, 82
Drysdale, Don, 100
Duncan, Dave, 21, 23, **25, 157**
Duren, Ryne, 144
Durocher, Leo, 124, 136

Eastwick, Rawley, 10, 11, 59, **77**-80, 82, 145-146, 149, 171
Eckersley, Dennis, **118**
Edwards, Johnny, 84
Ellis, Dock, 162
Epstein, Mike, 24, **25,** 28
Evans, Dwight, 10, 12, **13,** 17, 174

Face, Elroy, 144
Feeney, Charles "Chub", 55, 124
Ferguson, Joe, 36-37
Ferrick, Tom, 147
Fidrych, Mark, **100**
Figueroa, Ed, 162, 165, 167, 180
Fingers, Rollie, 21, 23, 25, 30, 32, 34, **35,** 36-**37,** 38, 57, 59, 132, 145, 148, 158-**159**
Finley, Charles O., 19-41, **18, 25, 35,** 41, 52, 123, 131, 153
Fisk, Carlton, **4-5,** 7, **8,** 9, 12, 13-**15,** 86, 89-90, 98, 174, 178, **179**
Flanagan, Mike, 140, 175
Flood, Curt, 44-47
Flynn, Doug, 76
Foli, Tim, 134
Forbes Field, 102
Fosse, Ray, 32, 36, **62**
Foster, Alan, 126
Foster, George, 10, 11, **64-65, 69,** 73, 76, 77, 80, 81
Freehan, Bill (*Behind the Mask*), 54

Gaherin, John, 53
Gamble, Oscar, **60**
Garagiola, Joe, 46, **91,** 94, 100, 101
Garber, Gene, 146
Garland, Wayne, 57-59
Garrett, Wayne, 34
Garvey, Steve, 60, 132, **135**-136, 166, 179-180
Gerard, Lou, 89
Geronimo, Cesar, 9, 10, 13, 17, 64, 69, 75, **76,** 81, 112, **142-143**
Giannoulas, Ted (San Diego Chicken), 99, 116, **117**
Gibson, Bob, 43, 100
Giusti, Dave, 73
Goldberg, Arthur, **45**
Gomez, Preston, 129
Gordon, Joe, 20
Gossage, Rich "Goose", 59, **60, 93, 144,** 146, 149, 152, 167, 171, 178, 179, 180
Grammas, Alex, 129
Greenberg, Hank, 46
Green, Dick, **21,** 36
Grich, Bobby, **56,** 57, 58, 132, 161-162
Griffey, Ken, 7, **9,** 10, 12, 13, 16, 64, **73,** 75, 81, 112
Griffith, Calvin, **57,** 58, 129
Grimsley, Ross, 73, 75
Grote, Jerry, **75**
Guidry, Ron, 167, **173,** 175, 176-**177,** 178, 180, 181
Guisti, Dave, 73, **147**
Gullett, Don, 16, 50, **55,** 57, 59, **60,** 74, 77, 82, 161, 167, 170, 180
Gura, Larry, 167

Haller, Bob, **160**
Harrelson, Bud, 74-75
Harrelson, Ken, 100
Hart, Jim Ray, 154
Hebner, Richie, 73, 115
Helms, Tommy, 69, 70

Henderson, Rickey, 113
Hendrick, George, **32,** 158
Hendricks, Elrod **140**
Hernandez, Keith, 126
Herzog, Dorrel "Whitey", 21, 112-113, 114, 122, **128,** 129, 156
Hickman, Jim, 63
Hiller, John, **146,** 147
Hisle, Larry, 57, 59
Hobson, Butch, 174
Hofheinz, Roy, 107
Holland, John, 43
Holtzman, Ken, 22, 25, 29, 32, 37, 57, 73-74, 145
Hooton, Burt, 167-170
Hough, Charlie, **147,** 170
Houk, Ralph, 21
Howsam, Bob, 58, **64,** 65-67, 69, 75, 82, 108
Howser, Dick, 124-125, 165, 171, 175
Hrabosky, Al, **149,** 152
Hunter, Billy, 125
Hunter, James Augustus "Catfish", 21-22, 23, 25, 26-**27,** 28, 29, 30, 32, **35,** 36, 37, **38, 53,** 56, 73-74, 104, 145, 152, 155, 158, 161, 162-163, 170, 173, 175, 180

Jackson, Grant, 146
Jackson, Keith, 90, 100
Jackson, Reggie, 7, 19, 22-**23,** 25, 28, 32-33, 34, **35,** 36, 37, **38,** 57, 59, 60, 65, 90, 95, 100, 102-**105, 160-**180, 176
Jenkins, Ferguson, **53**
Johnson, Cliff, 166
Johnson, Darrell, 6, 10
Johnson, Davey, **101**
Johnson, Deron, 32, 155
John, Tommy, 135
Jones, Cleon, **33**
Jones, Randy, 112

Kaline, Al, 100, 156
Kauffman, Ewing, 58
Kaye, Danny, **133**
Kern, Jim, **157**
Killebrew, Harmon, 26
King, Clyde, 129
Kingdome, 107
Kingman, Dave, **60**
Kison, Bruce, **101**
Kluszewski, Ted, 68
Knowles, Darold, 24, **34, 145**
Konstanty, Jim, 144
Kravec, Ken, **93**
Kroc, Ray, 57, 132, **133,** 158
Kubek, Tony, 81, 100
Kuhn, Bowie, 34, 37-38, 45-**46,** 54, 55, 92, **133**

LaGrow, Lerrin, 28
Landis, Kenesaw Mountain, **44**
Lasorda, Tommy, 134-**135,** 136
Lau, Charlie, 23, 113-114, 115
Lee, Bill "Spaceman", 16, 65
Lefebvre, Jim, 108
Lemon, Bob, **123,** 162, **172,** 173

Lemonds, Dave, 113
Leonard, Dennis, 167
Linblad, Paul, 30, **38**
Littell, Mark, 167
Locker, Bob, 145
Look, Bruce, 26
Lopat, Eddie, 102
Lopes, Davey, **95,** 135-136
Lucchesi, Frank, **124,** 125, 129
Luzinski, Greg, 81, **98**
Lyle, Sparky, 54, **92, 145,** 146, 148-149, 152, 162, 167, 168, 171, 176, 180
Lynn, Fred, 6, **7**-8, **9,** 10, 11, 16,

McCarver, Tim, 100
McCovey, Willie, 40
McDonald, Joe, **129**
McEnaney, Will, 11, 16, **17, 77**-80, 145
McGraw, Tug, 33, **146,** 147
McKeon, Jack, 129
McLain, Denny, 19, 25, 54
McMillan, Roy, **129**
McNally, Dave, 24-25, **52-**53
McNamara, John, 23, 24, **122-**123
McRae, Hal, 73, 113, 114, 156, 162 109, 174, 178
Maddox, Garry, 81
Madlock, Bill "Mad Dog", 97, **109,** 126, 134
Mantle, Mickey, 54, 167
Marberry, Firpo, 144
Marshall, Mike, 148, 150-**151**
Martin, Billy, 19, 28, 30, 92, **99,** 122, **124,** 125, 128-129, **160-**181
Mascots, 99, 116-**117**
Mathewson, Christy, 112
Matlack, Jon, 48
Matthews, Gary, 96
Mauch, Gene, 70, 115, 129, 134, **137,** 150
Maxvill, Dal, 28
May, Carlos, 155
May, Lee, 68, 69, 70, 156
Mays, Willie, 33, 43, 74
Mazeroski, Bill, 109
Menke, Dennis, 69, 73
Merritt, Jim, 68-69
Messersmith, Andy, **52-**55, 56
Millan, Felix, **75**
Miller, Marvin, 45, **47-**50, **51,** 52-53, 55
Miller, Ray, 138, 156
Mincher, Don, 24
Mitchell, Paul, 37
Monday, Rick, 21, **22,** 23, 30, 102
Moore, Wilcy, 144
Moose, Bob, 73
Moreland, Keith, 96
Moreno, Omar, 110
Moret, Roger, 10, 16
Morgan, Joe, 8, 9, 10, 12, 13, 16, **17, 32, 64-65,** 69-72, 70-**71,** 73-74, 75, 76, 77, 80, 81, 82, 107, 112
Moss, Les, 128

Munson, Thurman, 162-163, 165, 167-170, 168-**169,** 171, 173, 178, 179, 180-181
Murray, Eddie, 156
Murtaugh, Danny, 128, 131, **134**

Napp, Larry, **140**
Navin, Frank, 44
Nettles, Graig, 92-93, 162-163, **165,** 167, 179, 179-180, **181**
Nixon, Russ, 96, **142-143**
Nolan, Gary, 7, 29, 75-76, **82**
North, Billy, 32, 35, 38, 123

Oakland Alameda County Coliseum, 30-**31**
O'Brien, Danny, 132
O'Connell, Dick, 51, 57
Odom, John "Blue Moon", **21, 28,** 29, 30, 34, 36, 73-74, 145
Oliva, Tony, 26, **153,** 155
Oliver, Al, 73, 131
Olympic Stadium, 107
O'Malley, Walter, 56, 130
Osmond, Herb, 56
Otis, Amos, 63, **109,** 112, 113
Ozark, Danny, 122, **130**

Palmer, Jim, 24-25, 34, 138-**141**
Parker, Dave, 59, 110, **125,** 126, 131-134
Parker, Wes, 51
Patek, Freddie, **113,** 156
Paul, Gabe, 50, 129, 165, 173
Pepitone, Joe, 54
Perez, Marty, **61**
Perez, Tony, 8, 16, 64, **66,** 68, 72, 73, 74, 75, 77, 78, 82, 112
Perry, Gaylord, **98,** 158
Peters, Hank, 21
Petrocelli, Rico, 10, 12, 100
Piniella, Lou, **165,** 167, 173, 178, 179, **180**
Pinson, Vida, 66-67
Players' strike, 47-51
Powell, Boog, **140**
Pryor, Greg, 109

Quilici, Frank, 129

Radatz, Dick, 144
Randle, Lenny, 124, 125
Randolph, Willie, 162, 166, 167, 170, **174**
Reed, Ron, 146
Reese, Rich, 26
Remy, Jerry, 174, 178
Rettenmund, Merv, 16
Rice, Jim, **7**-8, **156-**157, 164, 175
Richards, Paul, 152
Rigney, Bill, 130
Riverfront Stadium, 78-**79,** 107
Rivers, Mickey, 162, **167,** 170, 178, **179**
Robertson, Bob, 115
Robinson, Bill, 110, 131-134
Robinson, Brooks, 68, 100, 112
Robinson, Frank, 43, **91,** 155

Robinson, Jackie, 46
Romero, Enrique, 146
Roseboro, John, 26
Rosen, Al, 172
Rose, Pete, 9, 12, 16, 29, 32, **62,
64-65,** 66-**67, 68,** 72, 73-74, **75,**
76-77, 78, 80, 81, **82**
Royals Stadium, 107
Rudi, Joe, 21, 23, **35,** 36, 37, **38,**
57, 58, 132
Russell, Bill, **95,** 135-136, 179
Ryan, Connie, 125, 129
Ryan, Nolan, 43, 59-60

Sambito, Joe, 70
Sanders, Ken "Daffy", 147
Sanguillen, Manny, **72,** 73, 131
Schmidt, Mike, **59, 60,** 81, 96, 112
Schueler, Ron, **61**
Scully, Vin, 99-100
Seaver, Tom, 33, **47,** 74, 78, 100,
142-143
Seghi, Phil, 58
Seitz, Peter, 53, 55
Shecter, Leonard, 54
Shepard, Larry, **142-143,** 146-147
Short, Robert, 46
Show, Eric, 78
Siebern, Norm, 21
Simmons, Ted, 86
Smith, Ozzie, 158
Smith, Reggie, 135, 136
Sosa, Elias, 170
Stanky, Eddie, 125
Stanley, Bob, 178
Stargell, Willie, 73, **86,** 110, 115,
126-**127,** 131-134
Staub, Rusty, **47, 156,** 157
Stearns, John, 125
Steinbrenner, George, 57, 60, 104,
123, 128-129, 132, 149, 161-181
Stello, Dick, 9, **131**
Stewart, Jimmy, 69
Sutter, Bruce, 146, **148,** 152-153
Sutton, Don, 126, 136
Swoboda, Ron, 154
Symington, Stuart; on Charlie Finley,
19

Tanner, Chuck, 122-123, 125, 130-
131, 134, **136**
Tekulve, Kent, 146, **149**
Tenace, Gene, **28, 29, 35,** 36, 38,
57, 59, 132
Thomas, Gorman, 102
Three Rivers Stadium, 107, 110-**111**
Tiant, Luis, 6, **7,** 8, 10, **42,** 124-125,
175
Tolan, Bobby, 68, 72, 75
Torrez, Mike, 37, 167, 175-178
Trillo, Manny, 34
Turner, Ted, 52, 54, 56, 93, **124,**
132

Uecker, Bob, 100

Veeck, Bill, 19, 93, 118
Veterans Stadium, 107
Virdon, Bill, 73, 123, 128-129, 148
Vukovich, John, 76

Walker, Harry "The Hat", 125
Ward, Robert, 163
Washington, Herb, 154
Weaver, Earl, 102-104, **120-121,**
122, 138-140
Welch, Bob, 104
Westrum, Wes, 130
White, Bill, 100
White, Frank, 113, 118-119, 156, 173
White, Roy, 166, 175
Wilhelm, Hoyt, 144
Williams, Dick, 19, 24, **25, 28,** 32-33,
34, 122-123, 145, 153
Williams, Ted, 67, 122
Willis, Mike, 175
Wills, Bump, 124
Wills, Maury, 154
Wilson, Willie, 114-**115**
Winfield, Dave, **94,** 158
Wise, Rick, 13
Wohlford, Jim, 113
Woodling, Gene, 168
Wood, Wilbur, 130
World Series; 1960, 48; 1964, 54;
1969, **140;** 1970, 68, 70, 81, 112;
1971, 24, 48, 92, **101,** 110, 115-
116; 1972, 28, **29, 32,** 81; 1973,
33, 34; 1974, **39,** 150; 1975, 4-17,
80, **81,** 89, 98; 1976, 80, 81, 86,
161, 168; 1977, 104, **166-**170, 181;
1978, 104, 168, 173-180, 180; 1979,
126, 134, **149;** 1980, 82, 115; 1984,
132

Yastrzemski, Carl, **6,** 7, **8,** 12, 16-17,
43, 50, 156, 166, 174-175, **178,** 179
Young, Dick, 47-50

Zernial, Gus, 102
Zimmer, Don, **4-5,** 11-12, 123, **131,**
174, 178
Zisk, Richie, 59, 115, 132

Boldface indicates picture.

PICTURE CREDITS

Front cover: Bill Freehan & George Scott by Malcolm W. Emmons

Back cover: Willie Stargell by Anthony Neste

Back Matter
182-6 All: Ron Menchine Collection/ Renée Comet Photography

Four Hours of Magic
4-5 Dick Raphael; 6 (left) Ron Menchine Collection/Renée Comet Photography; 6 (right) Tony Triolo/ *Sports Illustrated;* 7 Walter Iooss, Jr./*Sports Illustrated;* 8 (left) National Baseball Library, Cooperstown, NY; 8 (right) John D. Hanlon/*Sports Illustrated;* 9 (top) Tony Triolo/*Sports Illustrated;* 9 (bottom) AP/Wide World Photos; 10 (left) National Baseball Library, Cooperstown, NY; 10 (right) Dick Raphael; 11 Dick Raphael; 12 Dick Raphael; 13 AP/Wide World Photos; 14 John D. Hanlon/*Sports Illustrated;* 15 AP/Wide World Photos; 16 Ron Menchine Collection/Renée Comet Photography; 17 (top) Dick Raphael; 17 (bottom) Walter Iooss, Jr./*Sports Illustrated.*

Charlie O. and the A's
18 Fred Kaplan; 19 Fred Kaplan; 20 Fred Kaplan; 21 (left) Fred Kaplan; 21 (top right) Ron Menchine Collection/ Renée Comet Photography; 21 (bottom right) The Harry Naiman Collection; 22 (left) Malcolm W. Emmons; 22 (right) Malcolm W. Emmons; 23 George Long/*Sports Illustrated;* 24 (left) National Baseball Library, Cooperstown, NY; 24 (right) Fred Kaplan; 25 (top) Fred Kaplan; 25 (bottom) Fred Kaplan; 26 The Harry Naiman Collection; 27 Fred Kaplan; 28 (top) Dick Raphael; 28 (bottom) Ron Menchine Collection/ Renée Comet Photography; 29 AP/Wide World Photos; 30 National Baseball Library, Cooperstown, NY; 31 (left) Neil Leifer/*Sports Illustrated;* 31 (right) Garibaldi Studios; 32 (left) Focus on Sports; 32 (right) Malcolm W. Emmons;

33 Walter Iooss, Jr./*Sports Illustrated;* 34 (left) National Baseball Library, Cooperstown, NY; 34 (right) Walter Iooss, Jr.; 35 (left) Walter Iooss, Jr./ *Sports Illustrated;* 35 (right) Neil Leifer/*Sports Illustrated;* 37 (left) Fred Kaplan/*Sports llustrated;* 37 (right) UPI/Bettmann Newsphotos; 38 John Iacono/*Sports Illustrated;* 39 Walter Iooss, Jr./*Sports Illustrated;* 40 Anthony Neste ; 41 (top) Manny Rubio; 41 (bottom) Fred Kaplan.

Big Money
42 UPI/Bettmann Newsphotos; 43 The WOB Collection; 44 National Baseball Library, Cooperstown, NY; 45 (left) AP/Wide World Photos; 45 (right) Herb Scharfman/*Sports Illustrated;* 46 (left) Dick Raphael/*Sports Illustrated;* 46 (right) Louis Requena; 47 AP/Wide World Photos; 48 Lee Balterman; 49 (top) Walter Iooss, Jr.; 49 (bottom) AP/Wide World Photos; 50 (left) National Baseball Library, Cooperstown, NY; 50 (right) George Long/*Sports Illustrated;* 51 UPI/Bettmann Newsphotos; 52 (left) UPI/Bettmann Newsphotos; 52 (right) Malcolm W. Emmons; 53 (top) AP/Wide World Photos; 53 (bottom) Malcolm W. Emmons; 54 (both) The WOB Collection; 55 (left) Tony Triolo/*Sports Illustrated;* 55 (right) AP/Wide World Photos; 56 (left) National Baseball Library, Cooperstown, NY; 56 (right) AP/Wide World Photos; 57 Tony Tomsic/*Sports Illustrated;* 59 (left) Manny Millan/*Sports Illustrated;* 59 (right) Anthony Neste; 60 (left) Walter Iooss, Jr.; 60 (right) Anthony Neste; 61 UPI/Bettmann Newsphotos.

The Big Red Machine
62 UPI/Bettmann Newsphotos; 63 Ron Menchine Collection/Renée Comet Photography; 64 AP/Wide World Photos; 64-5 Neil Leifer/*Sports Illustrated;* 66 Neil Leifer; 67 (left) Malcolm W. Emmons; 67 (right) National Baseball Library, Cooperstown, NY; 68 AP/Wide World Photos; 69 (left) Dick Raphael; 69 (right) Anthony Neste; 70 Ron Menchine Collection/Renée Comet Photography; 71 (top) Tony Triolo/*Sports Illustrated;* 71 (bottom) Walter Iooss, Jr./*Sports Illustrated;* 72

Dick Raphael; 73 UPI/Bettmann Newsphotos; 75 Louis Requena; 76 (left) National Baseball Library, Cooperstown, NY; 76 (right) Dick Raphael; 77 (all) The WOB Collection; 78 Ron Menchine Collection/Renée Comet Photography; 79 (top) Focus on Sports; 79 (bottom) Kenneth Garrett/Woodfin Camp, Inc.; 80 Dick Raphael; 81 Dick Raphael; 82 (left) Dick Raphael; 82 (right) Heinz Kleutmeier/ *Sports Illustrated;* 83 Robert Riger; 84 Ron Menchine Collection/Renée Comet Photography; 85 (left) Kevin Fitzgerald; 85 (right) Malcolm W. Emmons; 86 (left) Malcolm W. Emmons; 86 (right) AP/Wide World Photos; 87 James Drake/*Sports Illustrated.*

Made for TV
88 Louis Requena; 89 Ron Menchine Collection/Renée Comet Photography; 90 Neil Leifer; 91 (left) AP/Wide World Photos; 91 (right) Fred Kaplan; 93 (top) Tony Inzerillo; 93 (bottom) Louis Requena; 94 (left) National Baseball Library, Cooperstown, NY; 94 (right) George Gojkovich; 95 Neil Leifer; 96 Ron Menchine Collection/Renée Comet Photography; 97 (left) Focus on Sports;97 (right) Malcolm W. Emmons; 98 (left) National Baseball Library, Cooperstown, NY; 98 (right) Anthony Neste; 99 (left) UPI/Bettmann Newsphotos; 99 (right) Ron Menchine Collection/Renée Comet Photography; 100 Tony Tomsic; 101 UPI/Bettmann Newsphotos; 102 Ron Menchine Collection/Renée Comet Photography; 103 (top) Anthony Neste; 103 (bottom left) AP/Wide World Photos; 103 (right) Manny Millan/*Sports Illustrated;* 104 Fred Kaplan/*Sports Illustrated;* 105 (top) Walter Iooss, Jr.; 105 (bottom) Louis Requena.

The Artificial Game
106 Louis Portnoy/Spectra-Action, Inc.; 107 Astro Turf Industries Inc./ Renée Comet Photography; 108 Herb Scharfman/*Sports Illustrated;* 109 (left) AP/Wide World Photos; 109 (right) Nancy Hogue; 110 Ron Menchine Collection/Renée Comet Photography; 111 Gary Quesada/Balthazar Korab Ltd.; 112 (left) National Baseball

ACKNOWLEDGMENTS

The author and editors wish to thank:

Peter P. Clark, Tom Heitz, Bill Deane, Patricia Kelly, Dan Bennett, Sara Kelly, Frank Rollins and the staffs of the National Baseball Hall of Fame and the National Baseball Library, Cooperstown, New York; Nat Andriani, Wide World Photos, New York, New York; Renée Comet Photography, Washington, D.C.; Bill Mead, Bethesda, Maryland; Jack Limpert, Washington, D.C.; Carol Ryder, Washington, D.C.; Joe Borras, Accokeek, Maryland; Kenneth E. Hancock, Annandale, Virginia; Dorothy A. Gergel, Springfield, Virginia; Dave Kelly, Library of Congress, Washington, D.C.; Karen Carpenter and Sunny Smith, Sports Illustrated, New York, New York; Elizabeth McLean, Decatur, Georgia; Julie Harris, Arlington, Virginia; Maria F. Negron, Falls Church, Virginia; Ed Milner AstroTurf Industries, Inc., Dalton, Georgia

FOR FURTHER READING

Tom Clark, *Champagne and Baloney: The Rise and Fall of Finley's A's,* Harper and Row, 1976.

Jim "Catfish" Hunter and Armen Keteyian, *Catfish: My Life in Baseball,* McGraw-Hill, 1988.

Dick Lally, *Pinstriped Summers,* Arbor House Publishing, 1985.

Ed Linn, *Steinbrenner's Yankees,* Holt, Rinehart & Winston, 1982.

Graig Nettles and Peter Golenbock, *Balls,* G.P. Putnam's Sons, 1983.

David Quentin Voight, *American Baseball, Volume III: From Postwar Expansion to the Electronic Age,* The Pennsylvania State University Press, 1983.

World of Baseball is produced and
published by Redefinition, Inc.

WORLD OF BASEBALL

Editor	Glen B. Ruh
Design Director	Robert Barkin
Production Director	Irv Garfield
Senior Writer	Jonathan Kronstadt
Text Editor	Sharon Cygan
Picture Editing	Rebecca Hirsh
	Louis P. Plummer
Picture Research	Catherine M. Chase
Design	Edwina Smith
	Sue Pratt
	Collette Conconi
	Monique Strawderman
Copy Editing	Ginette Gauldfeldt
	Carol Gardner
Copy Preparation	Anthony K. Pordes
Production Assistant	Kimberly Fornshill Holmlund
Editorial Research	Janet Pooley
	Mark Lazen
	Ed Dixon
Illustrations	Dale Glasgow
Index	Lynne Hobbs

REDEFINITION

Administration	Margaret M. Higgins
	June M. Nolan
Fulfillment Manager	Karen DeLisser
Marketing Director	Harry Sailer
Finance Director	Vaughn A. Meglan
PRESIDENT	Edward Brash

CONTRIBUTORS

Randy Rieland is a senior editor at *The Washingtonian* magazine, where he coaches and plays left field for the office softball team. He has worked as a reporter and editor with *The Pittsburgh Press, The Baltimore Sun* and *Pittsburgh Magazine.* His fondest memory of the 1970s is of attending the last game played in Forbes Field.

Henry Staat is Series Consultant for World of Baseball. A member of the Society for American Baseball Research since 1982, he helped initiate the concept for the series. He is an editor with Wadsworth, Inc., a publisher of college textbooks.

Ron Menchine, an advisor and sports collector, shared baseball materials he has been collecting for 40 years. A sportscaster and sports director for numerous radio stations, he announced the last three seasons played by the Washington Senators.

The editors also wish to thank the following writers for their contributions to this book: Robert Kiener, Washington, D.C.; Leonard Hochberg, Falls Church, VA; David Hoff, Washington, D.C.; Eliot Cohen, Washington, D.C.; Andrew Keegan, Alexandria, Virginia.

Library of Congress Cataloging-in-Publication Data
The new professionals/Randy Rieland.
    (World of Baseball)
    includes index.
    1. Baseball—United States—History.
I. Title. II. Series.
GV863.A1R527 1989 89-28292
796.357'0973—dc20
ISBN 0-924588-05-5

This book is one of a series that celebrates America's national pastime.

Redefinition also offers a World of Baseball Top Ten Stat Finder.

For subscription information and prices please write:
Customer Service, Redefinition, Inc.,
P.O. Box 25336,
Alexandria, Virginia 22313

Printed in the U.S.A.
10 9 8 7 6 5 4 3 2 1

The text of this book is set in Century Old Style; display type is Helvetica and Gill Sans. The paper is 70 pound Warrenflo Gloss supplied by Stanford Paper Company. Typesetting by Intergraphics, Inc., Alexandria, Virginia. Color separation by Colotone, Inc., North Branford, Connecticut. Printed and bound by Ringier America, New Berlin, Wisconsin.